Acknowledgements

NASB. Texts credited to NASB are taken from *The New American Standard Bible,* copyright © The Lockman Foundation 1960, 1962, 1963, 1968, 1971, 1972, 1973, 1975. Used by permission.

NEB. Texts credited to NEB are taken from the *New English Bible.* © The Delegates of the Oxford University Press and the Syndics of the Cambridge University Press, 1961, 1970. Used by permission.

RSV. Unless otherwise stated, the Scripture quotations throughout the volume are from the *Revised Standard Version of the Bible,* copyrighted 1946, 1952, © 1971, 1973.

Contents

Issues in the Book of Hebrews

Daniel and Revelation Committee Series

DANIEL AND REVELATION COMMITTEE SERIES

Volume 4

Issues in the Book of Hebrews

Editor
Frank B. Holbrook

Biblical Research Institute
General Conference of Seventh-day Adventists
Silver Spring, MD 20904

Printed in the U.S.A. by the
Review and Herald Publishing Association
Hagerstown, Maryland 21740

Library of Congress Cataloging-in-Publication Data

Issues in the book of Hebrews.

   (Daniel and Revelation Committee series ; v. 4)
   Includes bibliographical references and index.
   1. Bible. N.T. Hebrews—Criticism, interpretation, etc. I. Holbrook,
Frank B. II. Series.
BS2775.2.I84 1989   227'.8706   88-63901
ISBN 0-925675-03-2 (Volume 4)
ISBN 0-925675-05-9 (7 Volume Set)

Abbreviations

AB	Anchor Bible
ANET	*Ancient Near Eastern Texts,* Pritchard, ed.
Ant.	*Antiquities of the Jews,* Josephus
ASV	American Standard Version
AUSS	*Andrews University Seminary Studies*
BA	*Biblical Archaeologist*
BDB	F. Brown, S. R. Driver, and C. A. Briggs, *A Hebrew and English Lexicon of the Old Testament* (Oxford, 1952)
Bell.	*Bellum Judaicum*
Bib	*Biblica*
BZ	*Biblische Zeitschrift*
CJT	*Canadian Journal of Theology*
ERV	English Revised Version
EvQ	*Evangelical Quarterly*
ExpTim	*Expository Times*
HAL	*Hebräisches und aramäisches Lexikon zum Alten Testament*
HNT	Handbuch zum Neuen Testament (Tübingen)
HThR	*Harvard Theological Review*
IB	*Interpreter's Bible*
ICC	International Critical Commentary
Int	*Interpretation*
JBL	*Journal of Biblical Literature*
JTS	*Journal of Theological Studies*
Leg. Alleg.	*Legum Allegoriae (Allegorical Interpretation)*
LXX	Septuagint
Macc	Maccabees
MT	Massoretic Text
NASB	New American Standard Bible
NEB	New English Bible
NICNT	New International Commentary on the New Testament
NICOT	New International Commentary on the Old Testament
NovT	*Novum Testamentum*
NTS	*New Testament Studies*
RB	*Revue biblique*
RevQ	*Revue de Qumran*
RSV	Revised Standard Virsion

SBL	Society of Biblical Literature
SBT	Studies in Biblical Theology
SJT	*Scottish Journal of Theology*
TDNT	*Theological Dictionary of the New Testament,* Kittel and Friedrich, eds.
TDOT	*Theological Dictionary of the Old Testament,* Botterweck and Ringgren, eds.
THAT	*Theol. Handwört. z. AT,* Jenni and Westermann, eds.
TNTC	*Tyndale New Testament Commentary*
TOTC	*Tyndale Old Testament Commentary*
VT	*Vetus Testamentum*
ZAW	*Zeitsch. für die alttes. Wiss.*
ZNW	*Zeitsch. für die neutes. Wiss.*

Transliteration Of Hebrew and Greek Alphabets

1. Hebrew Alphabet

Consonants

א = '	ד = $\underline{d}$	י = y	ס = s	ר = r
ב = b	ה = h	כ = k	ע = '	שׂ = $\acute{s}$
בּ = $\underline{b}$	ו = w	כ = $\underline{k}$	פ = p	שׁ = $\check{s}$
ג = g	ז = z	ל = l	פ = $\underline{p}$	ת = t
ג = $\underline{g}$	ח = $\d{h}$	מ = m	צ = $\d{s}$	ת = $\underline{t}$
ד = d	ט = $\d{t}$	נ = n	ק = q	

Masoretic Vowel Pointings

- = a	(vocal shewa) = e	· = $\bar{o}$
, = $\bar{a}$	' , ' - = $\hat{e}$	= o
-ː = a	· = i	' = $\hat{o}$
ː = e	' · = $\hat{\imath}$	·· = u
·· = $\bar{e}$	' = o	' = $\hat{u}$

2. Greek Alphabet

α = a	ζ = z	λ = l	π = p	φ = ph
β = b	η = $\bar{e}$	μ = m	ρ = r	χ = ch
γ = g	θ = th	ν = n	σ = s	ψ = ps
δ = d	ι = i	ξ = x	τ = t	ω = $\bar{o}$
ε = e	κ = k	ο = o	υ = u	' = h

To the Reader

Four books of the Bible—Leviticus, Hebrews, Daniel, and Revelation—have contributed to Seventh-day Adventist understanding of Christ's priestly ministry in the heavenly sanctuary. Since the Committee's assigned task centered largely on issues relating to the Sanctuary doctrine, study was given also to Hebrews, although not a book of prophecy.

Hebrews provided our pioneers with the initial insights to resolve the dilemma of the 1844 disappointment. The Epistle pointed them not to the church or the earth as the sanctuary to be cleansed in the Christian era but to the heavenly sanctuary, the counterpart of the Israelite tabernacle/temple. By faith they beheld the Saviour as their high priest entering upon the second phase of His priestly ministry, corresponding to the Most Holy Place ministration in the typical sanctuary on earth.

Strange as it may seem, the book that brought great joy to our pioneers has caused other Adventists to withdraw from the church. The charge is that Hebrews denies the Adventist belief that Christ mediates in a two-phased priestly ministry (the antitype of the daily and yearly ministrations in the earthly sanctuary) with the latter ministry beginning in 1844. It is asserted that according to Hebrews Christ ascended after His death and resurrection to the Most Holy Place in the heavenly sanctuary and began a one-phased, intercessory ministry. In 1844 nothing happened in terms of His assuming an additional ministry.

Consequently, the issue addressed by the Committee was delimited to a twofold question: (1) Does Hebrews explicitly teach Christ's two-phased priestly ministry? (2) Does Hebrews deny Christ's two-phased priestly ministry? Eventually the Committee rendered a negative response to both questions.

It is evident that the author of Hebrews makes no attempt to detail the antitypical significance of the Levitical sanctuary. Instead he restricts his objective to noting its predicted demise and to exposing its inherent weakness (as a shadow-type) to purge the soul from sin. On the positive side he emphasizes the efficacy of Christ's once-for-all-time sacrifice and the new and living way into the very presence of God that has resulted from the merits of Christ's better blood and priesthood. Consequently, the two-phased ministry of Christ is not within the purview of the author's purpose, although he says nothing that would deny the validity of such a ministry.

The argument for the Adventist doctrine is drawn from the sanctuary types which present in sequence two major divisions of priestly ministration. It is legitimate to infer such a ministry since the Levitical priests are said to serve "a copy and shadow of the heavenly sanctuary" in which Christ now ministers as high priest (Heb 8:1, 5).

For the author of Hebrews the argument is drawn from the fact that the sanctuary ritual-types are inadequate in themselves "to take away sins" (Heb 10:4) and thus provide a free and direct access to God. Hebrew Christians, tempted to return to the worn-out Levitical system, needed to be warned of its limited nature.

The themes of Hebrews that stress direct access to God through the priestly mediation of Christ and the all-sufficiency of His blood to cleanse from sin appear to be sketched in part against the backdrop of Day of Atonement imagery. These are themes the modern church needs to hear today as much as did the first century believers.

Although Ellen White taught the two-phased ministry of Christ in the heavenly sanctuary, on occasion she referred to the major motifs in Hebrews. She saw no contradiction between these two basic applications of the Levitical system. We note two citations:

"Thank God for the bright pictures which He has presented to us. Let us group together the blessed assurances of His love, that we may look upon them continually: The Son of God leaving His Father's throne, clothing His divinity with humanity, that He might rescue man from the power of Satan; His triumph in our behalf, *opening heaven to men, revealing to human vision the presence chamber where the Deity unveils His glory*; the fallen race uplifted from the pit of ruin into which sin had plunged it, and brought again into connection with the infinite God, and having endured the divine test through faith in our Redeemer, clothed in the righteousness of Christ, and exalted to His throne—these are the pictures which God would have us contemplate."—*Steps to Christ*, p. 118 (emphasis added).

"Still bearing humanity, He ascended to heaven, triumphant and victorious. He has taken the blood of the atonement into the holiest of all, sprinkled it upon the mercy-seat and His own garments, and blessed the people. Soon He will appear the second time to declare that there is no more sacrifice for sin."—*Signs of the Times,* April 19, 1905.

The many papers prepared for the Committee provide grist for its discussions, but do not necessarily result in publication. This enables all viewpoints to be heard fairly. From its discussions on Hebrews the Committee prepared a consensus report which forms the first chapter in this volume (formerly printed in *Adventist Review,* February 7, 1985, pp. 5-9; *Ministry,* April 1985, pp. 12-16, 21). Some of the studies deemed to be of general worth are herewith published in permanent form with the report. A few studies on this topic are not included—either because they are in part duplicatory, too technical to be readable by a general audience, or they expressed views the Committee eventually did not adopt.

Two useful articles relating directly to the discussions are reprinted from *The Sanctuary and the Atonement* (a publication of the Biblical Research Institute). Two short articles that involve technical terms, appearing earlier in *Andrews University Seminary Studies,* have been placed in Appendixes as a reference for those familiar with Greek and Hebrew.

This present volume, therefore, is not intended to be a verse-by-verse study of the book of Hebrews. However it does deal seriously with one of the weighty issues that is of tremendous importance for the identity and well-being of the Seventh-day Adventist Church and its mission. A discerning reader may see individual differences on some points of interpretation, but the Committee did not attempt to reconcile these. Room is left for continued study of the message of Hebrews. Instead, the Committee stayed with the major question: Does the book of Hebrews invalidate the two-phased priestly ministration of Christ which the sanctuary types and other passages of Scripture indicate?

We express our appreciation to the several invitees who contributed to this discussion and to the authors whose contributions appear in the present volume:

Richard M. Davidson	Herbert Kiesler
William G. Johnsson	Alwyn P. Salom
Alberto R. Treiyer	

Daniel and Revelation Committee
General Conference of Seventh-day Adventists

Chapter I

Daniel and Revelation Committee Report

Historical Setting

A **sound interpretation of Hebrews** relies on an understanding of the times in which the Epistle was written and the needs of the persons to whom it was first addressed. Information provided by the Epistle itself and by the other NT writings enables us to be fairly certain of the particular situation in the first century Christian church to which Hebrews speaks. We review the external and internal evidence briefly:

External Historical Background

The death, resurrection, and ascension of Jesus Christ gave birth to the Christian church on Pentecost. Thousands of converts joined the apostles and their early associates at that time (Acts 2:5, 41, 47). Eventually "a great company of the priests" (6:7) and many from "the sect of the Pharisees" (15:5) as well as the common people swelled the ranks of the infant movement (4:4). These were all Jews, and they met great opposition from their countrymen in Judea (1 Thess 2:14; cf. Heb 10:32, 33). Standing as they were at the transition point between two great dispensations, it was difficult for many of these Hebrew Christians to detach themselves totally from the Temple and its prescribed worship. Apparently they did not sense that type had met antitype in Christ's appearance, atoning death, and priestly ministry in heaven (Matt 27:50-51). As the church rapidly enlarged its ranks by a new mission to the Gentiles, some Hebrew Christians urged the necessity of their participation in the Mosaic rituals.

The Jerusalem Council (A.D. 49) reaffirmed, however, the truth that sinners—whether Jew or Gentile—obtain salvation from sin by faith in Jesus Christ alone (Acts 15:7-11). The council excused Gentile Christians from any required participation in the Temple worship (vss. 13-21, 28, 29). But the matter of Hebrew-Christian observance was not addressed (cf.

1

Rom 14:5-6), and considerable numbers remained attached to the Temple.

Nearly ten years later (A.D. 58) the Jerusalem leadership informed the apostle Paul that there were "many thousands of Jews . . . which believe; and they are all zealous of the law" (Acts 21:20). Eight years later the outbreak of war between the Jews and their Roman overlords would occur (A.D. 66). This tragic clash of arms would culminate in the destruction of the Temple and the ruin of the nation (A.D. 70) as Jesus had foretold (Matt 23:38; 24:1, 2, 15-19; Luke 19:41-44; 21:20).

Internal Evidence

As this terrible crisis in Jewish history approached, the Epistle indicates that the spiritual condition of many Hebrew Christians was seriously deteriorating. Gradually losing confidence in the Lord's promised return, they tended to neglect the salvation He had provided and to forget the ringing affirmations of the gospel (Heb 10:35-37; 2:1-3).

There was danger that these once-earnest Christians would lapse into the unbelief of their forebears in the Exodus migration to the Promised Land (3:6-19; 4:1, 11) and under the pressures of many trials and discouragements (12:3-13) would fall away in open apostasy from the Christian faith (6:4-9). Already they were tending to forsake the assemblies of their Christian brethren (10:25) and to turn back to Judaism (13:13), from which they apparently had never fully separated.

Purpose of the Epistle

It is evident, therefore, that the Epistle to the Hebrews is written from *the perspective of a deep pastoral concern for these Christians,* who—in a crucial period of Jewish history—were in serious danger of making shipwreck of their faith. Its purpose was to revitalize their wavering experience (10:23) by focusing the faith and attention once again on their ascended Lord, "the author and finisher" of their faith (12:2). It attempted to lift their sights from the inadequate rites involving animal blood to Christ's true sacrifice for sin and His ministry in the true sanctuary in heaven. The emphasis was on the good news—the gospel—that is truly available through a transcendent high priest who ever ministered for them in the presence of God.

The salient points of the pastoral message may be summarized as follows:

1. God, who established the Levitical priesthood with its typical sanctuary system, intended at a given point in time to displace it by the real

2

priesthood of Jesus Christ (foreshadowed by the former, 8:4, 5) who now functions as a king-priest in the heavenly sanctuary (after the dual-office arrangement of the ancient king-priest Melchizedek (5:5, 6; 7:11, 12, 18, 19; 8:1, 2).

2. The Levitical sanctuary (designed to teach the gospel by type and symbol, 4:1, 2) provided in itself only a *limited access to God* (9:6, 7), and *was repetitious* in operation (vss. 25, 26; 10:1-3) because it *was unable to take away sin* and thereby to purge the conscience of the penitent sinner (10:4, 11).

3. But by virtue of *Christ's priestly office* the believer has free access to God at any time (4:16), for the Saviour (ever touched by his needs, vs. 15) intercedes in the presence of God for him (7:25; 9:24). Furthermore, in the mediation of the merits of *Christ's once-for-all-time sacrifice,* the believer finds the only available cleansing from the defilement of sin (9:14; 10:10-14).

This appeal to the first century Hebrew Christians is worked out in the Epistle by comparing and contrasting in broad strokes the Levitical sanctuary sacrifices and priestly ministry with Christ's efficacious sacrifice and heavenly priesthood. *There is no attempt to give an exposition of the typical significance of the two-apartment phases of priestly ministry.* (For example, although allusions are made to the Day of Atonement, there is no discussion of the scapegoat and its significance in that important ritual.)

Instead, the appeal to these first century Christians to hold fast their faith in Christ (3:6, 14) is underscored by emphasizing the *superiority* of Christ's person, His atoning death, and priestly ministry over the now-worn-out rituals. These belivers are assured that in their exalted Lord they have *a better sacrifice/blood,* and a *better priest,* who mediates for them in *a better sanctuary* in connection with *a better covenant.*

Some Questions Addressed

In the light of the Epistle's historical setting and purpose, the committee felt that a number of problems resolve themselves. The following were some of the questions addressed:

Language

How should the language employed by the inspired author of Hebrews be construed?

The language of Hebrews should be understood in its natural, literal sense. It should not be construed allegorically. In his argument the author compares in a straightforward manner the sanctuaries and priesthoods of the old and new convenants (8:1-13; 9:1).

1. The Epistle indicates clearly that there is a *heavenly reality* designated as "the real sanctuary, the tent pitched by the Lord and not by man" (8:1, 2, NEB). It asserts a vertical link between the heavenly sanctuary and its counterpart on earth. The earthly sanctuary is viewed as a "copy" and a "shadow" (shadow-type) of the heavenly (vss. 1-5; 9:11, 23, 24). Naturally, the Bible writers must speak about the heavenly sanctuary—the celestial reality as it is represented to them—in the limited terms of human speech. Consequently, direct one-to-one correspondences between the two sanctuaries may not always be possible to draw, inasmuch as celestial realities far exceed human comprehension and expression.[1] It is essential, therefore, to look for the big ideas emphasized in earthly types.

2. Literal language may employ idioms and figures of speech. For example, the general expression "seated at the right hand of God/throne" (cf. 1:3; 8:1) is an idiom. The Messiah is always portrayed in this manner (cf. Ps 110:1; Acts 2:33; 5:31; Rom 8:34; Eph 1:20; Col 3:1; 1 Pet 3:22, etc.). The idiom is used even at the second coming of the Saviour (Matt 26:64). A similar expression is made with regard to the redeemed (Rev 3:21). The expression *does not refer to location.* Rather, as an idiom, it indicates Christ's full authority, His dignity and rank, His exaltation and supremacy. The expression "within the veil" is probably also being used in a figurative manner to denote access to God. See discussion below under Hebrews 6:19, 20.

Hebrews 9:8

Does this passage teach that the *first apartment* of the earthly sanctuary was intended to represent the Mosaic era, whereas the *Second Apartment* represents heaven itself and the Christian era?

Hebrews 9:1-7 contains a linguistic phenomenon in that *each* apartment in the earthly sanctuary is referred to as a "tabernacle" or "tent" (vss. 6, 7). However, it is also true that the *entire* sanctuary is viewed as a "tabernacle" or "tent" (cf. 8:2; 9:11). Consequently, the expression "first tabernacle," or "first tent," in chapter 9:8 is interpreted by some scholars to mean the first apartment of the Israelite sanctuary, whereas others understand it to mean the first tabernacle inaugurated by Moses at Sinai.

The committee considers that the *context* (which begins with chapter

---

1 Cf. *The Great Controversy,* p. 414.

4

8:1, 2) is determinative and clearly resolves this question. The context indicates that the author is comparing the entire sanctuary of the *first covenant* with the entire sanctuary of the second, or "new covenant" (8:1, 2, 6-13; 9:1, 11, 24). Thus the reference to "the first tabernacle" is to be understood as a reference to the Sinai tabernacle-sanctuary. The committee rejected the argument that the author is using the "first tabernacle/ tent" (= first apartment) as a symbol for the *whole* Mosaic tabernacle (a part for the whole) inasmuch as the sense of the argument in the full context suggests a simple comparison of the two sanctuaries: the earthly and the heavenly.

The New English Bible translates Hebrews 9:8 as follows: "By this the Holy Spirit signifies that so long as the earlier tent still stands, the way into the sanctuary remains unrevealed." Thus, the sense of the passage is simply that as long as "the earlier tent," that is, the earthly sanctuary, had a viable function as a type (until Christ's first advent), our Lord's priestly ministry in the heavenly sanctuary was not operative.

Ta Hagia ("Holy Places")

How should this expression be translated in Hebrews? The term, functioning in the context of Hebrews as a noun, is derived from the adjective *hagios,* meaning "holy." The word occurs ten times in Hebrews 8-13 (8:2; 9:1-3, 8, 12, 24, 25; 10:19; 13:11). It is generally conceded to appear in these passages in the form of a *neuter plural noun* except in chapter 9:1, where it is written as a neuter singular noun.

The use of this plural form (*ta hagia*) as a designation for the entire sanctuary is common in the Septuagint (the LXX, Greek translation of the Hebrew Bible made in the third and second centuries B.C.). This may be significant, since the author of Hebrews consistently draws his citations of the OT from this version. (In the apocryphal book of 1 Maccabees [within the LXX] *ta hagia* is also used to designate the whole Temple. Judas Maccabeus says, "Let us go up to cleanse [*ta hagia*], and dedicate the sanctuary" [see 1 Macc 4:36, 41, 43, 48]). However, the practice of the author of Hebrews is not fully consistent, because in two clear instances he uses the plural form to denote a single apartment (9:2, 3).

In the light of these facts—and the overall context of Hebrews 8-10— the committee believes that *ta hagia* should be regarded as a general term that should be translated in most instances as "sanctuary" unless the context clearly indicates otherwise (such as in chapter 9:2, 3). The committee rejects the evident bias of the translators of *The New International*

Version, who, after taking the position that the expression should be rendered "Most Holy Place" in chapter 9:8 ("that the way into the Most Holy Place had not yet been disclosed"), have rendered every subsequent reference to the heavenly *ta hagia* with the phrase "the Most Holy Place." A more neutral rendering is that of *The New English Bible,* which translates *ta hagia* with "sanctuary" in each instance except chapter 9:2, 3 (in these cases the obvious meaning of "holy place" and "Most Holy Place" is given).

Hebrews 6:19, 20 ("Within the Veil")

Should this be understood to mean that Christ entered the Most Holy Place at His ascension? If so, does this invalidate the two-apartment, or two-phase, ministry of Jesus in the heavenly sanctuary as taught by the church?

Some scholars note that the entire two-apartment sanctuary was viewed by Israel as God's dwelling (Exod 25:8) and that the author was aware of the fact that a veil hung before each apartment (Heb 9:2, 3). They suggest, therefore, that the phrase "within the veil" is an allusion to the first veil and means simply that Christ has entered "within the heavenly sanctuary, into the presence of God."

On the other hand, there are scholars who believe that the author of Hebrews had "Day of Atonement" imagery in mind (cf. 9:7; Lev 16:3), and that he was thinking of Christ's entry into the Most Sacred Place of the sanctuary. Thus, they suggest that the phrase "within the veil" refers to the second veil and that the allusion heightens the thrust of the author's argument that the believers' transcendent high priest has opened a new and living way to the very heart of God.

The committee agrees that the author is contrasting *the limited approach to God* that Israel had in the Levitical priesthood (Heb 9:6, 7) with the *direct access* all believers now have in Christ Jesus, who ministers as high priest *in the very presence of God* for them (vs. 24). Any believer may come directly and "boldly unto the throne of grace" (4:16) "by . . . [the] new and living way" (10:20)—by virtue of the Saviour's accomplishments and mediation. Ellen White has applied the veil imagery of chapter 6:19, 20 to both apartments.[2]

It may be admitted that if the author is using Day of Atonement imagery in chapter 6:19, 20 (a view held by most scholars), it does indeed heighten

---

2 Cf. *The Great Controversy,* pp. 420-21, first apartment; *Present Truth* (March, 1850), p. 64 *(Review and Herald* reprints, p. 11), Second Apartment.

and sharpen the message he wished to convey to his readers that by virtue of Christ's death and priesthood they now had direct access to God. Through the ministry of their ever-living high priest they could draw near to God "in full assurance of faith" (7:25; 10:19-22). His efficacious blood would be mediated for them in the very presence of the Deity (9:14, 24).

It is the conclusion of the committee that if the author of Hebrews had Day of Atonement imagery in mind (in chapter 6:19, 20), his application neither exhausts the meaning of the Day of Atonement ritual nor negates a two-apartment priestly ministry of Christ in the heavenly sanctuary. In view of the author's evident purpose, Day of Atonement imagery would simply underscore the point that Christ had opened the way to the immediate presence of God, that every barrier between them and God had been removed. Hope in Christ, their living high priest in God's presence, could be to them "an anchor of the soul, both sure and steadfast" (vs. 19).

Day of Atonement Type and Calvary

Does Hebrews teach that the Day of Atonement type was fulfilled at Calvary? Does Hebrews 9:11-14 with its reference to "bulls" and "goats" indicate this?

The committee noted that the author of Hebrews alludes to a variety of sanctuary rituals and not to just one. For example, he alludes to the daily service (7:26, 27; 10:11, 12) as well as to the yearly service (Day of Atonement, 9:25; 10:3). He refers to the sprinkling of the water of purification made from the ashes of a red heifer (9:13; cf. Num 19) and to the administration of animal blood at the ratification of the covenant at Sinai (Heb 9:18-21). With one broad reference he includes all the varied sacrifices of the sanctuary ritual: "almost all things are by the law purged with blood; and without shedding of blood is no remission" (vs. 22).

It is true that a bull and a goat were sacrificed on the Day of Atonement, but they were offered on many other occasions as well (see Num 28, 29). The phrase "bulls and ... goats" in Hebrews 9:13 means the same thing as "goats and calves" in verse 12. But it is evident that the similar expression ("calves and ... goats") in verse 19 is a reference to the sacrifices made at the ratification of the covenant and not to those made on the Day of Atonement. There is scholarly acknowledgment that "bulls and goats" became a stereotyped expression denoting sacrifices in general (cf. Ps 50:9-13; 66:15). Consequently, the phraseology does not necessarily carry Day of Atonement imagery.

Be that as it may, it is important to keep in mind that *the cross is the true*

7

fulfillment of all typical sacrifices. Thus it may be said correctly that the cross (antitype) did indeed fulfill *the sacrificial aspect* (the offering of the Lord's goat) of the Day of Atonement (type).

However, it is the committee's conviction that the allusions to the Day of Atonement, as well as to the daily rites, were not intended to provide a complete interpretation of its antitypical significance. Rather, the purpose of the author is to underscore by contrast *the repetitious and ineffectual nature of animal sacrifices to save from sin, whether they are daily or yearly* (10:4). By contrast, he presents the better blood of Christ's supremely better sacrifice offered once for all time (9:25-28). The merits of His blood alone can purge the conscience (vss. 11-14) and provide genuine "redemption" from transgression in the covenantal relationship, whether it be under the first or second covenants (vs. 15).

Cleansing the Sanctuary

Does Hebrews indicate that Christ's atoning death in A.D. 31 cleansed (1:3, "purged") the heavenly sanctuary (9:23-26)? If so, there would be no need for a cleansing/Day of Atonement fulfillment of the type in 1844.

It is important to note that two ideas are intertwined in the author's thought when he speaks of sacrifice and its accomplishments: (1) the *sacrifice* itself (the shedding of blood), and (2) the *application or mediation of the blood* (= the application of the merits of the sacrifice). The two parts form a unit. A sacrifice never stood alone. Whether mentioned or not, the ministering, or application, of the blood was always an essential part of the sacrifice. These two facets of sacrifice may be seen in the author's descriptions in chapter 9:

1. Verses 12, 13
    a. *Blood* of goats/calves/bulls (= sacrifice)
    b. "Sanctifieth to the *purifying* of the flesh" (= application/mediation)
2. Verse 14
    a. *"Blood* of Christ"—"offered himself" (= sacrifice)
    b. *"Purge* your conscience" (= application/mediation)
3. Verses 18-21
    a. *Blood* of calves/goats—Sinai covenant (= sacrifice)
    b. *"Sprinkled"* book and people (= application/mediation)
4. Verse 22
    a. *"Shedding of blood"* (= sacrifice)
    b. *"Purged," "remission"* (= application/mediation)

5. Verse 23
   a. *Earthly sanctuary* ("patterns of things in the heavens")
      (1)*"These"* ([animal sacrifices understood] = sacrifice)
      (2)*"Purified"* (= application/mediation, at whatever times called for)
   b. *Heavenly sanctuary* ("the heavenly things themselves")
      (1)"Better *sacrifices"* (= Christ's sacrifice at Calvary)
      (2)"Should be purified" ([understood] = application/mediation)

It is evident that there is only *one* atoning sacrifice for sin, the atoning death of Christ. If that event had in itself "purified" the heavenly sanctuary, there would be no reason for the Saviour to function there in a priestly ministration. But a sacrifice never stood apart from the application of its merits. Consequently, it is understood that *there are many applications of the merits of the one cross event.*

All the "work" of Heaven is done on the basis of Calvary and is an application of its significance. Hebrews 9:23 (in context) contains both the ideas of Christ's efficacious death and the application of its merits—whether such is to be applied at the justification of a sinner who accepts God's salvation or whether applied in the final judgment to reaffirm the true believer and to vindicate God's authority and sovereignty before the universe. The cross event did not cleanse the heavenly sanctuary at the moment of the Saviour's death, but it did provide the basis upon which Christ, as man's high priest, could mediate His merits and bring about a total reconciliation of the universe (cf. Eph 1:10; Col 1:20) and thus restore the heavenly sanctuary and government of God "to its rightful state" (Dan 8:14, RSV).

Judgment and Day of Atonement

Another question commonly raised when the book of Hebrews is discussed (although not based on it) was touched on briefly by the committee. If, according to John 12:31, judgment took place at the cross, would not this be a fulfillment of the Day of Atonement type? Is it not also true that a person is judged when he hears the gospel and rejects it (3:18)?

It is evident, on the face of these passages, that the term judgment is being used in an accommodated, or modified, sense. Satan was indeed exposed and condemned in the eyes of the loyal universe at the cross, but he nevertheless continues to reign. The sinner who turns from the gospel invitation abides under divine condemnation (vs. 36), but he may again repent when the Spirit woos.

9

The point is that neither of these statements deals with the *final judgment*. The Day of Atonement ritual removed in a total manner all sin that had been transferred to the sanctuary. As a result the sanctuary, the people, and the camp were regarded as cleansed.

The Day of Atonement ritual is, therefore, analogous to the final judgment in its three phases (preadvent, millennial, executive), for only the final judgment completely resolves the sin problem and removes its effects from the universe. The Scriptures are clear that the final judgment will involve all humanity, including the professed followers of God (Acts 17:31; Rom 14:10-12; 2 Cor 5:10; Matt 22:9-14; Eccl 12:14; etc.). Thus, the Day of Atonement type—in terms of the final judgment—was not fulfilled at the cross.

Value of Hebrews

For the Sanctuary Doctrine

The book of Hebrews provides no detailed exposition of the Israelite sanctuary ritual because its pastoral concerns move in another direction. However, it furnishes some important keys for understanding the significance of the sanctuary and its main emphases. For example:

1. It indicates that there is a vertical link between the earthly and heavenly sanctuaries. The earthly is viewed as the counterpart of the heavenly and is designated a "copy" and "shadow" of the heavenly reality.

2. As a *teaching device,* the earthly sanctuary is described as a "parable" (9:9, "figure" = Greek, *parabolē* = English, "parable"). As a *parable,* the earthly sanctuary serves to illustrate major points in the gospel/plan of salvation (4:1-2).[3]

3. The earthly sanctuary and its rituals are also referred to as a "shadow," or type (8:1-5; 10:1). A shadow-type is like a prophecy; it foreshadows "things to come" (10:1). It is evident from Hebrews that the sanctuary rituals were intended to foreshadow the atoning, sacrificial death of Christ and His priestly ministry in the heavenly sanctuary (8:1, 2; 9:11-14).

4. The book of Hebrews makes certain applications of the sanctuary types to demonstrate the inadequacies of animal blood and human mediation to care for the sin problem. At the same time it seeks to lift the attention of its readers from the Temple and rituals as ends in themselves

---

3 Cf. *Christ's Object Lessons,* p. 133.

to focus faith on the grand Substance of all the shadows, Jesus Christ Himself, His atoning death and priestly ministry for them in the presence of God.

Other NT writers also apply sanctuary type in a general manner to a variety of topics such as the Incarnation (John 1:14), the church (2 Cor 6:16), and to the individual believer (1 Cor 6:19, 20). However, none of these applications, including that of Hebrews, exhausts or limits further application of the sanctuary types.

Seventh-day Adventist understanding of the two phases of Christ's priestly ministry is based on the two major ministries of the priests in the earthly sanctuary. The author of Hebrews has clearly underscored the fact that the Levitical priesthood served "a copy and shadow of the heavenly sanctuary" (8:5, RSV). It is only logical and reasonable, therefore, to examine these distinct labors of the typical priesthood for insights into the nature and scope of the Saviour's true priestly function in the heavenly sanctuary.

For Personal Experience

The same message that the inspired author of Hebrews conveyed to his readers in the first century is needed again in the closing years of human history. End-time Christians, jaded by affluence on the one hand or distracted by multiple cares on the other, are in danger of losing faith as they wait for their Lord's return. There is need to look in afresh on the living Christ, our High Priest, at the throne of God. As one of the committee members has expressed it so well:

"Our need, then, is to hear the same sort of message as the Hebrews. Someone must remind us of the reality of our religion, of its surpassing worth—must tell us again of the glory of our Head. And tell us in such a way that we can grasp it, that it brings us to our senses. Once more we must hear that because our religion is so great, we must take it seriously. Perhaps if we can grasp the magnificence of our salvation, if we can see the transcendent dimension, the divine realities of it, then we will cease to be so wishy-washy as Christians. Then we may stand up on our feet and look the world squarely in the eye. Then we shall know for sure who we are and what we are to be."

CHAPTER II

Hebrews: An Overview

William G. Johnsson

Editorial Synopsis. Seventh-day Adventists accept the unity of Scripture as a biblically supported principle because the Holy Spirit is the essential author of its documents. Thus, it is legitimate to synthesize the Bible's doctrinal teachings from the total corpus of Scripture (see Jesus' method, Luke 24:27, 44). On the other hand we recognize each book and letter of the Bible has its own standing, its own line of reasoning that must be respected. Individual passages must be understood first within the framework of the document's aim and perspective. Thus, the writer of this chapter takes the initial step toward understanding the teachings of Hebrews by inducting from the writing its purpose, structure, and nature—underscoring its relevance for Christians today.

Hebrews is more a tightly reasoned, carefully crafted sermon than a letter. A "word of exhortation" (13:22) is the apostolic author's own description. The book appeals to Jewish Christians in the first century A.D. whose spiritual energies are flagging and who are questioning the value of their faith in view of the once-held Jewish religion to which they seem to be drawn again.

The "sermon" alternates among four doctrinal expositions and four exhortations that arise in connection with the expositions. The expositions focus on the superiority of Christ's atoning death and high priestly ministry in the heavenly sanctuary as compared to the limited, repetitious, and ineffectual ministration of the Levitical priesthood and sanctuary. The four exhortations warn against neglect of and open apostasy from the great salvation made possible for them by Christ. It is suggested that these two lines of thought tie together naturally under a "pilgrim" motif or theme. The Christians addressed are viewed as a religious community—separated from their past and now God's people—on pilgrimage to the heavenly city in a "better country" (11:16).

In comparing and contrasting Christ with the OT worship system the apostolic writer rings the bells, as it were, with the concept, "better." Christ provides a better revelation of God than did the prophets (1:1-4). He has a better name than the angels (1:5–2:18) and is a better leader than Moses (3:1–4:16). He functions as a better priest (5:1–6:20) of a better priesthood (7:1-27) in a better sanctuary (8:1-6) and is the mediator of a better covenant (8:7-13). As our high priest He offers the merits of His better sacrifice in the presence of God for us (9:1–10:18).

The message of Hebrews is still important for the church today. It demonstrates that biblical theology is important to preaching and important to address human need. It indicates how Christians should relate to the apparent delay of Christ's return and draws attention to the living Christ and His priestly ministry in the heavenly sanctuary. "Hebrews is vital for its specific affirmations of a heavenly sanctuary and a heavenly ministry carried on by Christ our great high priest. Hebrews makes concrete what is pointed to by Old Testament types and New Testament (Revelation) symbols."

Hebrews uplifts Calvary as "the turning point in salvation history" and arouses the Christian pilgrim to persevere in his journey toward the promised goal. "For you have need of endurance, so that you may do the will of God and receive what is promised" (11:36).

Chapter Outline

I. Introduction
II. Purpose of Hebrews
III. Structure of Hebrews
IV. Nature of the Document
V. Relevance Today

* * * * * * *

Introduction

The enigmatic character of the Book of Hebrews is a commonplace among NT scholars. Apart from debates on the central meaning of the document, the basic questions of introduction—who wrote it? when? for whom? why? from where?—are subject to wide divergences of opinion.

"The Epistle of Paul the Apostle to the Hebrews" is the familiar title from the King James Version. But each part of this superscription has been,

14

and is, denied by certain students of the book. Such scholars argue that Hebrews is *not* a letter, Paul did *not* write it, and it was *not* addressed to readers out of a Jewish background.

These questions of introduction interlock. The answer we give to one impacts on others. For instance, the issue regarding the identity of the readers affects our understanding of the purpose of the document, as does, to a lesser degree, the question of the date of writing.

It is not the purpose of this chapter to canvass all the opinions and arguments concerning the various issues of introduction. Indeed, as has been demonstrated repeatedly in scholarly pursuits, where the data are scanty, theories proliferate. And for some of the questions about Hebrews—notably the authorship—the evidence is scant.[1] Rather, we seek to unlock those areas that most concern the thoughtful student of Hebrews: the purpose of the writing, the structure of the argument, the nature of the document, and its relevance to us. Fortunately, we do not need to rely on finely spun theories to gain access to these matters. Hebrews itself supplies the data and the answers.

Purpose of Hebrews

Recipients: The "Hebrews"

The earliest manuscripts read simply, *PROS HEBRAIOUS*—"To the Hebrews." The term "Hebrews" does not occur within the book itself.

"To the Hebrews" has four possible interpretations. The first two are the most obvious. "Hebrews," used ethnically, refers either to the Jews in general (thereby making the document an apology for Christianity to the Jewish people) or to Jewish Christians. A third way of understanding "Hebrews" would be in a spiritual sense. In this case, the document would address spiritual Jews, that is, the Christian church as the new spiritual Israel. Peter speaks about Christians in such terms.[2] C. Spicq[3] has suggested a fourth—a metaphorical—sense of "Hebrews." On the analogy of Deuteronomy 26:5 (in which the earlier Hebrews are described as

---

1 Erich Grässer's long review article, "Der Hebräerbrief 1938-1963," *TRu* 30 (1964): 138-236, is foundational for any discussion of the literature concerning Hebrews in the twentieth century. For update of Grässer's review see also William G. Johnsson, "Issues in the Interpretation of Hebrews," *AUSS*, vol. 15, No. 2 (1977), pp. 169-87; and William G. Johnsson, "The Cultus of Hebrews in Twentieth-Century Scholarship," *ExpT*, vol. 89, No. 4 (1978), pp. 104-8.

2 1 Peter 1:1; 2:4-9; 3:5-6; cf. Gal 3:29; 6:15-16.

3 C. Spicq, *L'Épître aux Hébreux*, 2 vols. (Paris, 1952); 1:269-80, esp. pp. 243-46; also "L'Épître aux Hébreux: Apollos, Jean-Baptiste, les Hellenistes et Qumran," *RevQ* (1958-59), 1:365-90.

wanderers) he holds that the title of our sermon signifies "To the Wanderers." His idea finds support in the references to journeying found especially in chapters 3, 4, 11, and 13.[4]

Jews. On the basis of clear-cut data within Hebrews itself we may quickly set aside this first suggestion. Although some students of the Book of Hebrews have argued that the readers were either non- or part Christian Jews, we may be sure they were "complete" Christians. The book calls Jesus "Lord" (2:3). Its readers had received His salvation mediated through the apostles (2:1-4) and had been blessed with the gift of the Holy Spirit (6:4, 5). Indeed, they had been Christians for a considerable period of time, because their service on behalf of the saints was well-known (6:9, 10), and formerly—at the time they became Christians—they had suffered hardship and loss because of their confession of Jesus (10:32-34).

Christian church. The third interpretation fails likewise. We do not find the writer applying the OT promises made to Israel in a spiritual sense to Gentile believers as Peter so obviously does. The book contains many references to the OT, but uses them in one of two ways—either without "spiritualizing," as in the descriptions of the sacrificial system, or Messianically.[5]

Metaphorical sense. Spicq's explanation of Hebrews as "wanderers" is ingenious. Unfortunately for the theory, however, we find no clear reference to Deuteronomy 26:5 within the text. It must therefore remain a conjecture. Perhaps Spicq was on the track of more than he realized, as we shall see when our understanding of Hebrews has run its full course.

Jewish Christians. We still have left the second possibility of Jewish Christians. For many students of Hebrews this answer already was obvious. They concluded that the extensive references to the OT priesthood and cultus presuppose a Jewish-Christian audience, one perhaps that feels the pull of the old Temple services or which faces the trauma of the loss of the Temple in the Roman destruction of Jerusalem in A.D. 70.[6]

The case is not watertight, however. The appeal to the sacrificial argumentation must face three curious bits of evidence in the text. On one hand, the writer does not reason from the services of the Temple supposedly current in his day. Rather, he argues from the sacrificial system of the wilderness Tabernacle (8:5; 9:1-8). That is, he does not work from

---

4 Heb 3:7–4:11; 11:8-10, 13-16, 27, 37, 38; 13:11-14.

5 Heb 1:5-13; 2:6-8, 12-13; 5:5-6; 7:1-3, 11, 17, 21.

6 This is the view set out in M. L. Andreasen, *The Book of Hebrews* (Washington, DC, 1948), pp. 21-31, 34-42.

contemporary Judaism but from the Pentateuch of the OT. On the other hand, he is not careful in his description of the OT sanctuary and sacrifices. For instance, he locates the golden altar in the Most Holy and merges the various sacrifices.[7] We wonder if such "lapses" would not have concerned a Jewish-Christian audience. The several appeals to the "living God" (3:12; 9:14; 10:31; 12:22) would have more significance if directed toward Gentile Christians.

We should add that much of the sacrificial argumentation would have added significance if the Jerusalem Temple were still erect and operating. On balance, then, the point of view that sees the readers as Jewish Christians has the stronger position, even if we do find some room for doubt.

Location. One verse, and only one, appears to shed some light on the location of the readers. In 13:24 we read, "those who come from Italy send you greetings [literally, 'those from Italy']." But even this is ambiguous. It can mean those resident in Italy, in which case Hebrews was composed and sent from Italy (many scholars think from Rome).[8] On the other hand the phrase may refer to certain *Italians traveling abroad* who send their greetings. In that case the author of Hebrews wrote to Christians in Italy (again, perhaps to Rome) from a country outside of Italy. Possibly we should prefer the latter on the basis of the Greek construction.[9]

The question of the identity of the Hebrews is interesting, but it is not the main issue. We do not have to know for sure whether they were Jewish or Gentile Christians before we can understand the document. More important is their spiritual profile, which readily emerges as we look at the instruction they received.

The Problem Addressed

As has been noted frequently, the Book of Hebrews alternates theological exposition with practical application or exhortation. In broad strokes[10] the pattern is as follows:

---

7 Heb 9:3-4. Despite many efforts scholars have advanced no convincing explanation. We note also the merging of "goats and bulls" (9:13), "calves and goats" (9:19), and "bulls and goats" (10:4). Exodus 24:3-8, the OT text to which Hebrews 9:15-22 alludes, mentions only "oxen."

8 William Manson, *The Epistle to the Hebrews: An Historical and Theological Reconsideration* (Edinburgh, 1951), most persuasively argued the case for Roman origin.

9 With B. F. Westcott, *The Epistle to the Hebrews* (Grand Rapids, 1965), pp. xliii-iv.

10 In the bridge passages, notably 4:14-16 and 6:19-20, the precise point of division between Exposition and Exhortation is debatable. More problematical is the place of chapter 11: Where does it belong? Although it is written almost entirely in the third person (instead of the first plural), the subject matter is quite different from that of the tight-knit passages which have comprised the Exposition to this point. It therefore fits better in the Exhortation.

Exposition 1:1-14
Exhortation 2:1-4
Exposition 2:5–3:6a
Exhortation 3:6b–4:16
Exposition 5:1-10
Exhortation 5:11–6:20
Exposition 7:1–10:18
Exhortation 10:19–13:25

By examining the writer's exhortations—by noting the spiritual dangers against which he warns—the problem of his readers emerges clearly.

In the first exhortation (2:1-4), the danger facing the readers is specified by the verbs "drift away" *(pararrein)* and "neglect" *(amelein)*. The former is a nautical metaphor meaning to "flow by, slip away, be washed away, drift away."[11] The latter term signifies "to neglect, be unconcerned about, disregard."[12] It is obvious that the "problem" to be avoided appears in this passage as a *gradual* falling away rather than a deliberate act of severance from the community.

The second hortatory passage (3:6b–4:16) both underlines and modifies this idea. On the one hand, the writer repeatedly warns against the danger of "hardening" *(sklērunein)*[13] the heart through the "deceitfulness," or "pleasures" *(apatē)*[14] of sin. Such an heart—an evil, unfaithful heart—leads to a dropping out *(apostēnai)*, from the community, just as the wilderness generation perished in the desert.

On the other hand, a more "active" type of danger is presented, one that comes to focus in the verbs, "to disobey" *(apeithein)*[15] and "to rebel" *(parapikrainein)*.[16] We see the danger threatening the community is that they may fail to realize the promised inheritance because of an unbelieving, unfaithful heart which may or may not be manifested in overt rebellion.

A third warning (5:11–6:20) maintains this distinction. The readers are rebuked for having become "dull of hearing" and are reminded that the blessings of God turn to a curse if no "fruit" is forthcoming. At the same time we are presented with a vivid picture of open rejection of the religious

---

11 William F. Arndt and F. Wilbur Gingrich, *A Greek-English Lexicon of the New Testament and Other Early Christian Literature* (Chicago, 1969), p. 627.
12 Ibid., p. 44.
13 Ibid., p. 763.
14 Ibid., p. 81.
15 Ibid., p. 82.
16 Ibid., p. 626.

values of the community: the apostates who fall away (*parapiptein*)[17] crucify (*anastauroun*)[18] on their own account the Son of God and expose Him to contempt (*paradeigmatizein*).[19]

We find the same sort of divide in the final exhortation (10:19–13:25). First, the danger lurks of "wavering," of neglecting the assembly, of forgetting the "former days" of Christian steadfastness, of "casting away" (*apoballein*) confidence, of lacking endurance, of shrinking back (*hupostole*). Second, the possibility exists that sin will be done deliberately (*hekousiōs*) when the Son of God is spurned, the covenant blood profaned, and the Spirit outraged (10:19-39).

In the final two chapters (12, 13) of the pamphlet we may again discern this differentiation of "gradual" and "radical" unfaithfulness. Thus, the danger is that the Christians will grow "weary" (*kamnein*)[20] or "lose heart" (*ekluesthai*),[21] that under the hardships of Christian life they may drop out, that they may neglect to show hospitality or to remember their fellows, that they may fall into idolatry, immorality, the love of money, or the snare of false teachings.

At the same time the warning example of Esau is introduced. He was "profane," "godless," "irreligious" (*bebēlos*),[22] so that at length he found no way to recover his inheritance. In the same way, the peril of rejecting or refusing God (*paraiteisthai*)[23] is always a fearsome possibility for Christians.

These passages have given us a fairly clear spiritual profile of the recipients of Hebrews. Their problem is not false teachers who have swept their young feet off the ground, as in Galatia. Nor is it a heady enthusiasm because of manifestations of the Spirit, as in Corinth. It is not the question of the failure of the Jews to receive the gospel, as in Romans. No, their problem is one of "tired blood." They have grown weary with waiting for the Lord's return, sluggish in their Christian identity, questioning the value of their religion, more so as hard times appear to loom on the horizon.

The apostle's message is that spiritual weariness is dangerous. Over and over he hammers home its fearful results. He suggests we may grow neglectful of our privileges, taking lightly what is of supreme value. Or we

---

17 Ibid.
18 Ibid., p. 60.
19 Ibid., p. 619.
20 Ibid., p. 403 (12:3).
21 Ibid., p. 242 (12:3, 5).
22 Ibid., p. 138 (12:16).
23 Ibid., pp. 621-22 (12:19, 25).

may defiantly reject the entire Christian faith, taking our place among the majority who do not confess Jesus as Saviour and Lord. One result is as dire as the other.

Solution

We find the above observations confirmed when we examine the "solution" which is held out by the author in the same passages.

The great need is "to pay attention," "give heed to," "be alert" (*prosechein*),[24] "to hold fast" (*katechein*),[25] "to grasp," "hold fast" (*kratein*),[26] to show "earnestness" (*spoudē*),[27] "to consider" (*katanoein*),[28] "to exhort" (*parakalein*),[29] "to recall" (*anamimnēskein*),[30] and to run with "endurance," "patience" (*hupomonē*).[31]

The conspicuous word, however, is "faith" or "faithfulness" (*pistis*). It was "faithfulness" (*pistis*) which characterized the life of Jesus, as of Moses (3:2). It was lack of faith (*pistis*) which led to the failure of the promise to the wilderness generation (3:19; 4:2). The famous eleventh chapter is built around this word: By their faith (*pistis*) the heroes of old time overcame all physical hardships and conquered all temptations. Even so will the readers of the pamphlet attain to the goal. Instead of being "sluggish" (*nōthroi*),[32] they are to be "imitators of those who through faith (*pistis*) and patience (*makrothumia*) inherit the promises" (6:12).

Here, then, is the purpose of the Book of Hebrews: to awaken tired Christians to the glorious privileges of belonging to the Christian community in order that they may persevere in faithfulness to the attainment of the promised inheritance.

How does the writer seek to achieve his object? This leads us to a study of the structure of the book.

Structure of Hebrews

Earlier we saw that the structure of Hebrews at its rudimentary level consists of an alternation between theological exposition and practical

---

24 Ibid., p. 721 (2:1).
25 Ibid., pp. 423-24 (3:6, 14; 10:23).
26 Ibid., pp. 449-50 (4:14; 6:18).
27 Ibid., p. 771 (6:11; 4:11).
28 Ibid., p. 416 (3:1).
29 Ibid., pp. 622-23 (3:13; 10:25; 13:19, 22).
30 Ibid., p. 57 (10:32).
31 Ibid., p. 854 (10:36; 12:1).
32 Ibid., p. 549 (6:12).

application. In this section we shall look more closely at each of these elements and then endeavor to find an overarching principle of structure for the book.

Exposition

It is not quite accurate to suggest that Hebrews juxtaposes theology and exhortation, inasmuch as the passages containing the latter are rich in theological content.[33] At the same time, however, a study of the passages we labeled "Exposition" reveals a concentration on theology and a developing theological argument that together give these sections of Hebrews distinct characteristics. Furthermore, the author himself customarily signals to us his intention to shift to application by injecting "since . . . therefore . . ." (2:1; 10:19) and changing from the third person to the first plural.

With what, then, is the "Exposition" concerned? Four features may be noted:

1. High priestly Christology. Hebrews is unique among the NT writings for its presentation of this motif. Elsewhere we find, at the most, hints, such as in Romans 8:34 or 1 John 2:2, or allusive imagery as in Revelation, chapters 1, 4, and 5. In Hebrews, however, Jesus as high priest is a dominant idea, and the book works it out in great detail.

Although the expression "high priest" appears first in 2:17, the entire argument to that point has been building for the disclosure. *Because* Christ is fully God (argued in 1:5-14) and fully man (argued in 2:5-16), He can *become* our high priest.[34] Subsequent passages elaborate on the two high priestly characteristics specified in 2:17—His faithfulness (in 3:1-6a) and His mercifulness (in 5:1-10). The seventh chapter shows how Jesus, a Judahite, nevertheless qualifies to be a high priest—in fact, He is a priest of a superior order.

Thus we reach the high priestly summit of 8:1, 2—"Now the point in what we are saying is this: we have such a high priest, one who is seated at the right hand of the throne of the Majesty in heaven, a minister in the sanctuary and the true tent which is set up not by man but by the Lord."

2. Cultic terminology. The Book of Hebrews, particularly in the passages we described as "Exposition," is replete with references to taber-

---

33 Examples: the treatment of faith, apostasy, pilgrimage (we will elaborate on this later in the chapter).

34 That is, in His person Jesus is unique; He is the *only* true high priest in history. The close reasoning of Hebrews 5:1-10 has this thrust.

21

nacles, sacrifices, priests, blood, and ablutions. Indeed, the very theological argumentation rests upon a cultic framework and cannot be grasped apart from it.

As I will show in chapter 5 of this book,[35] in the "Exposition" the human "problem" and its "solution" are markedly different from the presentations under the Exhortations. Here *defilement* rather than *unfaithfulness* calls for redress. Christ's work is to provide purification rather than to furnish a model of, and grace for, persevering effort.

3. A systematic presentation of theological argument. The writer thought out the whole work before he wrote the first word. He introduces each idea in its correct place, then develops and rounds it off. Each motif blends into the total argument to produce a composition of great logical force. Apart from its spiritual powers, the document is a masterpiece of ordered thinking.

For instance, we notice the following ideas:

a. Purification: introduced at 1:3; developed in 9:1–10:18.

b. High priest: introduced at 2:17, 18; expanded in 4:4-16 and 5:1-10; fully expounded with 7:1–10:18.

c. Angels: introduced at 1:4; developed in 1:5-14; terminated in 2:16.

d. Covenant: introduced at 7:22; developed in 8:6-13; rounded off with 9:18 and 10:16-18.

e. Faith: introduced at 2:17; expanded in 3:1-6; fully developed in 11:1-39.

4. Climax of the argument. The theological plan of Hebrews reaches its full development in the long passage 7:1–10:18, with 9:1–10:18 marking its summit.

The seventh chapter is concerned with Christ as high priest after the order of Melchizedek—an order which is superior to the Levitical order because it brings with it "perfection" (*teleiosis*). However, not only is the order superior, but Christ Himself surpasses the Levites by virtue of His moral character, His endless life, the oath of His office, and His priestly act. This then is the thrust of the seventh chapter: *a better priest.*

In chapter 8 the writer states that he has now arrived at the "chief point" (*kephalaion*) of his argument: Christ is high priest over a better sanctuary, even the heavenly. At the same time He is mediator of a better covenant—a covenant prophesied by Jeremiah. The eighth chapter, therefore, estab-

---

35 I have dealt with this topic extensively in my Ph.D. dissertation, *Defilement and Purgation in the Book of Hebrews* (Vanderbilt University, 1973).

lishes the following: *a better sanctuary and a better covenant.*

This prepares the ground for a discussion of Christ's work. Already 7:27 had thrown out the hint: Christ offered Himself once for all time. Chapters 9, 10 will pick up this thought and explicate it. Yet it would be a grave mistake to see chapters 9, 10 as forming merely the climax of the cultic argumentation of 7:1–10:18. There are numerous earlier anticipations of the passage, even as there are reflections upon it in the subsequent chapters.

The "when he had made purification for sins" clause (1:3b) is a direct announcement of the argument to be presented in detail only in the ninth and tenth chapters. In a similar manner the presentations in 2:5-18 (the priesthood of Jesus rooted in his humanity), 4:14–5:10 (Jesus a priest by virtue of His sufferings and the divine call), and in 6:19, 20 (Jesus the high priest as forerunner) look toward the more extended exposition in 7:1–10:18.

With 10:18 we reach the peak. The remainder of the book is to be comprehended under the "therefore" (*oun*) of 10:19. The immediate counsel comes as a dire warning. Then follow the exhortations to emulate the faithfulness of the old "heroes" and to "draw near" in the fulness of the access to the divine presence which the blood of Christ has provided.[36]

It is striking in these chapters after the peak of 10:18 to see the emphasis placed on the "blood" of Christ. In fact, the term "blood" (*haima*) does not occur in a cultic sense before chapter 9. After 10:18, however, it occurs seven times. Five times it signifies Christ's "blood."[37] In all of these seven occurrences there is an obvious looking back to the discussion of chapters 9, 10.

It seems apparent, therefore, that the ninth and tenth chapters of Hebrews place us, as it were, at the Everest of the pamphlet. This is true whether we consider the argumentation related to the sanctuary worship alone or whether we seek to trace the overall discussion of the author.

Exhortations

Already in this chapter we have given consideration to the content of the hortatory passage of Hebrews. Two further remarks are appropriate at this point:

1. The exhortations do not reveal the tight-knit, interlinked relation-

---

36 The warning, 10:26-31; the emulation of heroes of old, chapter 11; the invitation to draw near, 12:18-29.

37 With reference to the sanctuary rites, 11:28; 13:11; with reference to Christ's blood, 10:19, 29; 12:24; 13:12, 20.

ship of the theological argument; nor do they move forward with the same pursuit of a goal. Nevertheless we may discern direction in their presentation. In general they move from concern about *neglect* of the privileges of Christianity to dire warnings against overt *rejection* of Christ and the community. Eventually they focus on faith (*pistis*) as the character attribute most needed by the Hebrew Christians.

2. The exhortations skillfully proceed from the theological discussion and echo it. Examples: The first exhortation (2:1-4) builds on the superiority of Christ to angels (1:5-14) to argue the greater sinfulness of neglecting the good news that came through Jesus than the Torah given by angel ministration at Sinai. At 5:10 the writer's exposition of Christ as high priest after the order of Melchizedek breaks off sharply as he turns to rebuke the readers for their failure to grow in the Christian life and, hence, for their incapacity to understand the theological point he is making.

Sequence

An Outline of Hebrews[38]

A. The proem, 1:1-4

B. Christ superior to the angels, 1:5-14

C. First exhortation, 2:1-4

D. Christ's temporary inferiority to angels—the necessity of the incarnation, 2:5-18

E. Christ superior to Moses, 3:1-6a

F. Second exhortation—"Rest," 3:6b–4:16
   1. Lessons from Israel, 3:6b-19
   2. Application to Christians, 4:1-16

G. Characteristics of high priests, 5:1-10

H. Third exhortation, 5:11–6:20
   1. Rebuke, 5:11-14
   2. Warning, 6:1-8
   3. Encouragement, 6:9-20

I. Jesus Christ: high priest and sacrifice, 7:1–10:18
   1. Better order of priesthood, 7:1-28
   2. Better sanctuary, 8:1-5
   3. Better covenant, 8:6-13

---

38 The structure suggested here has parallels with, and differences from, that proposed by A. Vanhoye, *La Structure litteraire de l'Épître aux Hébreux* (Paris, 1963). In my judgment the content of Hebrews does not altogether match the literary forms he perceives in the document.

4. Better sacrifice—"better blood," 9:1–10:18
   a. Brief description of the earthly sanctuary, 9:1-5
   b. Limitations of the old cultus, 9:6-10
   c. Summary of the new cultus, 9:11-14
   d. "Objective" benefits of the new cultus, 9:15-28
   e. "Subjective" benefits of the new cultus, 10:1-18
J. Fourth exhortation, 10:19–13:25
   1. Response in view of Christ's work, 10:19-39
   2. Examples of faith, 11:1-39
   3. Encouragement and warning, 12:1-29
      a. Example of Jesus, 12:1-11
      b. Encouragement, 12:12-14
      c. Warning, 12:15-17
      d. Blessings, 12:18-24
      e. Warnings, 12:25-29
   4. Concluding exhortations, 13:1-25

A Holistic View of Hebrews

Our discussion of the structure of Hebrews has shown how theological exposition and practical application alternate and interweave throughout the document. At the same time it has exposed an apparent problem in its unity of thought: There appear to be two theological schemas operative.[39]

The first and major theme forms the exposition. It highlights the human problem of defilement and sets out Christ's work as one of making purification through His blood. It points to the *present* benefits made available to the believer through that work.

The second and minor theme runs through the exhortations. Here the focus is on the danger of apostasy, with faithfulness as the needed quality of life. The concern is *future*-directed: how to preserve the present quality of life and to enter into the future inheritance.

Can these two schemas be brought together under one principle? Yes. The *pilgrimage* concept[40] produces the theological holism in Hebrews.

---

39 The manner in which exposition and exhortation are integrated is the long-standing problem in determining the theological framework of Hebrews: See Grässer, "Der Hebräerbrief 1938-1963."

40 I have explored this idea at some depth in "The Pilgrimage Motif in the Book of Hebrews," *JBL*, vol. 97, No. 2 (1978), pp. 239-51. The concept of pilgrimage has become increasingly remote to Western man; the term itself now is inexact. In an attempt to lend precision to the term, I have drawn upon the model of pilgrimage developed by H. B. Partin, *The Muslim Pilgrimage: Journey to the Center* (Ph.D. dissertation, University of Chicago, 1967). Partin finds four essential elements to pilgrimage: (1) a separation, leaving home; (2) a journey to a sacred place; (3) a

The Christians of Hebrews are viewed as a *religious community on the move*. Each of the two parts of the picture is vital: a cultic or religious community and movement toward the sacred place.

It is because Hebrews sees Christians as a religious community that the "separation" idea is so strong in the document. Christians are "holy," "sanctified," "perfected," "purified"[41]—all cultic terms. They are God's people, even now. It is out of such a self-view that the dire warnings of 6:4-6; 10:26-31; and 12:15-17 become understandable. Because they are a religious community, they are *now* "clean," *now* have access to God, *now* have their consciences purged, *now* have Jesus as high priest. The time frame is past-present. The work of Jesus on Calvary (past) has placed them in full communion with God (present).

But they are also on the march. The pilgrim community (each pilgrim group) is not content merely to separate from home. It sets out on a journey with a definite goal. Although already consecrated and separated, it seeks the center of the universe, the very (actually realized) presence of God. Just so the people of God in Hebrews are on the move.

This theological alternation between cult and exhortation in Hebrews has not been clearly seen by students of the work, inasmuch as the cultus has been generally neglected and/or weakly grasped. The view of Hebrews in terms of the harmonized metaphors of cult and pilgrimage is able to account for these shifts in thought, however.

The defilement-purification concept looks back to their past separation from the world and highlights their present status before God as Christians. The unbelief-faithfulness "set" looks to the future, with particular awareness of perils in the present which may cause the goal to be lost. One may not merely fail to attain the promised "rest"; he may also fall away from the community of God's people.

In similar fashion we may see more clearly how Christ is both "high priest" (*archiereus*) and "pioneer/leader" (*archēgos*), and why the cultic argument points up the "already" and "now," whereas the exhortations call attention to the "not yet" of Christianity. Thus, the recognition of the pilgrimage motif of Hebrews opens up a holistic view of the document.[42]

---

fixed purpose; and (4) hardship. I have tested the data of Hebrews relative to pilgrimage against Partin's model and found close correspondence.

41 Heb 3:1; 13:24; 2:11; 9:13; 10:10, 14, 29; 13:12; 5:14; 7:19; 9:9; 10:1, 14; 11:40; 12:23; 7:11; 12:2; 1:3; 9:14, 22, 23, 10:2.

42 This interpretation of Hebrews in terms of the harmonized metaphors of cult and pilgrimage builds on the work of previous students of the document. It extends the insights of Käsemann, whose *archēgos* ("pioneer/leader") Christology did not give due weight to the *archiereus* ("high priest")

Nature of the Document

In most respects the letters of the NT follow a similar pattern to ours. When Paul, for instance, writes to Christians in Galatia, Rome, Philippi, Colossae, or Corinth, or to his friend Philemon, we find words of greeting, personal wishes, and discussion of items as they come to mind. A stylized closing marked by mention of individuals, and a Christian benediction concludes the correspondence. Such documents resemble letters a Christian pastor today might write to a congregation he previously shepherded, or to a church member. The only significant difference is the beginning. Whereas we commence with the person(s) addressed ("Dear John . . .") and close with the writer's name ("Yours truly, Agnes"), Paul immediately identifies himself: "Paul, an apostle of Jesus Christ, . . . to the church at . . ."[43]

But Hebrews is different. We find no identification of the author, no mention of the recipients, no word of greeting. Instead, the document plunges headlong into a profound theological statement: "In many and various ways God spoke. . . ." Nor does the writing show that spontaneous, itemized character, taking up topics, problems, or questions in turn, that we expect in a letter. Instead it follows the form of a measured argument that rolls on in a calculated, steady flow. It is not, we might say, the mountain stream, with rapids, crosscurrents, side eddies, even whirlpools, of the letter form, but the broad reaches of a river cutting its inexorable track to the sea.

The writer himself calls Hebrews a "word of exhortation" (13:22). Our studies of the purpose and structure of the book show how accurate is this description. Hebrews is not a work of systematic theology per se, although it contains theology systematically worked out. Rather, theology and exhortation blend and dovetail: The writer advances theology in the service of the exhortations, while the exhortations arise out of the theology.

Hebrews, then, is best described as a sermon. Unlike a letter, which may

---

motif and who looked primarily to the expositions for the understanding of *hamartia* ("sin"). See *Das wandernde Gottesvolk,* 1938, pp. 19-27. The essay by C. K. Barrett, "The Eschatology of the Epistle to the Hebrews," in *The Background of the New Testament and Its Eschatology,* eds. W. D. Davies and D. Daube (Cambridge, 1956), sought to relate the "now" with the "not yet"; I have endeavored to show how the concept of a cultic community on the move toward a goal holds these ideas together.

43 Rom 1:1, 7; 1 Cor 1:1-3; 2 Cor 1:1-2; Gal 1:1-5; Eph 1:1-2; Phil 1:1-2; Col 1:1-2; 1 Thess 1:1; 2 Thess 1:1-2; 1 Tim 1:1-2; 2 Tim 1:1-2; Titus 1:1-4; Philm 1-3; cf. James 1:1; 1 Pet 1:1; 2 Pet 1:1; Jude 1. Notice the personalized closing also, such as in Rom 16:1-27; 1 Cor 16:5-24; Gal 6:11-18; Phil 4:14-23; Col 4:7-18; 2 Tim 4:9-22; Titus 3:12-15; Philm 23-25.

emerge out of deep emotion and be written at feverish pace, a sermon results from careful planning. Yet it is not written in isolation from life—it continually has in mind its hearers and their needs. So, in the sermon to the Hebrews, the theological reasoning, for all its complexity, serves a specific, practical end in the lives of its original recipients.

What the theme of that sermon is has become abundantly clear during the course of this chapter. It is the greatness of Christianity, whose Lord is Jesus Christ, our Sacrifice and High Priest, and who has prepared an eternal home that those who live by faith will receive. It is "salvation so great" (2:2), absolute confidence in the presence of God because of the access and purification provided by Jesus, and at last eternity with Him.[44]

The first four verses of the book sound these triumphant strains in an overture of grandeur and resonance. They confront us immediately with the preeminence of Christ: the magnificence of His person as the divine Son—eternal beam of the divine glory and stamp of the divine essence, and with the magnificence of His work—Creator, Upholder, Purifier of sins, regnant King.

Hebrews abounds in superlatives; its key word is "better."[45] Without wresting the development of the book we may set out its pattern around this word as follows:

The better revelation	1:1-4
The better name	1:5–2:18
The better leader	3:1–4:16
The better priest	5:1–6:20
The better priesthood	7:1-27

---

44 Edmund Gosse, in a magnificent passage from *Father and Son,* has captured the force of the language and ideas of Hebrews. " 'The extraordinary beauty of the language—for instance, the matchless cadences and images of the first chapter—made a certain impression upon my imagination, and were (I think) my earliest initiation into the magic of literature. I was incapable of defining what I felt, but I certainly had a grip in the throat, which was in its essence a purely aesthetic emotion, when my father read, in his pure, large, ringing voice, such passages as "The heavens are the work of Thy hands. They shall perish, but Thou remainest, and they shall all wax old as doth a garment, and as a vesture shalt Thou fold them up, and they shall be changed; but Thou art the same, and Thy years shall not fail." But the dialectic parts of the epistle puzzled and confused me. Such metaphysical ideas as "laying again the foundation of repentance from dead works" and "crucifying the Son of God afresh" were not successfully brought down to the level of my understanding.... The melodious language, the divine forensic audacities, the magnificent ebb and flow of argument which make the Epistle to the Hebrews such a miracle, were far beyond my reach, and they only bewildered me' " (quoted in James Moffatt, *A Critical and Exegetical Commentary on the Epistle to the Hebrews* [Edinburgh, 1924]).

45 We read of a better name (1:4), a better hope (7:19), a better covenant (7:22), better promises (8:6), better sacrifices (9:23), a better country (11:16), a better resurrection (11:35), and better blood (12:24).

The better sanctuary	8:1-6
The better covenant	8:7-13
The better sacrifice	9:1–10:18
The better country	10:12–12:2
The better city	12:3–13:25

Relevance Today

Our study of Hebrews has shown how valuable this ancient sermon may be to Christians approaching the close of the second millennium after Christ. Our condition, our need, our preaching—it illumines all of them.

The portrait of the recipients of Hebrews seems strikingly modern. If the passage of the years troubled those early Christians—the seemingly relentless flow of time, uninterrupted by divine event—how much more so today. It is a sad fact that a great many Christians abandoned the hope of the Second Coming long ago.

Modern theories—the evolution of the race, the uniform processes of change, decay, and new life, the inevitability of progress—have shaped twentieth century thought. Indeed, in our age the scientist has become high priest, and the nostrums of the psychologist and sociologist provide balm (apparently) for every malady. When man has been, as it were, analyzed, dissected, and probed, when he seems to fit in with and conform to the natural order, what room remains for a specifically religious dimension?

Then we have the continual pressure of a secular way of thought and life. Christendom, if ever it existed, collapsed with the onset of World War I. We have entered a new Dark Ages for the Christian church, with enormous threats to a truly Christian way in the world. Its temptations are subtle, its allurements beguiling. The high dropout rate among Christians, especially teenagers, should not surprise us, even if it does distress us.

Drop out—or slowly dry up. That is the second danger, as real today as when the writer penned his sermon. Worship becomes a form, prayer a lifeless ritual, church membership a ticket in the Christian "club." One may choose to come and go, to leave and rejoin, almost willy-nilly.

Our need, then, is to hear the same sort of message as the Hebrews. Someone must remind us of the reality of our religion, of its surpassing worth—must tell us again of the glory of our Head. And tell us in such a way that we can grasp it, that it brings us to our senses. Once more we must hear that because our religion is so great, we must take it seriously.

Perhaps, if we can grasp the magnificence of our salvation, if we can see the transcendent dimension, the divine realities of it, then we will cease to be so wishy-washy as Christians. Then we may stand up on our feet and look the world squarely in the eye. Then we shall know for sure who we are and what we are to be.

Absolute confidence—surely here is our need. In the face of the man-centered confidence of the secular age, in defiance of its nonchalant passing by of God and His Word, we need absolute confidence in Him and His rule. We need absolute confidence of our own standing before Him, in the certainty of the triumph of His kingdom.

And suddenly the world is not so sure of itself. Human progress no longer seems inevitable. The close of the second millennium comes with dark prophecies of gloom from the scientists and futurologists as they see the world running out of fossil-fuel energy, clean air, fresh water, food. A secular apocalyptic fills the air. That world also needs to hear the message of absolute confidence borne by Hebrews.

Preachers who read this book will learn much. The writer tells us, first of all, that *theology* is important in preaching. To work and talk revival is meaningless unless it has its necessary theological accompaniment. Likewise, merely to tell the people what they ought to be and do is not enough—to harangue with exhortation is a failure. Perhaps preachers have served up milk for too long. Maybe they themselves need first to dig deeply into the mine of the Word and bring forth, like Matthew's scribe, treasures old and new. Only as the people receive solid food can we expect changes.

The writer's emphasis on the place of rigorous theological effort is shown in a passage that has puzzled exegetes who have struggled to grasp its logic: 5:11–6:2.

In 5:1-10 he embarked upon a careful consideration of the high priesthood of Jesus, bouncing the discussion off the Aaronic priests. He arrives at the point of Jesus' Melchizedekian priesthood—and abruptly stops. In fact, he does not get back to Melchizedek until the end of the next chapter. "About Melchizedek we have much to say," he writes, "much that is difficult to explain, now that you have grown so dull of hearing" (vs. 11, NEB). Then follows the rebuke that they are still infants instead of mature Christians.

In view of his statement in verse 12 that they need "milk" instead of solid food, we would expect him to bring out the baby's bottle. Apparently they will not be able to digest the heavy doctrine about Melchizedek. So in 6:1 we expect him to say, "Let us then go back to the elementary ideas of Christianity. Since you aren't ready for solid food, we'll have to leave Melchizedek alone!" But instead he says just the opposite: "Let us then stop discussing the rudiments of Christianity" (6:1, NEB).

It is the conjunction "then" or "therefore" (*dio*) that makes his logic so curious. We must not dilute its force. In essence, the apostle reasons, "You aren't ready for solid food, but only for milk; therefore let us leave aside milk and give you solid food."

And that is just what he does. After the exhortations of chapter 6, he launches into the most convoluted logic of the whole sermon as he argues about Melchizedek, Abraham, and Jesus. Likewise, 8:1–10:18, while not quite so involved, develops the priestly ministry and sacrifice of Jesus in a highly complex argumentation.

How shall we account for the *therefore* in 6:1? Some scholars have suggested two groups among the Hebrews—one spiritually retarded and the other developed. The writer rebukes the first in 5:11-14 and then goes on to give the advanced teaching about Melchizedek and Christ's ministry to those who are able to appreciate it. The problem with this interpretation is that it entirely lacks support in the text. The author directs his counsels toward all his hearers—we have no hint of a differentiation such as the one suggested.

When we meditate long enough on 5:11–6:2, its logic at last strikes home. The apostle, aware of the spiritual problems of his hearers, has thought through carefully to a solution. They have failed to grow and still are ready only for milk—*but milk will not help them any longer.* Their situation is serious. If they are to be saved from the perils of neglect or rejection, they must take solid food. The *therefore* suggests that *their only hope* is in what he is about to lay before them.

His emphasis upon intellectual activity is unique among the writings of the NT. The apostle declares that theology—even difficult theology—aids Christian growth. In at least some cases of stagnation, the *only hope* will come through the solid food of theology.[46]

Likewise, preaching must address a need. We must carefully think through the spiritual problems of the people and pray and study until we

---

46 Compare this observation from Ellen G. White: "The agency of the Spirit of God does not remove from us the necessity of exercising our faculties and talents, but teaches us how to use every power to the glory of God. The human faculties, when under the special direction of the grace of God, are capable of being used to the best purpose on earth. Ignorance does not increase the humility or spirituality of any professed follower of Christ. The truths of the divine word can be best appreciated by an intellectual Christian. Christ can be best glorified by those who serve Him intelligently."—*Counsels to Parents, Teachers, and Students,* p. 361.

know how to meet them with a blend of theology and exhortation. Too many "sermons" are lectures, interesting discourses. Few arise out of a burning conviction and desire to address human need.

Thus, Hebrews is relevant—highly relevant—to all Christians today. But to Adventists it has special significance.

First, because it directly addresses the problem of the apparent delay in the return of Jesus. It exhorts us not to be "of those who shrink back and are destroyed, but of those who have faith and keep their souls" (10:39). It promises:

> "For yet a little while, and the coming one shall come and shall not tarry" (10:37).

It grounds the hope of the Second Coming squarely in the fact of the first coming:

> "Christ, having been offered once to bear the sins of many, will appear a second time, not to deal with sin but to save those who are eagerly waiting for him" (9:28).

And it bridges the gulf of the years, showing that Christ and heaven are still active on our behalf, as the ministry in the heavenly temple goes forward to its completion.

Second, because it provides the biblical foundation for the doctrine of the heavenly sanctuary. That doctrine is a construct that draws from many biblical sources, but from four books in particular: Leviticus and Hebrews, and Daniel and Revelation. Hebrews is vital for its specific affirmations of a heavenly sanctuary[47] and a heavenly ministry carried on by Christ our great high priest.[48] Hebrews makes concrete what is pointed to by OT types and NT (Revelation) symbols.

Third, because it lifts up Calvary as the "consummation of the ages" (9:26, NEB), the turning point in salvation history that provides for thoroughgoing purification and guarantees that the future will be God's. This emphasis is distinctive of Adventist proclamation: We are preachers of the gospel in the setting of "the hour of his judgment is come" (Rev 14:7).

Fourth, because in Hebrews the gospel comes as promise. God's people are strangers and pilgrims, separated for God, on their way to the heavenly country. Already their blessings are many and large; but they have not yet arrived at the goal. For this reason, in Hebrews as in no other book of the

---

47 See my essay, "The Heavenly Sanctuary—Figurative or Real?" chap. 3 in this volume.
48 See my essay, "Day of Atonement Allusions," chap. 6 in this volume.

Bible, words of resounding assurance confront severe warnings of rejection, and "once-saved-always-saved" is ruled out of court peremptorily.

So the author of Hebrews still speaks, and speaks to Adventists especially. Just as to those first century Christians, so the word rings in our ears: "Today, when you hear his voice, do not harden your hearts" (3:7).

Chapter III

The Heavenly Sanctuary —
Figurative Or Real?

William G. Johnsson

Editorial Synopsis. How shall we regard the references to the heavenly sanctuary in the book of Hebrews? Does the heavenly sanctuary have an objective existence, or is it only an idea? The writer suggests that references to the heavenly sanctuary have been regarded in one of three ways:

1. In a metaphorical manner. This view denies any objective reality; concrete terms are given spiritualized meanings.

2. In a literalistic manner. This perspective would argue that each term has "hard value." The heavenly reality is construed in all aspects to be exactly like the earthly structure.

3. In a literalizing manner. In this view "the reality of the heavenly sanctuary and ministry [is] maintained as safeguarding the *objectivity* of the work of Christ, but precise details of that sanctuary would not be clear to us." This view affirms the *reality* of the heavenly sanctuary, but confesses that we have little data about the appearance of the celestial entity. Most Adventists would accept the latter view.

While Catholic scholars have generally read into the Epistle their liturgical interests, Protestant scholars have tended to neglect the message of Hebrews which focuses on Christ's priesthood. More serious, however, has been the stance to regard Hebrews as only a sustained metaphor. Sacrifices, priests, temples, and the like are taken as "code"—mere metaphorical sanctuary "talk" which in turn must be spiritualized along the line of Philo's view of the cosmos.

The present writer discounts any connection between Philonic thought

---

Reprint of "The Heavenly Cultus in the Book of Hebrews—Figurative or Real?" Arnold V. Wallenkampf and W. Richard Lesher, eds. *The Sanctuary and the Atonement* (Washington, DC: Biblical Research Institute, 1981), pp. 362-79.

and that of Hebrews by demonstrating that the *concepts* expressed in the Epistle are contrary to those entertained by Philo. The passages appealed to are shown to provide no support for the Philonic claim.

The language of the Israelite sanctuary pervades the book and should be taken at its face value. It addresses the very real human problem of sinful defilement. The essential religious need of humanity is a need for purification from sin. The Epistle to the Hebrews does not deal with the cosmological concerns of a Philo but with the great themes of human redemption through the sacrifice and priesthood of Jesus Christ—a redemption foreshadowed, but never accomplished, in the ritual types of the earthly sanctuary.

To that end, the Epistle to the Hebrews "sets out a series of bases for Christian confidence—*real* deity, *real* humanity, a *real* priest, a *real* covenant, a *real* sacrifice, *real* purification, *real* access, and in keeping with these, a *real* heavenly sanctuary and ministry."

Chapter Outline

I. Introduction
II. The Metaphorical Interpretation
III. Critique of the Metaphorical Interpretation
IV. The Realistic (Literal) Interpretation

* * * * * * *

That the book of Hebrews is impregnated with the language of sanctuary, priest, and sacrifice is apparent to even the superficial reader. As I have shown elsewhere,[1] the expressions—which we may term the cultic language of the document—extend beyond the formal theological argumentation. As the original text is searched, the cultic references are seen to pervade the entire work, entering into the exhortations as well as the theology. For example, the verb *proserchomai* ("approach"), used in the exhortations at 4:14-16 and 10:19-22, is a cultic word signifying the approach of the high priest into the very presence of God.[2]

The modern study of Hebrews has not dealt adequately with its cultic language.[3] Protestants in general—perhaps due to their distaste for

---

1 William G. Johnsson, *Defilement and Purgation in the Book of Hebrews* (Ph.D. Dissertation, Vanderbilt University, 1973), chap. 1.
2 See also Heb 7:25; 10:1; 11:6; 12:18, 22.
3 Johnsson, *Defilement and Purgation,* chap. 2; see also Id., "The Cultus of Hebrews in Twentieth-Century Scholarship," *ExpTim* 89/4 (January, 1978): 104-8.

ritual—have tended to neglect the concerns of Hebrews that focus on Jesus as high priest. This is indubitably a major weakness, for thereby the avowedly chief point or pith (*kephalaion,* Heb 8:1-2), of the book is passed over. On the other hand, Catholic scholars throughout this century have manifested a keen interest in the cultus of Hebrews. Very often their works reflect dogmatic concerns, as when writers look for allusions to the Mass in Hebrews.[4] Thus, the question of the interpretation of the cultic language of Hebrews has not come to the fore; it has remained a hidden issue.[5]

Yet the matter is even more involved. Along with the general Protestant neglect of the cultic concerns of Hebrews, there has often been an *implicit* interpretation of the cultic language, which effectively demolishes the force of that language. It is held that the talk of priests, temples, and sacrifices is only a sustained metaphor to explicate the work of Christ.[6] In other words, Hebrews sets out a code, as it were, and we should decipher the code to see the intent of the writing. To dwell only on the language of priest, sanctuary, and sacrifice is to miss the purpose of the document. The talk of a heavenly sanctuary, for instance, does not refer to an actual place in heaven but is to be understood along Philonic lines.[7] Nor are we to visualize an actual priestly work by Christ, or of His blood, as a heavenly sacrifice. These terms are but part of a consistent illustration, or model, of the transcendent work of Christ.[8]

This issue is significant for the Seventh-day Adventist Church when we recall the place that a *realistic* heavenly sanctuary and ministry have in our heritage. Our pioneers and Ellen White long ago looked to the book of Hebrews as strong support for *an actual heavenly sanctuary* and *an actual heavenly work* by Jesus Christ, our *actual High Priest.* To dissolve these realities into metaphorical speech must surely transform Seventh-day

---

4 See William G. Johnsson, "Issues in the Interpretation of Hebrews," *AUSS* 15/2 (1977), Nos. 67-71, for a bibliography of recent Catholic works on Hebrews.

5 Ibid., pp. 169-87.

6 For Jerome Smith (*A Priest for Ever* [London, 1969]) the entire argument of Hebrews is extended metaphor.

7 The most prominent scholars who lean toward this view are James Moffatt (*A Critical and Exegetical Commentary on the Epistle to the Hebrews* [New York, 1924]); E. Käsemann (*Das Wandernde Gottesvolk* [Göttingen, 1939]); F. J. Schierse (*Verheissung und Heilsvollendung: Zur Theologischen Grundfrage des Hebräerbriefes* [Munich, 1955]); E. Grässer (*Der Glaube im Hebräerbrief* [Marburg, 1965]); G. Theissen (*Untersuchungen zum Hebräerbrief* [Gütersloh, 1959]); C. Spicq (*L'Épître aux Hébreux,* 2 vols. [Paris, 1952]); and J. Héring (*The Epistle to the Hebrews* [London, 1970]).

8 Cf. Moffatt, p. xxxi: "The author writes from a religious philosophy of his own — that is, of his own among the NT writers. The philosophical element in his view of the world and God is fundamentally Platonic."

Adventist doctrine. It will reorder our understanding of heavenly reality and our place in the divine flow of events, with the important significance accorded to 1844.

Let me pause to quote just a few of the references to Hebrews in the writings of Ellen White that show a realistic interpretation of the cultic language.

"By virtue of His [Jesus'] death and resurrection He became the minister of the 'true tabernacle, which the Lord pitched, and not man.' Heb. 8:2. Men reared the Jewish tabernacle; men builded the Jewish temple; but the sanctuary above, of which the earthly was a type, was built by no human architect. 'Behold the Man whose name is The Branch; . . . He shall build the temple of the Lord; and He shall bear the glory, and shall sit and rule upon His throne; and He shall be a priest upon His throne.' Zech. 6:12-13.

"The sacrificial service that had pointed to Christ passed away; but the eyes of men were turned to the true sacrifice for the sins of the world. The earthly priesthood ceased; but we look to Jesus, the minister of the new covenant, and 'to the blood of sprinkling, that speaketh better things than that of Abel.' 'The way into the holiest of all was not yet made manifest, while as the first tabernacle was yet standing: . . . but Christ being come an high priest of good things to come, by a greater and more perfect tabernacle, not made with hands, . . . by His own blood He entered in once into the holy place, having obtained eternal redemption for us.' Heb. 12:24; 9:8-12."[9]

"Christ Jesus is represented as continually standing at the altar, momentarily offering up the sacrifice for the sins of the world. He is a minister of the true tabernacle which the Lord pitched and not man. The typical shadows of the Jewish tabernacle no longer possess any virtue. A daily and yearly typical atonement is no longer to be made, but the atoning sacrifice through a mediator is essential because of the constant commission of sin. Jesus is officiating in the presence of God, offering up His shed blood, as it had been a lamb slain. Jesus presents the oblation offered for every offense and every shortcoming of the sinner."[10]

"The question, What is the sanctuary? is clearly answered in the Scriptures. The term 'sanctuary,' as used in the Bible, refers, first, to the tabernacle built by Moses, as a pattern of heavenly things; and, secondly,

---

9 *The Desire of Ages*, pp. 165-66.
10 *The SDA Bible Commentary*, vol. 6, p. 1077.

to the 'true tabernacle' in heaven, to which the earthly sanctuary pointed. At the death of Christ the typical service ended. The 'true tabernacle' in heaven is the sanctuary of the new covenant. And as the prophecy of Daniel 8:14 is fulfilled in this dispensation, the sanctuary to which it refers must be the sanctuary of the new covenant."[11]

"Such was the service performed 'unto the example and shadow of heavenly things.' And what was done in type in the ministration of the earthly sanctuary is done in reality in the ministration of the heavenly sanctuary. After His ascension our Saviour began His work as our high priest. Says Paul: 'Christ is not entered into the holy places made with hands, which are the figures of the true; but into heaven itself, now to appear in the presence of God for us.' Hebrews 9:24.

"The ministration of the priest throughout the year in the first apartment of the sanctuary, 'within the veil' which formed the door and separated the holy place from the outer court, represents the work of ministration upon which Christ entered at His ascension. It was the work of the priest in the daily ministration to present before God the blood of the sin offering, also the incense which ascended with the prayers of Israel. So did Christ plead His blood before the Father in behalf of sinners, and present before Him also, with the precious fragrance of His own righteousness, the prayers of penitent believers. Such was the work of ministration in the first apartment of the sanctuary in heaven.

"Thither the faith of Christ's disciples followed Him as He ascended from their sight. Here their hopes centered, 'which hope we have,' said Paul, 'as an anchor of the soul, both sure and steadfast, and which entereth into that within the veil; whither the forerunner is for us entered, even Jesus, made an high priest forever.' 'Neither by the blood of goats and calves, but by His own blood He entered in once into the holy place, having obtained eternal redemption for us.' Hebrews 6:19, 20; 9:12.

"For eighteen centuries this work of ministration continued in the first apartment of the sanctuary."[12]

In contrast, the "metaphorical" or "spiritualizing" interpretation (we shall use these terms interchangeably in this chapter, as opposed to a "realistic" or "literal" interpretation) has the following outcome: (1) no actual heavenly sanctuary—"the heavenly sanctuary" is a metaphor for "the universe," (2) no actual heavenly *priesthood* of Christ—the language

---

11 *The Great Controversy,* pp. 417.
12 Ibid., pp. 420-21.

is interpreted eventually in subjective terms to mean the Christian *experience* of salvation (even some conservative interpreters eventually reach this position),[13] (3) no "cleansing" of the heavenly sanctuary; hence, no possibility of holding to 1844 as indicative of an objective heavenly event marking a new phase of an objective heavenly ministry by Christ.

It is possible that some Seventh-day Adventist students of Hebrews have been influenced toward the metaphorical school of interpretation. Of course, some might argue that such a viewpoint does not necessarily signal an abandonment of our historic sanctuary doctrine—they might appeal to Daniel and Revelation for that. It would seem, however, that if Hebrews were interpreted metaphorically, that doctrine must be seriously weakened; manifestly, it is Hebrews that, on the face of it, presents the strongest statements in the Bible in support of an actual heavenly sanctuary and ministry.

In this chapter, then, we shall address this most basic issue of understanding Hebrews: Is the cultic language of Hebrews to be interpreted metaphorically (spiritually) or realistically (literally)?[14] We shall proceed in three steps: (1) the case for a metaphorical interpretation, (2) a critique of the metaphorical viewpoint, and (3) the case for a realistic interpretation.

The Metaphorical Interpretation

The arguments in favor of this point of view may be classified as both conceptual and exegetical. That is, appeal is made on a broad front to the cosmology of Hebrews, whereas specific *verses* involving cultic language *are adduced* as clues to the metaphorical intent of the document. We will take up each view in turn.

The Conceptual Interpretation

It is held that the thought-world of hellenistic Judaism, and in particular the writings of Philo Judaeus,[15] furnish the backdrop for the cultic language of Hebrews. When Philo wrote of a heavenly sanctuary and liturgy,

---

13 Note, for instance, how F. F. Bruce in his commentary on Hebrews (*The Epistle to the Hebrews* [London, 1971]) appears to favor a realistic heavenly sanctuary in Hebrews 8:1-5, but by 10:19-22 he has allegorized the veil to denote the flesh of Christ.

14 Note: This chapter does *not* take up Ellen G. White's statements relative to Hebrews. These statements, which raise certain issues of their own, nevertheless obviously hold to a realistic heavenly sanctuary. Issues raised by these statements are handled by other chapters in *The Sanctuary and the Atonement*, eds. A. V. Wallenkampf and W. R. Lesher (Washington, DC, 1981).

15 The dates for Philo are uncertain: ca. 20 B.C. to ca. A.D. 50.

he had a cosmic view in which the *theios logos* ("divine word") was the priest: "The highest, and in the truest sense the holy temple of God is, as we must believe, the whole universe, having for its sanctuary the most sacred part of all existence, even heaven, for its votive ornaments of the stars, for its priests the angels who are servitors to His powers, unbodied souls, not compounds of rational and irrational nature."[16]

"It was determined, therefore, to fashion a tabernacle, a work of the highest sanctity, the construction of which was set forth to Moses on the mount by divine pronouncements. He saw with the soul's eye the immaterial forms of the material objects about to be made, and these forms had to be reproduced in copies perceived by the senses, taken from the original draft . . . and from patterns conceived in the mind. For it was fitting that the construction of the sanctuary should be committed to him who was truly high priest, in order that his performance of the rites belonging to the sacred office might be in more full accordance and harmony with the fabric."[17]

"An angel is an intellectual soul or rather wholly mind, wholly incorporeal, made (to be) a minister of God, and appointed over certain needs and the service of the race of mortals, since it was unable, because of its corruptible nature, to receive the gifts and benefactions extended by God. . . . (Therefore) of necessity was the Logos appointed as judge and mediator, who is called 'angel.'

"And a very clear proof of this is that the divine name is called upon the angel. And this is the most sovereign and principal (being) which the heaven and earth and whole world knows."[18]

Hebrews, it is claimed, shares this conceptual world. In support, it can be pointed out that the very terms used by Hebrews to describe the relation of the earthly sanctuary to the heavenly—*skia* ("shadow"), *eikōn* ("image"), and *hupodeigma* ("example," "copy")—have Platonic roots and are used by Philo in the same setting.[19] More importantly, however, Hebrews shares with Philo the Platonic cosmological dualism whereby the unseen is the ultimately real—the seen is transient. Hebrews 8:2 speaks of the *alēthinos*—the genuine, or real—whereas throughout chapter 11 the contrast is drawn between the earthly, which is temporary and ultimately

---

16 *De specialibus legibus,* I.xii.66 in LCL, *Philo,* VII:137, 139.

17 *De Vita Mosis,* II.xv.74 in LCL, *Philo,* VI:485, 487.

18 *Quaestiones et Solutiones in Exodum,* II.13, in LCL, *Philo,* Supp. II: 48, 51.

19 See Moffatt, xxxi-xxxiv, pp. 104-6, 135; also W. F. Howard, *The Fourth Gospel in Recent Criticism and Interpretation* (London, 1955), p. 115.

unreal even though seen, and the heavenly, which is permanent of God and ultimately real, though unseen.[20]

The idea of looking to Philo to provide the conceptual key for Hebrews has a strong tradition among commentators. Moffatt, in the ICC,[21] is probably the most influential. However, even where the relation to Philo is not directly acknowledged, exegetes of Hebrews often betray at least partial adherence to this interpretation.

A recent Harvard dissertation, L.K.K. Dey's *The Intermediary World and Patterns of Perfection in Philo and Hebrews,*[22] argues extensively for the Philonic-type world of Hebrews. Going beyond the old arguments based on chapters 8, 9, and 11, chapters 1-7 reason that the discussion of angels, Moses, "perfection," Aaron, and Melchizedek all proceed from a base in Philo's categories.[23]

If, then, the book of Hebrews is using the language of heavenly sanctuary and liturgy as Philo employs it (although in a Christianized sense so as to give Christ pride of place), it would be a grave misunderstanding of the document to understand an *actual* temple and work.

The Exegetical Interpretation

Several verses and expressions in the cultic argumentation of Hebrews 9:1–10:18 are said to give us clues to the cultic language.

1. The earthly sanctuary (*hagion kosmikon*), (9:1). The term *to hagion* in the LXX frequently means the whole sanctuary, as in Exodus 36:3 and Numbers 3:38.[24] What does *kosmikon* signify here? For Philo (and Josephus as well)[25] the earthly sanctuary was symbolic of the cosmos. The phrase *hagion kosmikon* would then be viewed as "a symbol of action worked upon the stage of this world to illustrate what was doing or to be done on a higher plane."[26] That is, *kosmikon* is here seen as a predicate use of the adjective, and the phrase *hagion kosmikon* should be translated "earthly tabernacle with a cosmic pattern."

2. The "first tent" (*skēnē hē prōtē*), (9:2). What is the precise referent of this term? Although it is clear in 9:2-4 that emphasis is upon the

---

20 See esp. Hebrews 11:1, 2, 6, 7, 10, 13-16, 26-27, 39-40.

21 See n. 7.

22 *SBL* Dissertation Series 25 (Missoula, MT, 1975).

23 It is significant that Dey does not attempt to embrace Hebrews 8-10 in his thesis.

24 A. P. Salom ("*ta hagia* in the Epistle to the Hebrews," *AUSS* 5 [January, 1967]: 60) holds that of 170 uses of *to hagion,* 142 refer to the sanctuary in general. See Appendix A for reprint of this article

25 *Ant.* III. 6:4; III, 7:7.

26 Moffatt, p. 113.

distinction between the first and second rooms of the tabernacle (shown by the discussion of the furnishings), it is held that we here have a clue to the nature of the heavenly sanctuary. The two tents (apartments) suggest the contrast between the earthly and the heavenly sanctuaries: the holy place with its mundane objects as a symbol of earth; the Most Holy Place is a symbol of heaven.

3. The "Holy of Holies" *(hagia hagiōn)*, **(9:3).** This is a reference to the heavenly sanctuary. In support of this viewpoint, reference is made to Hebrews 9:8-9, where the holy place is a symbol of the old age (the *kairos enestēkos*) and the Holy of Holies is a symbol of the new age (the *kairon diorthōseōs*).[27] According to this interpretation we see that Hebrews, although employing sanctuary terminology, is attaching allegorical significance to it.[28]

4. The "greater and more perfect tent" (9:11). The interpretation centers on the force of the use of the first *dia* ("through" or "by") in the sentence. It may be taken as instrumental and, indeed, is so used in verse 12.[29] This verse suggests that Christ obtained access to God through "a greater and more perfect tent, an instrument not made with hands," that is, His body. Then *skēnē* ("tent") corresponds to the earthly existence of Christ.

Elsewhere in the NT the body of Jesus is called a temple (Mark 14:58; John 1:14; 2:19; Col 2:9), and the book of Hebrews has earlier argued for the *necessity* of the incarnation (2:14-16; 5:7). That is, the body of Jesus becomes the instrument of God's salvation on earth. U. Luk further argues for this position on the basis of Hebrews 10:5 and onward, holding that Jesus in His existence as the "heavenly temple" brought the heavenly sanctuary to earth in His life. Thus His priestly service on the cross is carried out in His own body as temple; in the life and death of Jesus, heaven and earth meet dynamically.[30]

5. "The veil, that is His flesh" (10:19-20). The metaphorical interpretation looks to these verses for its strongest support. Whereas the earlier references required careful reasoning, here it is claimed we have evidence of a clear-cut spiritualizing intent—the veil of the heavenly sanctuary is identified with the flesh (or body) of Christ.[31]

---

27 So Schierse, pp. 29-33.

28 See also U. Luk, "Himmlisches and Irdisches Geschehen im Hebrärief," *NovT* (1963), p. 211.

29 Hebrews 9:11-12 form a continuous sentence; thus, it is argued *dia* should be used consistently throughout (i.e., instrumentally).

30 Luk, pp. 209-10.

31 It is interesting to notice how G. W. Buchanan (*To the Hebrews*, AB [New York, 1972]) handles this passage. His commentary rigidly opposes the metaphorical view throughout, arguing for an

Just as the curtain is the border between access and nonaccess to God in the Jewish temple, so the existence of Jesus marked a border point between heaven and earth.[32] However, a curtain hides as well as gives access. So only upon the death of Christ was the veil removed and His true role as priest revealed. Clearly, then, if the veil of the heavenly sanctuary is code for His flesh, we may likewise decode the entire sanctuary description and no longer see a realistic heavenly sanctuary and liturgy intended.

It is apparent, therefore, that a significant case for a spiritualizing interpretation of the sanctuary language of Hebrews can be made. Although most of the individual supports are small, the cumulative effect is weighty. Therefore, let us now engage this interpretation in a critique.

Critique of the Metaphorical Interpretation

We shall proceed in a step-by-step examination of the above case, looking first at the conceptual data and then at the detailed exegesis.

Conceptual

Only in the most general sense can we hold that the thought-world of Hebrews conforms to that of Philo. We may agree that Hebrews, like Plato and Philo, locates the ultimately real outside the sensory realm. However, this idea of looking to the extrasensory, or heavenly, for the genuine is not the exclusive province of Plato and Philo.[33] It is a part of the biblical view of reality. This is succinctly stated in 2 Corinthians 4:18—"Because we look not to the things that are seen but to the things that are unseen; for the things that are seen are transient, but the things that are unseen are eternal."

In three aspects the sanctuary of Hebrews is especially noteworthy:

1. Hebrews insists that Christ enters into a *place* of heavenly ministry—4:14, He "passed through the heavens"; 4:15, we *have* a high priest; 4:16, the "throne of grace" supplies timely help; 6:19-20, Jesus has gone "into the inner shrine behind the curtain"; 8:1-2, "we *have* such a high priest ... a minister in the sanctuary and the true tent"; 8:6, "Christ has obtained a more excellent ministry"; 9:12, "He entered once for all"; 9:24, "Christ has entered ... heaven itself"; 10:12, "He sat down at the right hand of God."

This concern with place runs counter to the Philonic idea. The ulti-

---

extremely literalistic interpretation. Here, however, he suggests that phrase "that is, his flesh" is a later gloss—surely a weak response!

32 N. Dahl, "A New and Living Way," *Int.*, 5:401-12.

33 It belongs, in fact, to ancient Near Eastern thought in general.

mately real is accessible only by the intellect. To speak, as Hebrews appears to, of an actual entry into a place would be absurd.[34]

2. The *temporal* emphasis of Hebrews is a decisive blow to Philonic interpretation, and in my judgment, incontrovertible. Hebrews not only speaks of "the genuine," as opposed to the seen, but also argues that "the genuine" relates to a point in time. We note in 10:1 that "the law has but a *shadow of the good things* to come." By the Philonic model, the real eternally juxtaposes the transient, that which is *skia* ("shadow"); but here the ultimately real has a *coming* aspect. Is not this the entire thrust of the argument that runs from Hebrews 1:5–10:18? We are shown the necessity both for deity and for humanity of the Son, "so that he might become a merciful and faithful high priest" (2:17). The divine word of designation (5:5-6; cf. 7:20-21) is part of this pattern. Likewise in Hebrews 8:3, "Hence it is necessary for this priest also to have something to offer."

The net effect of this reasoning is to show that Jesus has *become* our heavenly high priest. The once-for-all affirmations[35] point to the all-sufficient sacrifice of Himself which Calvary affords. Because of that offering, all barriers are broken down between God and man, removing the need for animal sacrifices. Thus, Hebrews focuses on the *temporal* aspect: first, of the becoming-man of the Son (the Incarnation); and second, of the sacrifice of Himself on Calvary. Both of these fulfillments enable Him to *enter upon* His heavenly ministry.

With these ideas the sanctuary language of Hebrews diverges sharply from the Philonic model. We can no longer hold to an eternal, unchanged, and unchanging heavenly order, far removed from and untouched by events on this earth.[36]

3. The third point is even more drastic. "Thus it was necessary for the copies of the heavenly things to be purified with these rites, but the heavenly things themselves with better sacrifices than these" (Heb 9:23). The thought that there should be any need to modify heavenly things staggers the mind, even as it utterly confounds some commentators![37] The Platonic model alone is clearly inadequate here.

It seems then that Hebrews, although employing terminology and some concepts that parallel Philo's usage, has its own distinctive content of meaning. It should be studied on its own terms without reading in ideas

---

34 R. Williamson, "Platonism and Hebrews," *SJT* 16 (1963): 419.
35 Heb 6:4; 9:7, 26-28; 10:2; 12:26-27 (*hapax*); Heb 7:27; 9:12; 10:10 (*ephapax*).
36 Cf. Buchanan, p. 134.
37 Note, e.g., the response of Spicq at such a thought: "nonsense" (II:267).

from Philo. Some recent interpreters of Hebrews have reexamined the alleged Philonic relationship and have reached a negative verdict. Such was the conclusion of Ronald Williamson in his dissertation *Philo and the Epistle to the Hebrews,*[38] which took up this specific topic. A. McNicol, in *The Relationship of the Image of the Highest Angel to the High Priest Concept in Hebrews,*[39] likewise argues against a Philonic basis.

We must now take up the exegetical material. Granted that the conceptual framework of Hebrews diverges from Philo's, we must still test the cultic language to see whether it is being used in a spiritualizing manner. We shall take up in turn the passages previously noticed where such an intent is said to be evidenced.

Exegetical

1. The *hagion kosmikon* (9:1). The simplest way to understand this text is to see *kosmikon* as a substantival use of the adjective. Then *hagion kosmikon* is merely a reference to the tabernacle of the Jewish covenant, nothing more. The context surely points us in this direction.

In chapter 8 the discussion centers on the two covenants, with Jeremiah's citation giving the prediction of the new *diathēkē* ("covenant"). In 9:1 we read that "the first [covenant] had a worldly [or earthly] sanctuary," and the next nine verses elaborate on the statement. Verses 1-5 give a thumbnail sketch of that sanctuary, and verses 6-10 briefly describe its services, which are shown to be limited in *access* to the presence of God. Thus, *kosmikon* in 9:1 stands in contrast to *epouranios* ("heavenly"),[40] just as 9:1-10 sets the stage for the account of the *heavenly* ministry of Christ, which will be elaborated on in 9:11–10:18. Just as the first *diathēkē* has its sanctuary (the *kosmikon* or "earthly"), so the new *diathēkē,* inaugurated by the blood of Christ (9:15-18), has a sanctuary (the heavenly—9:24-26). Therefore, to bring in speculation about the cosmos at 9:1 is quite unwarranted from the context.

2. The *skēnē hē protē* (9:2). The term in context is clearly for the purpose of making a distinction between the first apartment and the Second Apartment of the earthly sanctuary. The brief account of the furnishings of each makes this point. The issue is whether to read allegorical significance into these two apartments, so that they have separate referents—*hē protē skēnē* signifying the first sanctuary/age/covenant and *hē deutera* ("second")

---

38 Leiden, 1970.
39 Ph.D. dissertation, Vanderbilt University, 1974.
40 Heb 8:5; 9:23 (see also 3:1; 6:4; 11:16; 12:22).

46

skēnē signifying the heavenly sanctuary/new age/new covenant. If this is the intent of the passage, it surely has been well disguised. We note:

a. How the discussion of the two apartments ends abruptly with *peri hōn ouk estin nun legein kata meros:* "We will not say more about this now." That is to say, we are discouraged from looking into the details of these two apartments for hidden significances.

b. Hebrews 9:6-10 immediately follows with a description of the services of the earthly sanctuary, not in a way supportive of the allegorizing view. The Second Apartment is not set forth as the place of unhindered access; indeed, the high priest could enter it only once a year and "not without blood" (9:7). In other words, the entire passage, 9:1-10, hangs together as a description of the old sanctuary and its services. *In toto,* the old cultus was inadequate in two points: the limited access and the lack of finality in its offerings (shown by its failure to "perfect" the *suneidēsis* ["conscience"] of the worshiper—see 9:9).[41]

c. The subsequent argument is that 9:11–10:18 shows how Christ's death and heavenly sanctuary ministry accomplish all that the old cultus could not. It both breaks down all barriers between God and man[42] and provides an all-sufficient, final sacrifice[43] so that no more reminder of sins is necessary.[44] In this long argumentation, although we do find occasional contrasting of the old cultus with the new,[45] we do *not* find the contrast made in terms of the two apartments of the earthly sanctuary.

Thus, the *entire* earthly sanctuary, not merely its first apartment, was a parable of the old era, at the time then present (*ton kairon ton enestēkota*), which fulfills God's purposes "until the time of reformation" (9:10).[46]

3. "The greater and more perfect tent" (9:11). To interpret *skēnē* as the bodily existence of Jesus is unwarranted. In all other references to *skēnē* in the book of Hebrews (8:1, 5; 9:2, 3, 6, 8, 21; 11:9; 13:10), the meaning is clearly the sanctuary. Nor is the noun *skēnē* ever used elsewhere in the NT for the body of Jesus. The point is a strong one because Hebrews in particular—perhaps as no other book of the NT—emphasizes the humanity

---

41 I have developed the exegesis of 9:1–10:18 in some detail in *Defilement and Purgation,* chap. 4 of my dissertation. See a briefer discussion in chap. 5 of this book.

42 Heb 4:14-16; 6:19-20; 9:6-12, 24-25; 10:19-22; 12:18-24.

43 Heb 2:17; 7:27; 8:3; 9:13-14, 15-24, 26-28; 10:4, 11-14.

44 Heb 9:9-10; 10:1-4, 15-18.

45 Heb 9:6-10, 13-14, 18-23; 10:1-4.

46 The same conclusion is reached by McNicol, pp. 153-58, and O. Hofius, "Das Erste und das zweite Zelt—ein Beitrag zur Auslegung von Heb 9:1-10," *Zeitschrift für die neutestamentliche Wissenschaft und die Kunde des Urchristentums* 61, Nos. 3-4 (1970): 274-75.

of Jesus. But the term is *sarx* (2:14; 5:7; 9:10, 13-14; 10:20; 12:9). In 8:2 Christ is called *leitourgos* ("minister") of the heavenly sanctuary, and the latter is immediately described as *tēs skēnēs tēs alēthinēs* ("of the true tent"). This reference alone would appear to negate the metaphorical interpretation of 9:11.

What, then, of the force of *dia* in verse 11? The oft-repeated argument for consistency—that is, since in verse 12 *dia* clearly has an instrumental sense ("through His own blood"), it must have the same sense earlier in the long sentence (that is, at the beginning of verse 11)—is not sound. It has been clearly demonstrated that elsewhere in the NT the same preposition may function in different senses even though in immediate succession.[47] Thus, *dia* in verse 11 is to be interpreted locally. We have a description of Christ ascending to the real sanctuary, the heavenly. The passage is parallel to 4:14, "a great high priest who has *passed through* the heavens"; to 6:19-20, "He *entered* within the veil"; to 8:1-2, "we have a high priest who is seated at the right hand of the throne of the Majesty *in heaven*"; and to 9:24-25, "Christ has *entered*, not into a sanctuary made with hands . . . , but *heaven itself.*"

4. **"The veil, that is, his flesh" (10:19-20).** Here the metaphorical interpretation seeks its final support. On examination, however, this view, which seems convincing to the casual reader of the KJV, is impossible. If we are to say that *katapetasma* equals flesh, what will we do with the earlier references to the veil? The "second veil" of 9:3 is indubitably a literal curtain, the divider between the holy place and the Most Holy Place in the OT sanctuary. The passage of 6:19-20, furthermore, is impossible to interpret allegorically. Christ, as our forerunner, has *entered* "within the veil . . . having become a high priest after the order of Melchizedek." By no stretch of the imagination can *katapetasma* ("veil") here equal Christ's flesh. A local use must be held, and notice the parallels between 6:19-20 and 10:19-20, 22:

6:19-20	10:19-20, 22
Confidence ("anchor of the soul")	Boldness
Christ entered	Christ inaugurated
High priest	Great priest
Veil	Veil
Forerunner	For us . . . let us draw near

---

47 O. Hofius, "Inkarnation und Opfertod Jesu nach Hebr 10, 19f.," *Der Ruf Jesu und die Antwort der Gemeinde,* ed. E. Lohse, C. Burchard, and B. Schaller (Göttingen, 1970), pp. 132-41.

How, then, are we to understand the expression "the veil, that is, His flesh"? We can understand it only by a restudy of 10:19-20 in totality. Simply because "that is, His flesh" immediately follows *katapetasmatos* does not *necessarily* mean that it must be attached to it in meaning. The alternative is to see *hodon* ("way") as the referent, as have the translators of the NEB—"So now, my friends, the blood of Jesus makes us free to enter boldly into the sanctuary by the new, living way which he has opened for us through the curtain, the way of his flesh" (10:19-20).

A further argument was supplied by Jeremias,[48] who has convincingly pointed out the *chiastic* structure of 10:19-20, which shows that *hodon* is indeed to be attached in meaning to *tout' estin tes sarkos autou* (that is of His flesh).

Verse 19	Verse 20
(a) "for entrance into" (*eis tēn eisodon*)	(a) "a way newly made and living" (*hodon prosphaton kai zōsan*)
(b) "the holies" (*tōn hagiōn*)	(b) "through the veil" (*dia tou katapetasmatos*)
(c) "by the blood of Jesus" (*en tō haimati Iēsou*)	(c) "that is of His flesh" (*tout' estin tēs sarkos autou*)

Thus, upon examination of each of the passages in Hebrews that are adduced in favor of a metaphorical interpretation of the heavenly cultus, we see that they do not provide the support that is often claimed.

The Realistic (Literal) Interpretation

We hardly need to add to our comments above. We have seen early in the chapter how cultic language permeates the book of Hebrews. So all-pervasive is this factor that we are warranted in stating that *unless we are given convincing indications in the writing that this language is not to be taken at face value, we are obliged to take it seriously.* Only if the cultic argumentation were to be meaningless in its own right could we be justified in jettisoning a literal interpretation of Hebrews.

But a realistic interpretation is in no wise meaningless! I have shown elsewhere[49] how man's "problem," defilement, is expressed in Hebrews in the most basic manner, proving that his religious need is purification. These ideas are at the very core of Hebrews, and they are cultic terms.

---

48 J. Jeremias, "Hebräer 10:20—*tout estin tēs sarkos autou.*" *ZNW* 62 (1971): 131. This article supports the conclusion previously reached by O. Hofius (n. 46).
49 Johnsson, *Defilement and Purgation.*

We may add in brief just two points to the above. First, the realistic interpretation is altogether in keeping with the homiletical purpose of Hebrews. That purpose, as shown by a study of the exhortations,[50] is to build up confidence in the work of Christ, to show the superiority of the Christian religion, to warn against either a gradual neglect or an overt rejection, and to encourage perseverance to the end. The document thus sets out a series of bases for Christian confidence—*real* deity, *real* humanity, a *real* priest, a *real* covenant, a *real* sacrifice, *real* purification, *real* access, and in keeping with these, a *real* heavenly sanctuary and ministry.

Second, we should not suppose that all Jews of the first century held a metaphorical view of the heavenly cultus. In fact, it is becoming more and more clear that many Jewish groups believed in a realistic heavenly sanctuary and liturgy. The apocalyptic writings of Judaism indicate such a conception, for example, "And in it [the heavenly tabernacle] are the angels of the presence of the Lord, who minister and make propitiation for the Lord for all the sins of the ignorance of the righteous and they offer to the Lord a sweet-smelling savor, a reasonable and bloodless offering."[51] "And may the Lord give to thee . . . to serve in His sanctuary as the angels of the presence and the holy ones."[52] "Draw near unto God and unto the angel that intercedeth for you, for he is a mediator between God and man."[53]

In showing these parallels, we do not wish to suggest that Hebrews is dependent on such nonbiblical sources. Indeed, the presentation of Hebrews is uniquely Christian and Christocentric. Instead of angelic ministers, it knows of only one High Priest—Jesus Christ. Instead of exalting Melchizedek, it shows that he merely typified Christ.[54] However, being aware of these other ideas relative to a heavenly cultus, concurrent with first-century Christianity, is helpful in at least two ways: (1) We are better able to understand the cultic language of Hebrews; while it partakes of conceptions found in the apocalypticists as well as Philo, it cannot be termed "Philonic" without serious qualification. (2) We are able to understand the concerns of Hebrews in taking up the role of angels and the role of Melchizedek.[55]

Finally, as seems clear, a realistic literal interpretation of the cultic

---

50 Heb 2:1-4; 3:7–4:16; 5:11–6:18; 10:32-39; 12:1–13:21.
51 *Test. of Levi* 3:5-7.
52 *Jubilees* 31:14.
53 *Test. of Dan* 6:2.
54 There is strong evidence of Melchizedek exaltation among the Qumran sect.
55 One of the Dead Sea Scrolls refers to a mediatorial role of Melchizedek in the heavenly sanctuary.

language of Hebrews is called for by the evidence of the text. How *literalistic* should we be? For example, when we read of the "blood" of Christ,[56] are we to understand His *actual* blood being offered in the heavenly sanctuary? We are led, therefore, to see three possible ways of interpreting Hebrews: (1) metaphorical or spiritual, which is deficient, as we have tried to show in this chapter; (2) literalistic, in which each term has hard value—for the heavenly sanctuary, the earthly would be a miniature in all respects; and (3) literalizing, in which the reality of the heavenly sanctuary and ministry would be maintained as safeguarding the *objectivity* of the work of Christ, but precise details of that sanctuary would not be clear to us.

In my judgment, the book of Hebrews does not help us decisively to resolve 2 and 3 as stated above. Although the argument does not necessarily exclude the possibility that the heavenly sanctuary is a glorified version of the earthly, we should note: (1) The *heavenly* is the genuine, the true, so we should see the earthly in light of the heavenly, rather than vice versa.[57] (2) In 9:24 we read merely of "heaven," surely a very general sort of description. (3) The lack of interest in drawing lines of comparison from the earthly to the heavenly is shown by the terse words in 9:5. And (4) the emphasis in 9:1–10:18 falls on the *work* Christ accomplishes; there seems to be no interest in giving details as to surroundings. It is therefore apparent that, while we may affirm the *reality* of the heavenly sanctuary in the book of Hebrews, we have comparatively little hard data about its appearance.

56 Heb 9:12, 14; 10:19, 29; 12:24; 13:12, 20.
57 Heb 8:1-5.

Chapter IV

An Exegesis Of Selected Passages

Herbert Kiesler

Editorial Synopsis. Seventh-day Adventists teach that the priestly ministry of Christ in the heavenly sanctuary consists of two distinct phases or ministrations. The nature and sequence of the daily and yearly services connected with the holy and Most Holy places of the typical earthly sanctuary provide the biblical basis for the belief.

This doctrine of Christ's priesthood entwines with Adventist understanding of certain prophecies in Daniel and Revelation and the church's origins. Arising out of the mid-nineteenth century interfaith Millerite movement in North America, Seventh-day Adventists came to believe through the study of the Scriptures that in 1844 (the close of the 2300 year prophecy—Dan 8-9) Christ began the second phase of His priestly service.

According to the sanctuary type, as well as the prophecies, this second and final phase of ministry constitutes a preadvent judgment, the initial phase of the final judgment (Lev 16; Dan 7:9-10, 13-14; Rev 14:6-7). Christ continues this ministry, along with His intercession in behalf of sinners, until the close of human probation when He returns the second time for His people in the glory of His kingdom as King of kings and Lord of lords (Rev 19:11-16; Heb 9:28).

From time to time opponents have suggested that the Epistle to the Hebrews denies the Adventist position of a two-phased priestly ministry for Christ. Hebrews, it is argued, teaches that Christ at His ascension was enthroned at God's right hand in the Most Holy Place of the heavenly sanctuary to begin His priestly work. Therefore, He could not have entered upon a second phase of ministry analogous to the Most Holy Place ministry in the earthly sanctuary in 1844.

The question then is whether the Epistle to the Hebrews does indeed deny the doctrine of Christ's two-phased priestly ministry which appears so evident from the sanctuary type. In this chapter the author examines the major passages in Hebrews that are central to the question.

It will be evident at once that biblical scholars are not in full agreement on the precise meaning of these passages, although their general thrust is clear. A pivotal text is Hebrews 9:8. Its translation will affect the reader's understanding of the author's subsequent argument. The translators of the *New International Version* inferred that the author was speaking about the Most Holy Place of the heavenly sanctuary and translated the passage as follows: "The Holy Spirit was showing by this that the way into the Most Holy Place had not yet been disclosed as long as the first tabernacle was still standing."

This interpretive translation of 9:8 led to the rendering of verse 12 in this manner: "He [Christ] did not enter by means of the blood of goats and calves; but he entered the Most Holy Place once for all by his own blood, having obtained eternal redemption."

On the other hand scholars who translated the *New English Bible* took an entirely different position on this crucial passage which they inferred to be speaking in general terms about the heavenly sanctuary: "By this the Holy Spirit signifies that so long as the earlier tent still stands, the way into the sanctuary remains unrevealed."

This led them to translate verse 12 thus: "The blood of his sacrifice is his own blood, not the blood of goats and calves; and thus he [Christ] has entered the sanctuary once and for all and secured an eternal deliverance."

While one group of scholars interpretively translates the Greek term to mean that Christ entered the *Most Holy Place* of the heavenly sanctuary upon His ascension, another group interprets the same terminology to mean simply that Christ entered *the heavenly sanctuary.*

This scholarly ambivalence suggests a certain ambiguity on the part of the author of Hebrews. The fact that he makes only general references to both the daily (7:27; 10:11-12) and the yearly rituals (9:25; 10:3) implies that he is not concerned to detail the meaning and significance of the two phases of priestly ministration. Rather, his focus is on the broader necessity to move dispirited Christians away from their trust in the worn-out rituals of the temple service. He desires to direct their attention to the reality of Jesus Christ, their Saviour, who alone can purge their sin.

Thus it appears that the author's objective is not to explain in depth the nature of Christ's priestly ministrations, but to underscore the inadequacy of the Levitical system so as to fasten the faith of believers on the living High Priest in God's presence who provided a better sacrifice and inaugurated a better priesthood in a better sanctuary of a better covenant.

Chapter Outline

*   *   *   *   *   *   *

Introduction

To Seventh-day Adventists the heavenly ministry of Jesus Christ is of vital importance. By comparing the teachings of Hebrews, Leviticus, and the prophetic statements of Daniel 7-9, Adventists have reached a unique understanding of Christ's role and function in the heavenly sanctuary.

In this present study we will not make a presentation of the sanctuary doctrine. Rather, we will attempt to determine the role and function of Jesus as our great High Priest from the data provided by the author of Hebrews. Thus we read to understand the message Hebrews conveyed to its original hearers as far as possible. Our appreciation of the historical situation will help us understand the author's Christological conception of Jesus as our high priest.

The main purpose for the writing of Hebrews was to bring encouragement to the readers.[1] Again and again, the author exhorts them to resist the temptation to fall away from their Christian commitment and urges them to continue their pilgrimage toward their eschatological goal. If they apostatize, they may once again become subject to the regime of the old covenant, which was inherently imperfect and of no duration. Therefore, in his argumentation the author tries to establish the true image of Christ in the minds of his readers. Some commentators hold that this was necessary because Jesus, in His earthly appearance and His shameful death on the cross, had become a stumbling block to them.[2]

In order to counter these negative sentiments the author develops a unique Christology of the high priesthood of Jesus. On the basis of the OT

---

1 H. Strathman, *Der Brief an die Hebräer* (Göttingen, 1953), p. 69.
2 Ibid., p. 68.

conceptions of the high priest, he brings out the unfamiliar features of Jesus as the great High Priest. Jesus is portrayed as a compassionate mediator between God and man and His high priesthood is closely linked to His atoning death for sin. Finally, the superiority of His priesthood over the Levitical system is clearly indicated; Jesus can assure them of the gift of divine salvation. In a negative sense the Christological conceptions of Jesus' priesthood indicate that Jewish concepts have been discharged as a possible temptation or threat to the readers.

Hebrews 8:1-6

Verse 1

In 8:1 the author introduces the superior high priesthood of Jesus with the phrase "Now the point in what we are saying is this"(*kephalaion de epi tois legomenois*).[3] The word *kephalaion* may be rendered in the sense of "the crown of the argument" or the main point,[4] rather than "summary." The context favors the idea of "main thing" or "main point."[5] Jesus is superior to the Levitical priesthood because He is seated at the right hand of the throne of the Majesty in heaven. Thus, in contrast with the Levitical high priests whose ministry is confined to this earth and who are subject to death (7:23), Christ's ministry is shown to be superior.

The phrase, "seated at the right hand of the throne of the Majesty in heaven," brings to mind passages such as Psalm 110:1-7, Hebrews 1:3, 13, also 10:12. It underlines the position and authority of Jesus, the status and honor of His high priesthood.[6] The expression "the Majesty in heaven," like the one in Hebrews 1:3, designates God Himself.[7] The word "throne" is a symbol in itself of authority.

In short, the author is saying that Jesus has been exalted and elevated

---

3 All citations are from the RSV unless otherwise stated.

4 For further discussion of this point see W. Manson, *The Epistle to the Hebrews* (London, 1951); and F. F. Bruce, *The Epistle to the Hebrews* (Grand Rapids, 1964). Both scholars prefer to translate *kephalaion* in terms of the crown of the argument with a forward thrust. Otto Michel, *Der Brief an die Hebräer,* vol. 13 of Kritisch-exegetischer Kommentar über das Neue Testament est. by Heinrich August Wilhelm Meyer (Göttingen: Vandenhoeck & Ruprecht, 1975), p. 287, points out that *toioutos* points back. Hughes maintains that the affirmation of vss. 1-2 constitutes the *leitmotif* of the whole epistle. Philip E. Hughes, *A Commentary on the Epistle to the Hebrews* (Grand Rapids, 1977), p. 50.

5 Michel, pp. 286-87. For the view, *epi tois legomenois* is a reference to the whole subject of Christ's high priesthood which is still under discussion, rather than to what has been advanced before, see B. F. Westcott, *The Epistle to the Hebrews* (Grand Rapids, 1950), p. 213.

6 Michel, p. 287; Hughes, p. 281.

7 Ibid.

to a position of eminence, authority, and rulership. Consequently, it would be futile to assume that the phrase denotes the mere act of sitting. It must be understood as a word of delegated power, of investiture with authority. The fact that this expression is linked with Christ's function as high priest in the presence of God is not to be overlooked.[8] It marks the beginning of the authority of Jesus as the heavenly high priest.

Verse 2

The phrase "a minister in the sanctuary and the true tent" (*tōn hagiōn leitourgos kai tēs skēnēs tēs alēthinēs*) expresses the fundamental idea of the whole Epistle.[9] The terms *ta hagia* (literally, "the holies") and *skēnē* ("tent/tabernacle") have given rise to considerable variation among commentators. From his study of *ta hagia* (in the light of the Septuagint [LXX]), Salom concludes that the expression refers to the sanctuary in general.[10] This means that this word is not a technical term for the Most Holy Place.

In Salom's opinion, this basic meaning of *ta hagia* as the "sanctuary" should be uppermost in the mind of the translator. He notes, however, that contextual consideration would allow the experts to be more precise than translators in determining what specific part of the sanctuary the writer may have had in mind.[11] In the context of Hebrews 8:2, Salom understands the expression as a generalized reference to the heavenly sanctuary.

Michel views the phrase "a minister in the sanctuary" (*tōn hagiōn leitourgos*) as a fixed hellenistic construction. He has no doubt that the author has the heavenly sanctuary in its totality in mind. He reasons that the existence of a heavenly high priest necessitates heavenly cultic action as well as a heavenly sanctuary.[12]

Some exegetes, however, are convinced that the expression *ta hagia* refers to the heavenly Holy of Holies. Hughes, for example, argues that the heavenly Holy of Holies is intended in the present context.[13] In his opinion, Jesus is conceived here (8:2) as having entered as our high priest into the heavenly Holy of Holies. On the other hand, the parallel word "tent" (*skēnē*), which is used to explain the *ta hagia*, clearly denotes the

---

8 H. Montefiore, *A Commentary on the Epistle to the Hebrews* (London, 1964), p. 132.

9 L. Sabourin, "Liturge De Sanctuaire Et De La Tente Veritable (Heb. 8:2)" *NTS* 18 (1971): 87-88.

10 A. P. Salom, "*Ta Hagia* in the Epistle to the Hebrews" *AUSS* 1 (1967): 65. See reprint in Appendix A of this book.

11 Ibid.

12 Michel, p. 288.

13 Hughes, pp. 281-82.

whole tabernacle or sanctuary rather than a part of it (8:2).

This heavenly sanctuary is said to be the "true tent," established by the Lord Himself and not by any human agent. The adjective "true" (*alēthinēs*) means "genuine," "real," in the sense of the reality possessed only by the antitype and not by its copies.[14] The true heavenly sanctuary is contrasted with the material one on earth.

Salom has cautioned us not to read back from earth to heaven too much detail regarding the nature and formation of the heavenly sanctuary.[15] However, it cannot be denied that the author's understanding of the role and function of the heavenly sanctuary was rooted in the earthly tabernacle. This is evidenced from his assertion that the earthly sanctuary was a "copy" (*hupodeigma*), a "shadow" (*skia*), and a "type" (*tupos*; "pattern" [RSV]) of the heavenly sanctuary (8:5). He drew the term for "type" (*tupos*) from the Septuagint translation of the Hebrew *tabnît* in God's instructions to Moses (Exod 25:40, LXX). These expressions give strong support to the view that the writer of Hebrews was indebted to the OT for his understanding of earthly-heavenly sanctuary correspondences.

Verse 3

Since Christ is said to function in the heavenly sanctuary, the question arises, What is the nature of His ministry? In Hebrews 5:1 the author has already indicated that every high priest is chosen from among men and "is appointed (*kathistēmi*) to act on behalf of men in relation to God, to offer gifts and sacrifices for sins." Therefore, it is necessary also for Christ as high priest to have something to offer (cf. 8:3).[16]

What is the nature of His offering? It should be noted that the offering is limited to a single sacrifice (indicated by the singular pronoun "something").[17] The author is obviously concerned to emphasize the sufficiency of the one-time sacrifice of Jesus Christ in contrast to the repetitious offerings of the Levitical system. This is evident in the original language by the tenses the author employs in verse 3: "Every high priest is appointed *to offer* [*prospherein*, present infinitive] gifts and sacrifices; hence it is necessary for this priest also to have something *to offer* [*prosenegkē*, aorist subjunctive]." The first "to offer" in the present tense denotes the continual, repetitive sacrificing of the earthly high priests. The second "to

---

14 Michel, pp. 289-90.
15 See chap. 9, p. 206-8 in this book.
16 Westcott, p. 215; Bruce, pp. 163-64.
17 Bruce, p. 164.

offer" in the aorist tense indicates the once-for-all-time nature of Christ's sacrifice on the cross.[18]

Verse 4

The contrary to fact condition introduces Hebrews 8:4 in a strong way for making a positive statement. ("If he were on earth, he would not be a priest at all.")[19] Jesus is high priest. His ministry must be exercised in the heavenly sanctuary. His priesthood belongs to a sphere that is not earthly and temporal.

The reason for His heavenly priesthood is given in the text (". . . since there are priests who offer gifts according to the law"). There is no possibility for Him to function in the earthly sanctuary because He does not belong to the order of Levi, a requirement of the Mosaic Law.[20] Jesus belonged to the tribe of Judah, "and in connection with that tribe Moses said nothing about priests" (7:14). As Michel has aptly pointed out, the heavenly High Priest does not fit into the structure of this time and world.[21]

Verse 5

Earthly priests served a "copy" (*hupodeigma*) and a "shadow" (*skia*) of the heavenly sanctuary. Thus, the question arises, How much detailed information concerning the heavenly sanctuary may be gained by comparing the two? Before a conclusion on this point can be reached, it is necessary to consider the significance of three key terms found in the text: *hupodeigma* ("copy"), *skia* ("shadow"), and *tupos* ("type"). According to Michel these three terms belong to the thought pattern or relationship of archetype ("original") to copy. This contrast is similar to the relationship of "shadow" (*skia*) to "true form" (*eikōn*) expressed in 10:1.

The term *hupodeigma* (8:5; 9:23) signifies a mere outline or copy.[22] According to Moffatt, the only analogous instance is in the LXX ("copy of the house," *hupodeigma tou oikou* [Ezek 42:15]). He suggests that the two terms "copy" and "shadow" in 8:5 form a hendiadys, giving the combined idea of a shadowy outline, that is, a second and inferior reproduction.[23]

In Exodus 25:40 (LXX), cited in verse 5, the *heavenly original* is called

---

18 Ibid.

19 A. P. Salom, "Exegesis of Selected Passages of Hebrews 8 and 9" (unpublished paper presented to Sanctuary Review Committee, Glacier View, August 1980), p. 6.

20 Bruce, p. 164.

21 Michel, p. 290.

22 Ibid., pp. 290-91.

23 J. Moffatt, *A Critical and Exegetical Commentary on the Epistle to the Hebrews* (Edinburgh, 1924), pp. 105-6.

tupos ("type"), whereas the *earthly* sanctuary is called the *antitupos* ("anti-type" [Heb 9:24]). In this instance the terms are switched. According to Goppelt the author of Hebrews has thus sought to characterize the heavenly high priestly ministry of Christ as a real counterpart to the ministry of the OT. So (in the light of Exodus 25:40), he argues that there is for the earthly sanctuary (the *antitupos,* "counterpart" [9:24] and *hupodeigma,* "copy" [8:5; 9:23]) a heavenly "original" (*tupos*).[24]

The writer's three terms in verse 5 suggest, therefore, that the earthly sanctuary is but a very shadowy representation of the heavenly reality. However, we would do injustice to the argument in Hebrews if we were to reject its thrust that there is a vital likeness and relationship between the earthly ministration of the Levitical priests and the ministration of Jesus in the heavenly sanctuary.

It should be pointed out that the *tupos* ("type") in Hebrews (citing Exodus 25:40, LXX) is at the same time the archetype ("the original") which means that the reality (in heaven) had existed before the copy and the shadow (on earth).[25] Thus, the earthly tabernacle built by Moses was constructed according to the pattern or *tupos* revealed to him on Mt. Sinai. Its purpose was to demonstrate in a typical manner deep truths concerning God's plan of salvation.

What can be said about the pattern which formed the basis for the Mosaic tabernacle? F. F. Bruce maintains, in the light of Exodus 25:40, that Moses did not simply receive verbal instruction but was shown a model or some other kind of representation.[26] From the Hebrew word *tabnît* in Exodus 25:40 (*tupos,* LXX) we may infer that the writer had a miniature model of the heavenly sanctuary or even the heavenly sanctuary in mind. Such a model would function as a pattern for the construction of the earthly sanctuary. The *tabnît-tupos* terms, therefore, reflect the original or prototype itself.[27] There seems to be good support for such a relationship.

The correspondences between the earthly and heavenly sanctuaries are limited to the essential aspects only. By making comparisons we must realize that the transcendental can never be contained within the finite categories of this world. On the other hand if we can assume that the ministration of the Levitical priests represents a reflection of the heavenly

---

24 L. Goppelt, "Tupos," *TDNT* (1972), pp. 256ff.

25 Ibid., pp. 257-58.

26 Bruce, p. 165.

27 R. M. Davidson, "Typology in Scripture," *Andrews University Seminary Doctoral Dissertation Series,* No. 2 (Berrien Springs, MI, 1981), p. 343.

archetype ("original"), the latter must have a two-phased heavenly ministration. The typological language of the author indicates that he must have had such a two-phased ministry of Christ in mind.

Verse 6

The introductory phrase, "but as it is" (*nuni de*), continues the thought of Christ's superior "ministry/service" (*leitourgia*). According to Hughes this introductory phrase emphasizes the fundamental contrast between the ministry of Christ and that of the old order.[28] Christ's ministry is superior because He is the mediator (*mesitēs*) of a superior covenant. The word *mesitēs* ("mediator") has its basis in Greek legal language. It can mean umpire, peacemaker, witness, guarantor. As mediator (*mesitēs*) Christ is in the position to settle disputes between two parties.

Michel points out that both concepts, "mediator" (*mesitēs*) and "covenant" (*diathēkē*), have neither hellenistic nor juridical meaning within the context of Hebrews but tie in with biblical and Jewish conceptions. Christ as the mediator (*mesitēs*) is greater than Moses (the phrase "mediator of the covenant" bringing to mind the parallel to Moses). Christ is the initiator of the new covenant and He is the one to guarantee that it will be carried through.[29]

The verb "has obtained" (*tugchanō*) denotes achievement, success, and victory, which, however, is not the result of one's own endeavors. It may be inferred, therefore, that Jesus has obtained the authority from His Father to minister as High Priest in the heavenly sanctuary. Christ's ministry, as the author of Hebrews states, is far superior to any earthly ministry because the covenant mediated by Him is better.

The "better" or new covenant is enacted on better promises. These promises are referred to in Jeremiah 31. They are better promises because they have been fulfilled in the cleansing of our conscience from guilt and sin and in the restoration of intimate fellowship with our Creator.[30]

The announcement of a new covenant implies the inadequacy of the old. In a sense, the teachings of the prophets lend support to the view that the new is indeed superior to the old. The author appears to be driving home the point that a transformation of heart and mind will take place, resulting in obedience to the commandments of God.

The concept of the new covenant gained particular significance in the

---

28 Hughes, p. 295.
29 Michel, p. 292.
30 Hughes, p. 297; also Bruce, p. 176; Montefiore, p. 133.

Qumran community.[31] There is, however, a fundamental difference between these sectarians and the views set forth by the author of Hebrews. The people of Qumran had their eyes fixed upon a material temple with its sacrificial service and duly appointed priesthood. On the contrary, according to the author of Hebrews, the new covenant focuses on the high priestly ministry of Christ in the heavenly sanctuary which completely displaces the worn-out sacrificial system.

Hebrews 9:1-8

In chapter 8 the author demonstrates the inadequacies of the old covenant and its priestly ministration. With 9:1 he turns to a description of the parts and function of the earthly sanctuary.

Verse 1

"Now even the first covenant had regulations for worship and an earthly sanctuary" (vs. 1). Some exegetes are of the opinion that "the first" (*hē prōtē*) in this verse refers to "the first tent," that is, the Mosaic tabernacle, rather than to the first covenant.[32] There is, however, no support for this position. The point in verse 1 is clear. The first covenant had its own regulations for worship and an earthly sanctuary.

Some exegetes, including Martin Luther, have been inclined to take *latreias* ("service/worship") as an accusative plural.[33] In this case, the text would read, "The first covenant had regulations, services, and an earthly sanctuary." Others, such as Moffatt, Riggenbach, and Hughes hold that it would be more natural to treat the term as a genitive singular, defining the word "regulations" (*dikaiōmata*).[34] Consequently, the text would read, "regulations of/for worship."

The use of the neuter singular noun *to hagion* ("the sanctuary") in the same verse carries the meaning of "sanctuary." It is not found anywhere else in the NT.[35] In the LXX, however, the term is used in Leviticus 16:2, 3, 16, 17, 20, 23, 27 for the Holy of Holies. But here in Hebrews 9:1 the term denotes the entire sanctuary.[36] On the other hand, there is considerable confusion among the translators on the correct rendering of the

31 Bruce, pp. 176ff.
32 Hughes, p. 304.
33 Ibid., n. 25, p. 305.
34 Ibid.
35 Westcott, p. 244.
36 Ibid.

plural form of this noun in the book of Hebrews (*ta hagia,* literally, "the holies"). The correct meaning of the word must be determined in the light of the context.

Verses 2-7

The use of *hagia,* a plural form without an article (literally, "holies"), in verse 2 is unique. It obviously refers to the first apartment, the "first" or "outer tent" (*prōtē skēnē*). The author names the furnishings that were located in it.

The expression *hagia hagiōn* (literally "Holies of Holies") is also used without an article. In this instance it refers to the Most Holy Place.

In 9:6 the author clearly delineates the role and duties of the priests in the holy place. The priests go in continually into the "outer" tent performing their ritual duties. Only the high priest goes into the second ("inner tent," understood) once a year, but "not without taking blood which he offers for himself and for the errors of the people" (Heb 9:7).

There can be no doubt that the high priest's role and function is seen within the context of the Day of Atonement. The fact that the high priest enters into the second tent (vs. 7) once a year and not without blood lends support to this argument.

In order to bring out the clear distinction between the two parts of the sanctuary the author uses in verse 6 *hē prōtē skēnē* ("the first tent"/"the outer tent") to designate the holy place in which the priests performed their daily services. The Second Apartment which the high priest enters once a year is designated *tēn deuteran* ("the second [tent]") meaning "the inner tent" (vs. 7).

Verse 8

While it is fairly easy to determine the meaning of *prōtē skēnē* ("first tent") in 9:2, 6, the situation seems somewhat ambiguous in 9:8. What is the meaning here? Does it refer to *the first apartment* as in 9:2, 6 or to the *first tabernacle,* the sanctuary that Moses erected at Sinai?

Westcott and others maintain that the expression must refer to the first apartment as in verse 2.[37] They cannot see why in verse 8 it suddenly should be applied to the first sanctuary, the Mosaic tabernacle.

More recently Young has argued that the *prōtē skēnē* ("first tent") in 9:8 refers to the outer tent rather than to the entire sanctuary.[38] He

---

37 Ibid., p. 252.

38 N. H. Young, "The Gospel according to Hebrews 9," *NTS* 27 (1981): 198-210.

attributes a *temporal* (time element) rather than spatial significance to the outer tent in verse 8 because of the use of *eti* ("as long as"/"while as"). In his opinion, the first or outer tent ceased to be of importance in the redemptive purposes of God the moment the cultic ritual of Judaism lost its validity. It was this daily round of offering sacrifices which blocked the way into the Holy of Holies.

At first sight these proposals appear convincing. On the other hand the position cuts asunder the two-apartment sanctuary symbolism. The question arises whether that equation of *prōtē skēnē* ("first tent") with the Mosaic age holds true. Is, in fact, the holy place alone—and not the entire sanctuary—symbolic of the old Jewish dispensation? At any rate, the total context of the book makes better sense to translate *hē prōtē skēnē* ("the first tent") in terms of the whole tabernacle as in 8:5; 9:11, 21 and 13:10.

The position that verse 8 refers to the Mosaic sanctuary as a whole is also supported by Héring. He correctly maintains that it is not only the first apartment of the earthly tabernacle which has lost its value and which ceases "to have a standing" (*echousēs stasin*), but the whole of the earthly sanctuary.[39] This observation ties in with Hebrews' conception of the covenant. The first covenant lost its importance the moment Christ became the mediator of "a new covenant." Likewise, the earthly tabernacle in its totality became obsolete at the moment of Christ's atoning death on the cross.

Before we get the full meaning of verse 8 however, it will be necessary to consider the word *ta hagia* (literally, "the holies") in verse 8. It appears that *ta hagia* here is the heavenly counterpart to *prōtē skēnē* ("first tent") or the earthly sanctuary. In this case the author is saying that access to the heavenly sanctuary was historically not available as long as the earthly sanctuary was still standing.[40] To say it differently, before the atoning death of Christ believers had only a very limited access to God because of the structure and ceremonial of the earthly sanctuary. At the death of Jesus the earthly sanctuary had fulfilled its purpose. Access was now made possible into the heavenly sanctuary.

Verses 9-10

The grammatical construction of verse 9 is a difficult one which, in Michel's opinion, allows for various grammatical and stylistic possibili-

---

39 J. Héring, *The Epistle to the Hebrews* (London), p. 74.
40 Hughes, p. 321.

ties.[41] The question is, What are the antecedents of the clauses introduced by its two relative pronouns ("*which* [*hētis*] was a figure for the time present"; "*in which* [*kath' hēn*] were offered both gifts and sacrifices," KJV)?

Windisch, for example, maintains that the first relative clause (*hētis*) refers to the whole preceding context,[42] while he connects the second relative clause (*kath' hēn*) to "the first tent" (*tēs prōtēs skēnēs*) in verse 8. Michel[43] and Bruce[44] hold that the antecedent of the first clause (*hētis*) may be the whole situation of verses 6-8. According to the latter, the relative pronoun "which" (*hētis*) is being attracted to the gender and number of *parabolē* ("symbol," "figure," "parable" in verse 9).

If Bruce and Michel are correct in their assumption that the antecedent of the first relative clause (*hētis*) is indeed the whole situation of verses 6-8, it means the author has deviated from the norm. In other instances he consistently refers back to a specific antecedent, gender, and number.[45] Thus for grammatical reasons it is better to consider "the first tent" (*hē prōtē skēnē*) in verse 8 as the antecedent of the relative clauses in verse 9. The author's point is that the rituals of the earthly sanctuary were composed of external rites that in themselves could not cleanse the conscience from sin. It was a temporary, limited system, designed to function until the coming of the Messiah.

Hebrews 9:11-14

This paragraph is composed of two long sentences in the Greek text. Verses 11-12 form the first sentence. The second sentence (vss. 13-14) is added to explain the phrase, "having obtained eternal redemption," which occurs at the close of the first sentence. We cite the opening sentence from the somewhat literal rendering of the NASB:

> But when Christ appeared as a high priest of good things to come, He entered through [*dia*] the greater and more perfect tabernacle, not made with hands, that is to say, not of this creation; and not through [*dia*] the blood of goats and calves, but through [*dia*] His own blood, He entered [*eiselthen*] the holy place [*ta hagia*] once for all, having obtained eternal redemption (Heb 9:11-12, NASB).

---

41 Michel, p. 307.
42 H. Windisch, *Der Hebräerbrief* (*HNT* 14) cited by Michel, n. 4, p. 307.
43 Michel, p. 307.
44 Bruce, n. 60, p. 195.
45 Young, pp. 201ff.

Verse 11

A textual variant in the first clause has led translators to render the participle connected with "good things" to mean either "good things *to come*" (*mellontōn,* like Heb 10:1) or "good things that *have come*" (*genomenōn*). The latter variant makes better sense in the context.[46] It underlines the fact that due to the atoning death of Christ, the "good things" have, indeed, arrived. The two "good things" brought by the present ministry of Christ which the old system could never provide are: (1) an efficacious sacrifice which can take away sin and cleanse the conscience, and (2) an ever living high priest who provides direct access to God.

How to understand and translate the three *dia* ("through") passages (see citation above)—especially the clause, "through the greater and more perfect tabernacle"—has proven a more serious challenge to interpreters.

Some have sought a solution by connecting the three *dia* ("through") phrases to the final verb, "entered" (*eiselthen*). This creates a redundancy, because it means that Christ went through "the more perfect tabernacle" to enter the heavenly sanctuary (*ta hagia*). Commentators clarify this somewhat by suggesting that the first *dia*-phrase should be understood in a locative sense (place) rather than in an instrumental sense (by means of). Consequently, the expression "through the greater and more perfect tabernacle" is construed as another way of saying that Christ crossed heaven to reach the throne of God.[47] However, the phrase used to describe this tabernacle—"not made with hands [*ou cheiropoiētou*], that is to say, not of this creation"—seems inappropriate and forced if applied as a reference to heaven.

A related proposal suggests that "the greater and more perfect tabernacle" refers to the heaven of angels or to the heavenly throng of angels through whom Jesus passed in order to come to the throne of God.[48] This innovative thesis can hardly be upheld.

Some commentators, following expositions of the early Church Fathers, have equated "the greater and more perfect tabernacle" with the body of Christ.[49] M. L. Andreasen took the position that the passage meant that Christ, by virtue of His perfect life—having made His body a fit and clean temple for the indwelling of the Spirit of God—appeared before God

---

46 Westcott, p. 255; Bruce, p. 199; W. G. Johnsson, "Defilement and Purgation in the Book of Hebrews" (Ph.D. Dissertation, Vanderbilt University), 1973, p. 290.
47 Héring, p. 76.
48 P. Andriessen, "Das grössere und vollkommenere Zelt (Heb. 9:11)," *BZ* 15 (1971): 76-92.
49 Ibid., pp. 77ff.

bringing His own blood. This gained Him entrance into the sanctuary above.[50]

While there may be some merit in the patristic attempt to solve the linguistic construction in this passage, it raises questions. The difficulty imposes itself once more when the phrase, "not made with hands, that is to say, not of this creation," is applied to Christ. This is not only a strange manner in which to speak about the Saviour, but it runs counter to the author's view that Christ is *human* (Heb 2:14-17; 5:7) as well as divine. A variant of this view equates the "more perfect tabernacle" with the Eucharistic body of Christ.[51]

A recent commentator suggests that "the greater and more perfect tabernacle" should be equated with the new covenant arrangement by which sin is purged and access to God is made available.[52] But an abstract conception of the meaning of "the more perfect tabernacle" does not seem justified. The descriptive phrase, "not made with hands, that is to say, not of this creation," seems to be an unsuitable way in which to speak of the new covenant.

These attempts, and others that could be mentioned, are various endeavors to come to grips with the use of *dia* in verse 11. Some are hardly more than conjectural. While a linguistic problem (to us) appears in the passage, the broader context provides good support for identifying "the greater and more perfect tabernacle, not made with hands, that is to say, of this creation" with the heavenly sanctuary into which Christ entered at His ascension. Two passages demonstrate this:

> For Christ did not enter a holy place *made with hands* [*cheiropoiēta*], a mere copy of *the true one* [not made with hands, understood], but into heaven itself, now to appear in the presence of God for us (9:24, NASB).

> Now the main point in what has been said is this: we have such a high priest, who has taken His seat at the right hand of the throne of the Majesty in the heavens, a minister in the sanctuary, and in *the true tabernacle,* which the Lord pitched, *not man* [not made with hands, understood] (8:1-2, NASB).

The expressions "made with hands" and "not made with hands" (expressed or understood) tie 8:1-2; 9:11-12; and 9:24 together. It is evident

---

50 M. L. Andreasen, *The Book of Hebrews* (Washington, DC, 1948), pp. 335ff.
51 J. Swetnam, "The Greater and More Perfect Tent: A Contribution to the Discussion of Hebrews 9:11," *Bib* 45 (1966), pp. 91-106.
52 Young, pp. 201ff.

that the author of Hebrews is contrasting the earthly and heavenly sanctuaries. Thus, we may safely say that in this passage (vss. 11-12) the author of Hebrews portrays the superiority of Christ's high priesthood by describing His entrance into the "true tabernacle," the celestial sanctuary, to appear in the presence of God for us.

Since this seems to be the correct sense of the context, we suggest that the preposition *dia* ("through") in this instance (vs. 11) is carrying the nuance of "into." The other two occurrences would have an instrumental function. The passage would read:

> But when Christ appeared as a high priest of the good things to come, [He entered] *into* the greater and more perfect tabernacle, not made with hands, that is to say, not of this creation; and not through [by means of] the blood of goats and calves, but through [by means of] His own blood, He entered the holy place once for all, having obtained eternal redemption.

Verses 12-14

Many exegetes understand verses 12-14 as alluding to a Day of Atonement setting. Some reasons cited are as follows:

1. Christ functions as "a *high priest*" (vs. 11).

2. Christ entered into the *presence of God* (vs. 24). The distinctive aspects of the Day of Atonement were enacted in the Most Holy Place which on earth especially denoted His presence.

3. His entry into the celestial sanctuary was "once for all" which reminds us of the Aaronic high priest's entry into the Most Holy Place once a year on the Day of Atonement (vs. 25).

4. The reference to "goats and calves" (vs. 12) and "goats and bulls" (vs. 13) seem to allude to the Day of Atonement.[53] Goats and bulls were used on that day (Lev 16:3, 5, 14; Num 29:7-11).

5. A comparison of Hebrews 9:6-7 with 11-12 seems to support the view that the author of Hebrews had the setting of the Day of Atonement in mind. For example:

a. "Into the second only the *high priest* goes" (vs. 7).
"Christ appeared as a *high priest* of the good things that have come" (vs. 11).

b. "He but *once* a year" (vs. 7).
"Entered *once* for all" (vs. 12).

---

53 Andriessen, p. 82.

c. "not without *taking blood*" (vs. 7).
"*Taking* not the blood of goats and calves but *his own blood*" (vs. 12).

In the light of such considerations it is not at all surprising that there are commentators who view 9:12-14 against the background imagery of the Day of Atonement.

But others differ. In Gerhard Hasel's opinion, a Day of Atonement allusion puts unnecessary limitations on the achievements of Christ's superior sacrifice. He notes that whereas Hebrews 9:12-14 refers to two kinds of animals (bulls/goats), Leviticus 16 (the major OT chapter on the Day of Atonement) actually refers to three kinds: bull, goat, and ram. Hasel argues that Hebrews 9:12-14 really takes up the inauguration theme of the OT and applies it to the heavenly ministry of Christ.[54]

In this respect he is in line with F. F. Bruce who perceives the situation in terms of Christ's entrance into the presence of God. Bruce interprets Christ's entry into the heavenly sanctuary as a day of celebration in view of His accession as a priest-king—and not as a day of soul affliction and fasting, reminiscent of the Day of Atonement under the old covenant.[55] However, as we shall see, the author of Hebrews may have had a much broader perspective in mind than either the Day of Atonement or an inaugural scene.

For many commentators the reference to the blood of goats and bulls in verse 13 is sufficient evidence that the author is pointing to the sacrifices of the Day of Atonement.[56] On the other hand the linking of the cleansing ritual of the red heifer to the alleged Day of Atonement in the same verse seems rather strange. In Bible times the cleansing rite involving the ashes of the red heifer had no connection with the Day of Atonement rite.

Michel maintains that the participle, "sprinkling" (*hrantizousa*), has reference to "the water of sprinkling" prepared from the ashes of a red heifer and used in ceremonial cleansings (*hudor hrantismou* [Num 19:9, LXX]).[57] The water was commonly used to purify a person who had become defiled by contact with a corpse.[58] Michel does not link "sprinkling" with "blood" in verse 13.[59]

---

54 G. F. Hasel, "Some Observations on Hebrews 9 in view of Dr. Ford's Interpretation," unpublished manuscript, Andrews University.
55 Bruce, p. 199.
56 Hughes, p. 354; Montefiore, p. 154.
57 Michel, p. 313.
58 S. H. Horn, *SDA Bible Dictionary* (Washington, DC, 1979), p. 917.
59 Michel, p. 313.

However, other scholars make that linkage (see Heb 9:13, RSV). Hasel argues that if it should indeed refer to the blood, then the author of Hebrews does not have the Day of Atonement in mind. He suggests that Hebrews 9:13 can best be understood in terms of covenant making and red heifer rites.[60]

The introduction of the red heifer into the sequence of verses 11-14 underscores the conviction that the author of Hebrews is not attempting to explain the antitype of the ritual Day of Atonement. He has another purpose, more closely related to the problem he is addressing. That is, he is stressing the superiority of Christ's blood—His sacrifice—over animal blood and ritual cleansing. Only the blood of Christ can purify the conscience that sin has defiled (vs. 14). Furthermore, he is also emphasizing that Christ, as our high priest, has entered in once for all into the heavenly sanctuary—into the very presence of God by virtue of His own blood—having obtained our redemption.

In verse 12 the author of Hebrews asserts the eternal validity of Christ's sacrifice and accomplished redemption. This fact contrasts sharply with the temporary nature of animal sacrifices that could in themselves provide only ritual "purification of the flesh" (vs. 13). Westcott points out four ways in which the sacrifice of Christ is, indeed, superior to animal sacrifices: it was voluntary, rational, spontaneous, and moral.[61] Above all, the efficacy of the Saviour's sacrificial death has its basis in His eternal nature.

Hebrews 9:23, 24

In the verses preceding this passage (vss. 15-22) the author maintains the necessity for the sacrificial death of Jesus. In his first line of reasoning (vss. 15-17) he makes a play on the Greek word *diathēkē* which can mean either "covenant" or "will" ("testament"). He employs both meanings here. First he repeats that Christ is the mediator of the new covenant (vs. 15; 8:6). By means of the covenant the Lord draws us into a special relationship to Himself. But, the author observes, the covenant is also like a will or testament and becomes effective only on the death of the testator. So, in that sense, the death of Christ has established the covenant; His shed blood has made its redemptive provisions available.

In his second line of thought the author continues with the motif of sacrifice by stating that even the ratification of the Sinai covenant and the

---

60 Hasel, "Some Observations on Hebrews 9 . . ."
61 Westcott, p. 260.

inauguration of the tabernacle required sacrificial blood (vss. 18-21). This leads him to his summary: "Indeed, under the law almost everything is purified with blood, and without the shedding of blood there is no forgiveness of sins" (vs. 22). This is the setting for the passage under examination which we now cite:

> Thus it was necessary for the copies of the heavenly things to be purified with these rites, but the heavenly things themselves with better sacrifices than these. For Christ has entered, not into a sanctuary made with hands, a copy of the true one, but into heaven itself, now to appear in the presence of God on our behalf (vss. 23-24).

The question we address here is, How are we to understand the author's statement that heavenly things—the heavenly sanctuary understood—need cleansing? Scholars differ widely on this point.

In defining "the heavenly things" (*ta epourania*), Michel has argued that according to 9:24 the sanctuary where Christ serves God represents heaven itself.[62] Therefore the cleansing of the sanctuary could be understood as a kind of inauguration or consecration in heaven. However, he suggests that the cleansing would be better understood in the light of apocalyptic portrayals which describe Satan being cast out of heaven (Rev 12:7-9; Luke 10:18; John 12:31).

According to Windisch there is a definite need for the cleansing of the heavenly sanctuary because of its pollution through the sins of mankind.[63] Other exegetes infer that the "purification" of the heavenly things means the "inauguration" or "consecration" of the heavenly sanctuary by the "better" sacrifice of Christ.[64]

Since the days of Chrysostom a number of exegetes have argued that "the heavenly things" are a designation for the people of God who constitute the church, that is, God's temple. Thus, Bruce holds that "in order to be a spiritual house of this kind they must have experienced regeneration and cleansing by the 'sprinkling of the blood of Jesus Christ' (1 Pet 1:2, 19, 22f.)."[65] However, one can hardly see how such an explanation does justice to the text before us. As Hughes has rightly pointed out, such an interpretation requires an identification between the *heavenly* sanctuary (or even heaven itself) and the community of the redeemed.[66]

---

62 Michel, pp. 323-24.
63 Ibid., n. 2, p. 324.
64 Hughes, p. 380.
65 Bruce, p. 219.
66 Hughes, p. 381.

Seeking for a correct insight into the expression Westcott has rightly pointed out that "the necessity for the purification of the earthly sanctuary and its vessels came from the fact that they were to be used by man and shared in his impurity."[67] He continues this line of thought by saying that in harmony with this idea even " 'heavenly things' . . . contracted by the Fall something which required cleansing."[68] We may add that the very origin of evil in the heavenly reality would also make it necessary for the latter to be cleansed.

In our passage it is evident that the author is contrasting the two sanctuaries: (1) the earthly ("the copies of the heavenly things" [vs. 23]; cf. "They serve a copy and shadow of the heavenly sanctuary" [8:5]), and (2) the heavenly ("the heavenly things themselves," "the true one" [vss. 23-24]; "the heavenly sanctuary" [8:5]). The purification of the former is accomplished by animal sacrifices; the purification of the latter is accomplished by Christ's better sacrifice (vs. 23). Thus the author refers to the cross and alludes to his opening remark: "when he [Christ] had made purification for sins, he sat down" (1:3).

It is clear, therefore, that the purification of the heavenly sanctuary has to do especially with human sin. In the light of the context it should not be construed that the cross accomplished—at one stroke—this purgation in the sense of providing automatic universal salvation. Rather, it should be understood that the once-for-all sacrifice provided for the purification of sin as it would be worked out through Christ's priestly ministry (9:14; 7:25).

Hebrews 10:19-22

An ambiguity in the Greek of verse 20 affects the interpretation of this passage to some degree. The clause, "that is to say, his flesh," may be understood in two different ways. Grammatically (in the Greek) it is possible for the expression, "his flesh," to stand in apposition to either "veil/curtain" or "way." Two standard translations may be cited as examples:

> Therefore, brethren, since we have confidence to enter the sanctuary by the blood of Jesus, by the new and living way which he opened for us *through the curtain, that is, through his flesh,* . . . (RSV).
>
> So now, my friends, the blood of Jesus makes us free to enter boldly into the sanctuary by *the new, living way* which he has opened for us through the curtain, *the way of his flesh* (NEB).

---

67 Westcott, p. 270.
68 Ibid.

His Flesh

Westcott points out that the words "his flesh" (*tēs sarkos autou*) are taken by some to be grammatically dependent on "the veil/curtain" (*tou katapetasmatos*) in two possible constructions.[69] In both instances the flesh of Christ is understood as the veil, something He had to pass through, a curtain which for some time shut off any access to God.

Westcott, however, is opposed to the equation veil = flesh. In his opinion, one would not expect to find the flesh of Christ "treated in any way as a veil, an obstacle, to the vision of God in a place where stress is laid on His humanity." Furthermore, he argues that one would expect a complete parallelism to be preserved "between the description of the approach of Christ to God and the approach of the believer to God."

Bruce takes the opposite tack, stating that the expression "his flesh" explains the meaning of "the veil." This view is attractive because the word order is more natural than the construction that links "his flesh" to "the new and living way."[70] Furthermore, he argues that Westcott's objection to the equation, veil = flesh, is not a weighty one since the author uses other metaphors besides "flesh," such as "the body of Jesus" or "the blood of Jesus" (vss. 10, 19).

The flesh of Jesus Christ, then, would be a reference to His human life which He offered up as a sacrifice to God.[71] It would mean that Christ's incarnation and atoning death has made possible our access to God. In light of the context the view that the veil is the flesh of Jesus appears to be the most plausible one.[72]

The Veil

In the LXX *katapetasma* is a word used for a curtain of the tabernacle. It is important to note that it is sometimes used to refer to the curtain at the courtyard entrance, the curtain at the entrance of the sanctuary, as well as the curtain between the holy place and the Most Holy Place.[73]

In the Synoptic Gospels "the curtain of the temple" (*to katapetasma tou naou*) was torn at the moment of the death of Jesus (Matt 27:51; Mark 15:38; Luke 23:45). The question, of course, arises as to which curtain the

---

69 Ibid., p. 319.

70 Bruce, p. 247.

71 Ibid., p. 248.

72 For discussion of the equation, veil = way, see W. G. Johnsson, pp. 48-49, in this book.

73 See George Rice, "Hebrews 6:19: Analysis of Some Assertions Concerning *Katapetasma*," *AUSS*, 25 (1987): 65-71. See Appendix B in this book.

evangelists had in mind. Scholarly opinion is divided. Fiebig, Zahn, and others argue for the outer curtain at the entrance of the sanctuary. In their opinion, this alone could be seen by the people.

On the other hand the outer curtain, while it veiled the holy places from the people, seems to have had less cultic significance than the inner curtain which separated the holy from the Most Holy. Furthermore, the underlying theological conception that the death of Jesus opened up access to the Holy of Holies deserves careful consideration.

According to Schneider[74] the curtain in 6:19, 9:3, and 10:20 has a theological meaning and in each case refers to the inner curtain. He points out that this curtain is identified in 10:20 with Christ's flesh, suggesting that the earthly existence of Jesus has a twofold meaning: as a veil between the Holy of Holies and the congregation, and as the only possible way to the Holy of Holies.

More recently, Hasel has argued that the author of Hebrews employed the term *katapetasma* in a sense that includes collectively the veil before both the holy place and the Holy of Holies.[75] Christ's entry "within the veil" is seen as involving the dedication of the entire heavenly sanctuary. After such a dedication Christ would function as heavenly priest and high priest to apply the benefits of His blood and sacrifice. Through Christ as his heavenly priest and high priest the believer is able to enter within the veil and have access to God who is present in the whole sanctuary.

While this attempt to cast light on a difficult problem is very attractive, the question still remains whether the author of Hebrews had in mind Christ's dedication of the entire heavenly sanctuary when he speaks of the Saviour's entry "within the veil." Whether we understand the term *katapetasma* in this passage as the outer or inner curtain, it seems fairly certain that the author has conceived of it as that which hides the *divine* presence. But the good news is that through Jesus Christ the believer may now pass through the curtain into the very presence of God.

What is meant by *tōn hagiōn* (literally, "the holies")? Is it to be understood collectively as a reference to both the holy place as well as the Most Holy Place? In 9:8 as well as here, it may be rendered "sanctuary" (cf. NEB). Other commentators are convinced that the expression designates the innermost apartment of the sanctuary, the Most Holy Place. Nevertheless, the author's main concern in our passage is to show that Christians

---

74 C. Schneider, "Katapetasma," *TDNT* (Grand Rapids, 1965), p. 631.
75 Hasel, "Some Observations on Hebrews 9 . . ."

now have free and direct access to God in the heavenly sanctuary by virtue of their king-priest, Jesus Christ.

Hebrews 6:13-20

By appealing to the experience of Abraham, the author seeks to bring encouragement to his readers. Thus, he points to "two unchangeable things" that he considers the basis of their hope: (1) the promise of God, and (2) the oath by which His promise is confirmed. The particular promise referred to in the present context is the one God made with Abraham after his experience with Isaac on Mt. Moriah (Gen 22:16-18).

This promise, of course, is to be viewed as an elaboration of God's earlier promises to Abraham which were to result in the birth of a son, the emergence of a great posterity, and the coming of the world's Redeemer through his line (Gen 12:1-3; 15:3-6; 17:15-25). The author observes that after the patriarch's willing attempt to offer Isaac, God repeated His promise and confirmed it with an oath, thus making the promise doubly sure (vss. 16-17).

In the present passage, therefore, the readers are assured that God's promises for them are equally certain. Our hope, he maintains, which has its basis in God's immutable promise, is absolutely secure. Furthermore, it is like a sure and steadfast anchor of the soul, entering "into that within the veil" (*eis to esōteron tou katapetasmatos*).

The points at issue here are the phrases "within the veil/curtain" (*esō-teron tou katapetasmatos* [6:19]) and "through the veil/curtain" (*dia tou katapetasmatos* [10:19-20]) which we noted earlier. The term employed for veil/curtain is *katapetasma*. In the NT this word appears in Matthew 27:51, Mark 15:38, and Luke 23:45. In these passages the tearing of the veil is recorded as one of the accompanying signs of the death of Jesus on the cross.

According to Schneider, as we have observed earlier, the evangelists had the inner curtain in mind, since the outer one had no great significance. He also attributes a theological significance to the three references in Hebrews (Heb 6:19; 9:3; 10:20). There is no doubt in his mind but that these six NT references are to the inner curtain (*to esōteron tou katapetas-matos* [Lev 16:2, 12]) or "the second curtain" (*to deuteron katapetasma* [Heb 9:3]).

Schneider is convinced that *katapetasma* in Hebrews 6:19 applies to the curtain which separates the holy from the Most Holy Place, but as we have

75

noted earlier there is no scholarly consensus as to whether the term designates either the inner or the outer curtain.[76]

In the light of philological considerations, therefore, we may be hard pressed to determine whether the word *katapetasma* refers to the inner or the outer veil. It is quite possible that the author, who at times shows little concern for minutiae, may have had something broader in mind than just the "curtain" before the Holy of Holies. It is clear that the main thrust of his message is to show that Christ has entered upon a ministry which He performs in the presence of God.

It is in the presence of God in the heavenly sanctuary that he applies the benefits of His blood and sacrifice as the heavenly high priest after the order of Melchizedek. A comparison of Hebrews 6:20 and 9:24 seems to support the view that the phrase "into the inner shrine behind the curtain" (RSV) may be simply another way of stating that Jesus has entered "into heaven itself, now to appear in the presence of God on our behalf."

Summary and Conclusion

Like a master artist, the author of Hebrews has painted, in broad but not uncertain strokes, a profound picture of the nature and role of Christ's superior high priestly ministry and the absolute certainty of the believer's hope of salvation. The impression thus created cannot be captured by analytical work alone. To appreciate and understand his message it is imperative to listen to the text again and again.

This implies also that we should not ignore his objective to meet the needs of his readers who were in danger of apostasy. It seems certain that they faced some apparently insurmountable problems that tended to cause them to give up their Christian commitment. It is such a situation that prompted his masterly exposition.

The view that the author was indebted to Platonic-Philonic conceptions is unacceptable to us. One may be able to detect some Philonic influence upon his language, but the correspondence between the earthly and heavenly sanctuary is not a Philonic-Platonic mode of thinking.

The author's use of typological language, which points to the correspondence between the earthly and heavenly sanctuaries, allows us to assume that he must have had in mind a two-phased priestly ministry for Christ. Having said this, we realize that any comparison between the earthly and heavenly sanctuaries must take into consideration that the transcendental

---

76 Schneider, pp. 631-32.

can never be contained in the finite categories of this world.

We believe the expression *ta hagia* ("holies") is best understood as a general term for the entire heavenly sanctuary rather than the Most Holy Place alone, unless it is definitely qualified as in Hebrews 9:2-5. In this connection we have attempted to clarify the meaning of *protēs skēnē* ("first tent") in 9:8. In our opinion the phrase refers to the entire sanctuary of the old eon or the time of the old covenant. The reference to "the greater and more perfect tent" (*tēs meizonos kai teleioteras skēnēs*) in 9:11 is also envisioned by the author as the two-partite sanctuary in heaven. For syntactical reasons, however, we may not be able to recapture fully the author's intended meaning here.

In verses 11-14 the author comes to the heart of his message. Although some scholars believe he employs Day of Atonement language, it is evident that his ultimate objective is to emphasize the superiority of Christ's blood over animal blood. The latter could accomplish ritual cleansing, but the former alone could purge the conscience.

While some of the syntactical and linguistic problems posed by these texts may still puzzle us, their central message is clear. Again and again the readers are assured that the high priestly ministry of Christ in the heavenly sanctuary in their behalf is to be viewed as the ultimate reality. From a purely practical point of view the believer no longer has to perform rites which are at best symbolic of something greater to come. No longer does he have to rely upon the mediation of human priests. Now, through Jesus, his great high priest whose blood is able to remove the stains of sin and guilt, he is able to come into the very presence of God with confidence. Sin, therefore, no longer presents a barrier between God and man. Through the unique ministry of Jesus Christ in the heavenly sanctuary man is now able to enjoy a person-to-person relationship with God.

Chapter V

Defilement/Purification
and Hebrews 9:23

William G. Johnsson

Editorial Synopsis. It is Adventist understanding—based on the Levitical sanctuary types and the prophecies of Daniel—that Christ began in 1844 His second-apartment phase of priestly ministry in heaven. In biblical phraseology this ministry is referred to as "the cleansing of the sanctuary" (Dan 8:14, KJV). In the NT Hebrews 9:23 added an important insight to Daniel 8:14.

"Thus it was necessary for the copies of the heavenly things [the Israelite sanctuary] to be purified with these rites, but the heavenly things themselves [the heavenly sanctuary] with better sacrifices than these" (Heb 9:23).

In recent years it has been argued that this passage in Hebrews should lead us to conclude that Christ's work of purifying—or cleansing—the heavenly sanctuary was completed at the cross. Such an interpretation of the verse, if correct, would immediately invalidate Adventist teaching as summarized above. However, the present writer demonstrates that this interpretation rests on a defective exegesis, because it fails to consider the central theological argument of the book. Exegesis of isolated passages cannot lead to sound interpretation unless the passages are seen in relationship to the full theological perspective of the document.

The essential theological concern in Hebrews revolves around the problem of defilement and purification. This is evident both from the apostolic writer's choice of vocabulary and his progression of thought beginning with his opening summation of Christ's accomplishment on earth: "When he had made purification for sins" (1:3). Defilement/blood/purification terminology forms the theological core of concepts by which the apostolic writer describes humanity's dilemma and the way to its salvation.

His model must not be muted or collapsed by blending or confusing it

79

with other models. Defilement points to the stain, the blot, the corruption of person. As the writer observes, "One is not redeemed from defilement, just as one is not *forgiven* it, *reconciled* to it, or *justified* in spite of it. If one is defiled, he must be made clean—the stain, the corruption must be taken away." The means for that purification is blood, the blood of Christ Himself, the purifying agent par excellence.

Although the concepts of human defilement and the need for purification seem to be universally acknowledged, the apostolic author draws his concepts from the sanctuary pattern of defilement-blood-purification and works out his argument in this setting. God appointed the sanctuary ritual as an educative tool, but its repetitious animal-blood rites were in themselves inadequate to remove the defilement and stain of moral sin. Thus, the focus of the theological presentation of Hebrews 9-10 is Calvary. The Good News is that "once for all time" Christ "put away sin by the sacrifice of himself" (9:26); by His own shed blood He has provided the means for permanent purification.

In the light of the central theological argument it is evident that Hebrews 9:23 is not stating that the heavenly sanctuary was purified *when* Christ died on Calvary. On the contrary the passage reflects the theme given at the outset: "He . . . made purification for sins" (1:3). The time frame for the purification of the heavenly sanctuary is *not* in view here, but rather the necessity for the heavenly realities to be purified by the better sacrifice of Christ. This fact is underscored inasmuch as the apostolic writer envisions an ongoing priestly ministry for Christ who will apply the merits of His purifying blood to penitent seekers after God (7:25; 9:24).

The point of the book of Hebrews is precisely this: "The great Sacrifice, Jesus, provides what all animals could not—a solution to the sin problem, a sacrifice that is able to purify decisively. It does *not* address the time when the heavenly sanctuary is to be cleansed." Furthermore, the intent of the apostolic writer is not to show that Calvary is the antitype of the Day of Atonement, but that Calvary is the antitype of all the sacrifices of the OT. Only the *better blood* of Christ is able to provide genuine cleansing.

A time element enters the argument in this respect: at a point in time, Calvary provided God's single, all-sufficient Answer to sin. Hebrews does not take up the time for the cleansing of the heavenly sanctuary and the "investigative judgment"—two concepts that our Adventist pioneers tied together, supported by Hebrews 9:23. Although these concepts are not subjects of Hebrews, we affirm that the pioneers' basic insight was correct and their use of Hebrews 9:23 valid.

The central theological argument also sheds light on the book's concept of "perfection." In Hebrews the concept does not indicate growth in character nor a goal toward which to strive. On the contrary, perfection means that "the age-old problem of defilement has been met by a Sacrifice that provides thoroughgoing purification, throwing wide open the doors to the presence of God and bringing to an end all other sacrifices and human effort to find cleansing."

Chapter Outline

    I. Introduction
    II. Vocabulary of Defilement and Purification
    III. Theological Emphasis in Hebrews
    IV. Aspects of Interest to Adventists
    V. Conclusion

* * * * * * *

Introduction

The book of Hebrews has long been regarded as of particular significance by Seventh-day Adventists. Our pioneers looked especially to this work for the foundations of the distinctive Adventist doctrine of the heavenly sanctuary with Christ, its great high priest. Although Hebrews has been largely neglected by Protestant scholars during the twentieth century,[1] Adventist students of the Bible have been an exception in their concern to unlock the meaning of this masterfully reasoned document.[2]

During the past few years the Book of Hebrews has become a center of controversy in Seventh-day Adventist scholarship. Already, 80 years ago, A. F. Ballenger challenged the traditional Adventist view of the heavenly work of Christ, basing the argument principally on his interpretation of Hebrews 6:19-20.[3] In the recent years an appeal has been made to Hebrews—especially to the ninth and tenth chapters—as support for another reinterpretation of the sanctuary doctrine.[4] Since Hebrews is the one NT

---

1 William G. Johnsson, "The Cultus of Hebrews in Twentieth-Century Scholarship," *ExpT,* vol. 89, No. 4 (1978), pp. 104-8.
2 Apart from courses in this book offered over the years at Seventh-day Adventist colleges and universities, note, for example, M. L. Andreasen's *The Book of Hebrews* (Washington, DC, 1948).
3 Albion Foss Ballenger, *Cast Out for the Cross of Christ* (Tropico, CA, n.d.).
4 Desmond Ford, *Daniel 8:14, the Day of Atonement, and the Investigative Judgment,* a document

book where explicit and sustained interpretation of the OT cultus is given, it is regarded as fundamental to the proposed new schema.

I think it is fair to say that Hebrews has been more misunderstood than understood throughout the twentieth century. Roman Catholic writers—who have shown more interest in it than Protestants, with the exception of the past 10 or 15 years—often have "read in" ideas of the Mass and earthly priesthood.[5] Protestant scholars have found the cultic terminology and reasoning foreign and uncongenial to their way of thought and have passed over it.[6] And oftentimes Adventist students have been preoccupied with apologetic or polemical concerns, catching significant nuances but failing to trace the broad lines of argument, the progression of this magnificent theological treatise.

Central Argument

The theological argument of Hebrews centers in the cultus (the sanctuary worship system). And the cultus—as set forth in Hebrews—revolves around the problem of defilement and purification.[7] That is the point made in its opening statement, where the entire earthly career of the Son of God is summed up by the words, "when he had made purification for sins" (1:3). It is the point to which the reasoning returns again and again, especially in chapters 9 and 10, where the theological argument reaches its final outcome.

Yet it is a point not seen by most scholars of Hebrews. They have not been alert to this cultic language. They have tended instead to collapse the model of defilement-purification into other models such as redemption, forgiveness, or atonement. Even Adventists, who might have been expected to be attuned to the rhythm of the sanctuary ritual, have failed to appreciate fully what is "going on" in this, the larger scope of the argument of Hebrews.[8] An awareness of the book's central argument is important for Adventists on at least two counts:

First, the specific, isolated questions of Hebrews that concern the

---

prepared for the Sanctuary Review Committee, Glacier View, CO, 1980.

5 I have listed the books and articles on Hebrews by Roman Catholic authors in William G. Johnsson, "Issues in the Interpretation of Hebrews," *AUSS,* vol. 15, No. 2 (1977), pp. 169-87.

6 A striking example of this is shown by D. Bernhard Weiss, *Der Hebräerbrief in zeitsgeschichtlicher Beleuchtung* (Leipzig, 1910). Weiss devotes 32 pages to Hebrews 12:12–13:25 but only 12 pages to the entire cultic argumentation of 8:6–10:18!

7 This thesis is developed in my Ph.D. dissertation, *Defilement and Purgation in the Book of Hebrews* (Vanderbilt University, 1973).

8 A concentration on selected portions of the book rather than seeing the work as a whole, coupled with apologetic and polemical concerns, probably accounts for this failure.

interpretation at particular points—or the exegesis of certain key texts—can be resolved only as one has thoroughly grasped the overall structure of the theology of Hebrews. This means that the student of Hebrews must "get inside" the cult and explore its reason for existence.

Second, Adventists, at least at one level, have long been concerned with questions of defilement and purification. Working out of the KJV of Daniel 8:14 (in turn derived from the Septuagint and Vulgate), we have taught "the cleansing" of the heavenly sanctuary. It is curious that all along the book of Hebrews had much to say about defilement and purification, but we had been unable to grasp the full impact of its language. It is time to correct this omission—to see the contribution of Hebrews to the understanding of the cleansing of the heavenly sanctuary as we endeavor to be true to the overarching theological development of the book.

Three-Stage Study

Our study will proceed in three stages. The first will be descriptive. We will lay out the textual data of Hebrews to demonstrate that the reasoning of defilement-purification forms the matrix of the cultic argumentation. The second phase will be theological. We will reflect on the significance of the data presented. In the final part we will indicate the bearing of the discussion in Hebrews on the theological matters of particular Adventist concern. And here we must face squarely the issue: Does the presentation in Hebrews lead us to conclude that Christ's work of purification was completed at the cross, thus falsifying the Seventh-day Adventist teaching of the cleansing of the heavenly sanctuary commencing in 1844?

Vocabulary of Defilement and Purification

Theology is not done by counting the occurrences of words. Nevertheless, at the outset it is helpful to set out the lexical data.

Vocabulary of Defilement

Defilement is indicated specifically by the use of two Greek verbs: *koinoun and miainein* and related adjectives.

Koinoun (and related adjective, *koinos*) signifies to "make common or impure, defile in the ceremonial sense," or to "consider or declare (ceremonially) unclean."[9] The terms are used twice in Hebrews, the first time

---

9 William F. Arndt and F. Wilbur Gingrich, *A Greek-English Lexicon of the New Testament and Other Early Christian Literature* (Chicago, 1969), p. 439.

with reference to the OT cultus and the second time with reference to the new covenant:

> 9:13 "For if the sprinkling of *defiled* [*koinoun*] persons with the blood of goats and bulls and with the ashes of a heifer sanctifies for the purification of the flesh."

> 10:29 "How much worse punishment do you think will be deserved by the man who has spurned the Son of God, and *profaned* [*koinos*] the blood of the covenant by which he has sanctified, and outraged the Spirit of grace?"

Miainein signifies to "stain, defile," and can refer to either "ceremonial impurity" or "moral defilement by sins and vices."[10] It also occurs twice, both times with reference to Christians:

> 12:15 "See to it that no one fail to obtain the grace of God; that no 'root of bitterness' spring up and cause trouble, and by it the many become *defiled* [*miainein*]."

> 13:4 "Let marriage be held in honor among all, and let the marriage bed be *undefiled* [*amiantos,* negated adjective form]; for God will judge the immoral and adulterous."

By themselves, these four occurrences of terms pointing to defilement might seem of little significance. We begin to sense their force, however, when we realize that the counterpart of the concept they convey—purification—is given strong emphasis.

Vocabulary of Purification

The principal word used to signify purification is *katharizein* and its cognates. Two related terms also should be noticed: *louein* and *baptismos.*

Katharizein signifies to "make clean, cleanse, purify."[11] The verb form occurs four times, corresponding nouns twice, and the corresponding adjective once:

> 1:3 "He reflects the glory of God and bears the very stamp of his nature, upholding the universe by his word of power. When he had made *purification* [*katharismos*] for sins, he sat down at the right hand of the Majesty on high."

---

10 Arndt and Gingrich, p. 522.
11 Ibid., p. 388.

9:13   "For if the sprinkling of defiled persons with the blood of goats and bulls and with the ashes of a heifer sanctifies for the *purification* [*katharotēs*] of the flesh."

9:14   "How much more shall the blood of Christ, who through the eternal Spirit offered himself without blemish to God, *purify* [*katharizō*] your conscience from dead works to serve the living God."

9:22   "Indeed, under the law almost everything is *purified* [*katharizō*] with blood, and without the shedding of blood there is no forgiveness of sins."

9:23   "Thus it was necessary for the copies of the heavenly things to be *purified* [*katharizō*] with these rites, but the heavenly things themselves with better sacrifices than these."

10:2   "Otherwise, would they not have ceased to be offered? If the worshipers had once been *cleansed* [*katharizō*], they would no longer have any consciousness of sin."

10:22   "Let us draw near with a true heart in full assurance of faith, with our hearts sprinkled clean from an evil conscience and our bodies washed with *pure* [*katharos*] water."[12]

The data thus demonstrate that *prima facie,* the topic of defilement and purification in the book of Hebrews merits careful examination. But by listing the bare lexical data, we have only begun.

The terms we just have noticed do not represent discrete concepts. They are simply windows into the same cultic structure, a part of the matrix of the theological argument. We need also to take account of a related vocabulary. This vocabulary is extensive, but for the sake of simplicity we will confine it to those terms that may be associated most readily with defilement and purification.

---

12 We have not taken up the occurrences of *louein* ("to wash" or "bathe") or *baptismos* ("dipping" or "washing") since these terms do not enter into the cultic argumentation of Hebrews. The terms occur in Hebrews 10:22 ("Let us draw near with a true heart in full assurance of faith, with our hearts sprinkled clean from an evil conscience and our bodies *washed* [*louein*] with pure water"); 6:2 ("with instruction about *ablutions* [*baptismos*], the laying on of hands, the resurrection of the dead, and eternal judgment"); and 9:10 ("but deal only with food and drink and various *ablutions,* regulations for the body imposed until the time of reformation").

Related Vocabulary

Blood. The most important noun calling for consideration here is *haima* ("blood"). *Haima* is the middle term, so to speak, between defilement and purification. Just as defilement is the *problem* and purification is the *solution,* so blood is the *means* to obtain the latter.

Haima occurs no fewer than 21 times in Hebrews, with 14 occurrences in Hebrews 9-10.[13] We shall cite those that most clearly point to blood as the means of purification.

9:7   "But into the second only the high priest goes, and he but once a year, and *not without taking blood* which he offers for himself and for the errors of the people."

9:12   "He entered once for all into the Holy Place, *taking not the blood of goats and calves but his own blood,* thus securing an eternal redemption."

9:13-14 "For if the sprinkling of defiled persons with the *blood of goats and bulls and* with the ashes of a heifer sanctifies for the purification of the flesh, how much more shall the *blood of Christ,* who through the eternal Spirit offered himself without blemish to God, purify your conscience from dead works to serve the living God."

9:22   "Indeed, under the law almost everything is purified with blood, and without the *shedding of blood* there is no forgiveness of sins."

10:4   "For it is impossible that the *blood of bulls and goats* should take away sins."

10:19   "Therefore, brethren, since we have confidence to enter the sanctuary by the *blood of Jesus, . . .*"

10:29   "How much worse punishment do you think will be deserved by the man who has spurned the Son of God, and profaned the *blood of the covenant* by which he was sanctified, and outraged the Spirit of grace?"

12:24   "And to Jesus, the mediator of a new covenant, and to the *sprinkled blood* that speaks more graciously than the blood of Abel."

13:12   "So Jesus also suffered outside the gate in order to sanctify the people through his *own blood.*"

---

13 Heb 2:14; 9:7, 12, 13, 14, 18, 19, 20, 21, 22, 25; 10:4, 19, 29; 11:28; 12:4, 24; 13:11, 12, 20.

13:20 "Now may the God of peace who brought again from the dead our Lord Jesus, the great shepherd of the sheep, by the *blood of the eternal covenant. . . .*"

Verbs of removal. Three verbs are used in the cultic argumentation in connection with the sin problem—*anapherein, aphairein* and *periairein.* These point to "sin" (*hamartia*) as something that must be *removed* (in contrast to a debt to be paid, a relationship to be restored, and so on). As such, they parallel the concept of sin as defilement:

a. *Anapherein* signifies "to bring or take up ... to take away."[14] It is used in Hebrews of Christ's removal of sins:

9:28 "So Christ, having been offered once to *bear [anapherein]* the sins of many, will appear a second time, not to deal with sin but to save those who are eagerly waiting for him."

b. *Aphairein* signifies "to take away"[15] and is found in connection with the OT cultus:

10:4 "For it is impossible that the blood of bulls and goats should *take away [anapharein]* sins."

c. *Periairein,* signifying "to take away, remove,"[16] is found likewise in reference to the old services:

10:11 "And every priest stands daily at his service, offering repeatedly the same sacrifices, which can never *take away sins [periairein].*"

Having surveyed the terminology of defilement and purification in Hebrews, we need now to focus on where the terms occur in the argument—that is, on the relative significance accorded them by the author.

Defilement/Purification Argument

The following observations are pertinent:

1. The opening statement to the book of Hebrews is not merely an introduction. It is in reality programmatic of its theology and identifies Christ's achievement as *making purification* for sins (vs. 3). Indeed, the whole period of the Incarnation is comprehended here under this single rubric. By this statement the cultic treatment of this work is immediately

---

14 Arndt and Gingrich, p. 62.
15 Ibid., pp. 123-24.
16 Ibid., p. 651.

signaled and the view of sin—a defilement calling for purification—is indicated.

2. The occurrences of the defilement/purification/blood terminology cluster in the heart of the theological argument of the book—chapters 9 and 10. These chapters elaborate the statement of 1:3 that Christ has made purification for sin. They spell out in detail the efficacy of His work in comparison and contrast to the animal sacrifices provided by God for the OT nation of Israel. It seems incontrovertible that the exegete of Hebrews must come to grips with these concepts of defilement and purification, giving them their full weight in the argument, if he is to interpret aright these key chapters.

3. Not only do these terms (for defilement/blood/purification) *occur* in Hebrews 9-10, but they in fact form the logical and theological underpinning of the argument. Proof of this contention can be provided only by a full-blown exegesis, a task beyond the purview of this study. We merely provide the following examples as demonstration; a full presentation is available elsewhere.[17]

a. The chief theme of the chapters concerns blood, a term occurring, as we noticed, 14 times. As the writer argued earlier in terms of a better name (chap. 1), a better leader (chap. 3), a better priest (chap. 5), a better priesthood (chap. 7), a better sanctuary and a better covenant (chap. 8), so here his presentation is shaped around "better blood."

b. The argument, which at first sight moves away from blood in chapter 9 to sacrifice in chapter 10,[18] returns in its summary to the blood motif (10:19, 29).

c. The three "not without blood" affirmations (9:7, 18, 22) underscore the role of blood in the author's thought.

d. The logical structure is as follows:

(1) 9:22—The "blood rule." The axiom underlying all sacrifices, whether OT or NT.

(2) 10:4—The ultimate inadequacy of animal blood to solve the problem of sin.

(3) 9:13, 14—Comparison and contrast. The limited ability of animal blood contrasted with the ultimate ability of Christ's blood to effect purification.

---

17 See *Defilement and Purgation in the Book of Hebrews*.
18 See n. 13: After 10:4 instead of "blood" we read of "sacrifices and offerings" and "burnt offerings and sin offerings" (vss. 5-6), "sacrifices and offerings and burnt offerings and sin offerings" (vs. 8), "sacrifices" (vs. 11), "sacrifice" (vs. 12), "offering" (vs. 14), and "offering" (vs. 18).

e. The interrelations of defilement, blood, and purification (blood being the middle term, the means to effect the transition) are seen most clearly in 9:13-14, the passage that summarizes the involved reasoning of the two chapters.

> For if the sprinkling of *defiled* persons with the *blood* of goats and bulls and with the ashes of a heifer sanctifies for the *purification* of the flesh, how much more shall the *blood* of Christ, who through the eternal Spirit offered himself without blemish to God, *purify* your conscience from dead works to serve the living God.

We conclude, therefore, that the data of defilement and purification in the book of Hebrews—both the vocabulary employed and the role of the concepts in the progress of the author's thoughts—require us to engage in serious reflection on the meaning intended by the author. This will be our task in the following section.

Theological Emphasis

The data in Hebrews concerning defilement and purification suggest four observations:

Theological Unity of Concepts

The complex of ideas associated with the terms "defilement," "blood," and "purification" represents a logical and theological unity.

These ideas are not to be collapsed or translated into another theological "package" made up of terms that may be more familiar to us or more readily accessible to our grasp. When Hebrews describes the human dilemma as one of defilement, the problem is not a lack of righteousness before the law, so that we cry out for "right-wising." Nor is it a debt that we owe, so that we seek forgiveness; still less is it a will in bondage, with freedom seen as the ultimate blessing. No; defilement points to the stain, the blot, the corruption of person.

One is not *redeemed* from defilement, just as one is not *forgiven* it, *reconciled* to it, or *justified* in spite of it. If one is defiled, he must be made clean— the stain, the corruption must be taken away. And, argues the author of Hebrews, the means of that purifying and purification is blood, the blood of Christ Himself, the purifying agent par excellence.

In fact, studies in the religious literature[19] and practices of humankind

---

19 Note especially *Proceedings of the XIth International Congress of the International Association for the History of Religions,* vol. II: *Guilt or Pollution and Rites of Purification* (Leiden, 1968). I have gathered other data in *Defilement and Purification in the Book of Hebrews.*

demonstrate the fundamental nature of the portrayal of the human condition and the way provided by God for its restoration as set forth in the book of Hebrews. As scholars such as Paul Ricoeur[20] have shown, the most basic recognition of our lostness, our sense of falling short, is expressed by "I am dirty, unclean." That is a category reducible to no other and calling for a remedy appropriate to the need.

Such recognition is deeply rooted in the human psyche. It surfaces in hymns such as "Washed in the Blood of the Lamb" and "Whiter Than Snow." But even secular contexts show its persistence, show it despite modern education and psychology, in unconscious expressions such as "dirty politics," "dirty linen," "coming clean," and "dirty jokes."

Given the prominence of law in many presentations of theology, it is not surprising that the pattern of defilement/blood/purification has been passed over. Concentration on law leads logically to the model of the court: God is judge, mankind in the dock is guilty. The desire is for acquittal.

We do not denigrate the importance of this model and the theological systems that have developed from it. But it is necessary to point out that the court model, valuable as it is, is but one of the ways by which the human dilemma and Christ's work to solve it are set forth in the Scriptures. In Hebrews the law/court model is not present and should not be imported nor superimposed. To understand Hebrews we must let the argument reveal itself on its own terms as the Holy Spirit, who called it forth in the first century A.D., illuminates our minds today.

Sanctuary Setting

The question inevitably confronts us: Why Hebrews? Why here, of all the documents in the NT, should the work of Christ be portrayed in this manner?

It is true that Hebrews is the only NT book where the theological argument is built upon the pattern of defilement-blood-purification. While other books have occasional references to the model (for example, 1 John 1:9; Titus 2:14), in no other is it argued in the sustained, systematic manner of Hebrews.

But no other NT book revolves around the motif of the sanctuary as does Hebrews, either. Here and there we find hints of Christ's heavenly intercession (for example, Rom 8:34; 1 John 2:1), and Revelation employs sanctuary imagery and places the visions in the setting of the heavenly

---

20 Paul Ricoeur, *The Symbolism of Evil,* tr. Emerson Buchanan (Boston, 1969).

sanctuary. But only in Hebrews is Jesus explicitly called high priest, and only here is the existence of the heavenly sanctuary explicitly argued.[21]

Inevitably, we are led back to the sanctuary setting of the OT. Inevitably, we are led to reflect on the call to holiness, sounded over and over again in Leviticus. Inevitably, we are reminded of the mass of regulations designed to safeguard the purity of the wandering people of God—the laws of defilement and purification. The call to holiness of the people of God camped around the sanctuary was a call to protection from defilement, a call to purification. And the way of dealing with sin, the way of removing defilement, was the way of blood, through the sacrifice of animals.

The sanctuary!—here is the key. " 'Let them make me a sanctuary, that I may dwell in their midst,' " Yahweh had said (Exod 25:8). And this was His promise, the word of the covenant keeping God: "I . . . will be your God, and you shall be my people" (Lev 26:12). With that word, however, came this one also: " 'You are a people holy to the Lord your God; the Lord has chosen you to be a people for his own possession, out of all the peoples that are on the face of the earth' " (Deut 7:6). So in Leviticus, the book of the sanctuary, the God who dwells among His people says: " 'For I am the Lord your God; consecrate yourselves therefore, and be holy, for I am holy. . . . For I am the Lord who brought you up out of the land of Egypt, to be your God; you shall therefore be holy, for I am holy' " (Lev 11:44-45).

The correlation of "sanctuary" with "defilement/blood/purification" in both the OT and NT seems undeniable. Hebrews is the NT counterpart of Leviticus, elaborating and explaining its ideas in significant respects.[22] Thus in Hebrews we again find the call to holiness: "Strive for peace with all men, and for the holiness without which no one will see the Lord" (Heb 12:14). That is why the presentation of the work of Christ is found in Hebrews in the categories we have noticed: the model is the sanctuary, not the moral law or any other.

Effectual Work of Christ

The defilement/blood/purification complex of ideas points us to a distinctive presentation of the work of Christ.

---

21 In my judgment the attempt to view the sanctuary language of Hebrews as metaphor or illustration fails in the light of its use in the book. See William G. Johnsson, "The Heavenly Sanctuary — Figurative or Real?" chap. 3 in this volume.

22 While the sanctuary doctrine unique to Adventists finds brief mentions or hints in many books of the Bible, four in particular underscore it: Leviticus and Hebrews, Daniel and Revelation.

First, we see by means of the defilement idea the hopelessness of the human condition. In Hebrews 9-10 the accent falls on the inadequacy of the OT cultus. Despite its many educative features, it was strictly temporary, "regulations for the body imposed until the time of reformation" (9:10). The blood of animals could extend to the "purification of the flesh" (9:13), but no farther. It was "impossible" for sin to be dealt with in finality by such means (10:4). The same sacrifices, offered year after year, were unable to "perfect" the worshipers (10:1). Despite what individuals may have attained in religious peace (and no doubt many did), the very repetition of the sacrifices of Israel viewed in the corporate sense pointed up the lack of solution to the problem of defilement (9:6, 25; 10:2, 11).

We must be clear as to the argument of Hebrews: the author is not denigrating the OT cultus in toto. After all, God had given it! It was His way of salvation by faith for those times.[23] But in the final analysis, it was inadequate of itself. This is his point. The God who had provided the sacrificial system would, in His own time and through His own plan, provide a Sacrifice that would deal with the sin problem in a decisive, ultimate manner.

Sin is a moral problem, not to be removed by mechanical shedding of animal blood. It is a hideous defilement, separating us from God's holiness. Only God can supply the answer and bring radical purification. And this He did in the gift of Jesus Christ, He who is both Sacrifice and High Priest.

In contrast to the many, repeated sacrifices of animals, Christ's death was "once for all time" (7:27; 9:26, 28; 10:2, 12-13). The purification He provided was decisive—not merely of "the flesh (*sarx*)" but of the "consciousness (*suneidēsis*)." These terms (respectively *sarx* and *suneidēsis* in the Greek) are to be understood from the perspective of Israel as a whole rather than individual worshipers (see 9:9-10, 13-14; 10:2-3, 19-22).[24] They point on the one hand to the uneasy conscience of Israel, its continuing awareness of the lack of finality of the OT cultus, as shown by the round of sacrifices. On the other hand they underscore the all-sufficiency of the blood of Christ, which by one offering provides purification for all time and brings to a halt the need for animal sacrifices.

As we noticed in the first section of the study, in both the frequency of key terms and the structure of the argument, the author's emphasis falls on blood. His is a Christocentric argument, emphasizing the accomplish-

---

23 Note Heb 1:1-2: the same God spoke in both OT and Christ!
24 Note C. A. Pierce, *Conscience in the New Testament* (Chicago, 1955).

ment of Jesus on our behalf rather than the human predicament and resultant benefits. Thus, the focus of the theological presentation of Hebrews 9-10 is Calvary. The argument preeminently looks back to the cleansing means par excellence.

Uniqueness of Christianity

We see, lastly, the uniqueness of the Christian religion in this portrayal of the work of Christ. Throughout human history mankind has been troubled by a persistent sense of "numinous uneasiness,"[25] an awareness of being unclean, defiled. Many have been the means and the agents that have been enlisted to remove the defilement. Always the goal of the defiled person has been purification. But that goal has been elusive, fleeting, sought after but never attained, felt but never held fast. Humanity's religious experience has been an oscillation:

Defilement   many unsuccessful agents   →   Purification

← causes of defilement

But Christ, argues the book of Hebrews, has broken the terrible cycle. By Himself—by His own blood, He has provided the means of thorough-going, permanent purification. He alone is able to bring to an end mankind's driving quest for a way to be free of the corruption of person:

Defilement   Christ's blood   →   Purification

Our theological reflection in this section has highlighted the significance of Hebrews as a document centered in the sanctuary. It has shown how the OT sanctuary roots provide the complex of ideas of defilement, blood, and purification. These ideas are a logical and theological unity, pointing first to the terrible weight of the sin problem and then to the glorious means God has provided in Christ to escape it. This is a distinctive representation of Christ's work, not to be collapsed into any other schema or subsumed under the other religions of mankind.

The manner in which the theology of defilement, blood, and purification is worked out in the overall development of Hebrews cannot concern us here. Neither can we explore the relationship of the hortatory sections

---

25 The term is A. C. Bouquet's.

93

of the book (in which this theology is muted) to the high priestly argument. I have addressed these matters in a different study prepared for this volume.[26]

We turn now to the final section of this chapter and take up aspects of special concern to Seventh-day Adventists.

Aspects of Interest to Adventists

Four matters connected with the topic of this study are of special concern to Seventh-day Adventists: (1) the interpretation of Hebrews 9:23, (2) the time aspects of purification (Is Christ's work of purification already past?), (3) the role of blood, and (4) the teaching of the document concerning "perfection."

Interpretation of Hebrews 9:23

Hebrews 9:23 boggles the minds of most commentators on Hebrews: "Thus it was necessary for the copies of the heavenly things to be purified with these rites, but the heavenly things themselves with better sacrifices than these."

On the face of it, the text speaks of the necessity of purifying "the heavenly things"—meaning in context, the heavenly sanctuary, since the earthly sanctuary and its appurtenances were "copies of the heavenly things." The magisterial commentary of C. Spicq is repelled by such a thought ("non-sens"!),[27] as are almost all expositors. How, they argue, can things in heaven—the place of perfection—require purification?

Two lines of interpretation are usually found; each avoids the obvious meaning of the text:

1. The "heavenly things" refers, not to the heavenly sanctuary, but to the *suneidēsis* ("consciousness" or "conscience"). This reasoning is based on an alleged parallel with 9:14, where Christ's blood is said to purify the *suneidēsis*: "How much more shall the blood of Christ, who through the eternal Spirit offered himself without blemish to God, purify your conscience [*suneidēsis*] from dead works to serve the living God." This interpretation is false to both terminology and context, however.

First, as to the terminology. The book of Hebrews, expounding the person and work of the Son, has a great deal to say about "the heavenly things." It argues that the genuine, the real is in heaven (see 4:14; 7:26;

---

26 "Hebrews: An Overview," chap. 2.
27 C. Spicq, *L'Épître aux Hébreux*, 2 vols. (Paris, 1952).

8:1-5; 9:8, 11-12; 10:12, 19; 12:18-24). We have given reasons elsewhere[28] why we hold that the author of Hebrews believes in an *actual* heavenly sanctuary—that he is not using sanctuary language as metaphor.

To interpret "the heavenly things" at 9:23 as the *suneidēsis* ("consciousness/conscience") does violence to the total conceptual framework of the book. Further, it collapses the author's terminology in a manner not warranted by the context. We hold that the vocabulary of Hebrews exhibits a precision of choice and use that forbids us to make such an equation. The purification of the consciousness or conscience (*suneidēsis*) is a benefit to believers that flows from Christ's work—it is not that work itself.

The context is clearly against this interpretation as well. Hebrews 9:23 is a *transition* between a discussion of the OT cultus (vss. 18-22) and a discussion of the new, the heavenly (vss. 24-28). It takes the reader from "the copies" to "the heavenly things" themselves and to the "better sacrifices," Christ's own atoning death. Its point is, as throughout chapters 9-10, the "better blood" of Christ. Hence, verse 23 commences with "Thus (*oun*). . . ." And verse 24 follows with "For (*gar*) Christ has entered, not into a sanctuary made with hands, a copy of the true one, but into heaven itself. . . ." To interpret "the heavenly things" in 9:23 as human consciousness/conscience (*suneidēsis*) wrenches the context inadmissibly in view of the verses that follow immediately.

2. Another attempt to explain the purification of the heavenly things in 9:23 is to suggest that the concept carries the sense of "inauguration." This understanding has gained credence in some Adventist circles.[29] Its chief support is drawn from the context. Verse 18 speaks of the inauguration of the first covenant, and verses 19-21 describe that inauguration. Thus, it is argued that verse 23 may be seen as paralleling verse 18: "Hence even the first covenant was not ratified without blood."

We may reject this interpretation, however, for three reasons:

First, the parallel is not convincing. Whereas verses 19-21 do describe the inauguration of a sanctuary, verses 24-28 do not. They center in Christ and His work, not on the sanctuary itself. Christ appears in the presence of God on our behalf (vs. 24); He has "put away sin by the sacrifice of himself" (vs. 26). That is, the scope of the argument is much wider than the inauguration of the heavenly sanctuary. The passage is dealing with *mediation,* not inauguration!

---

28 See n. 21.

29 Some non-Seventh-day Adventist expositors also have advanced this interpretation.

Second, verse 22 is to be seen as a contextual break. "Indeed, under the law almost everything is purified with blood, and without the shedding of blood there is no forgiveness of sins." When we give this verse its due weight, the supposed parallel is weakened. Many exegetes of Hebrews have seen in this verse the so-called "blood rule," a critical plank in the author's argument. It clearly looks far wider than inauguration, since it is dealing with *aphesis* ("release," "pardon").[30] Verse 22, in fact, is summing up the role of blood in the OT. It is reaching back beyond verse 18 to embrace verses 1-21. Without the presence of this verse the suggested interpretation of inauguration would have strong contextual support; with it, the support collapses.

But the strongest argument against this view, in my judgment, is the author's terminology. He uses *katharizein* ("to purify") not *egkainizein* ("to inaugurate"). These terms are not equivalent; they are not to be collapsed together.

Our work on the book has shown the necessity of "listening" to the voice of Hebrews itself. We must avoid the mistake of importing or superimposing other categories on the language of the cult. In making this point we do not advocate a wooden literalness; we merely make a plea that the author be permitted to explain his meaning without our getting in his way. If taking his language at face value causes us a conceptual problem, we must be prepared to rework our concepts. Given the overall theological schema of defilement/blood/purification, such reworking will lead us to see a greater logical and theological unity in the overall development.

We hold, therefore, that Hebrews 9:23 is to be understood to mean what it appears to say—that the heavenly sanctuary itself requires purification. Just what such purification entails is not elaborated, either later in the chapter or elsewhere in the book.

The pioneers tied together the concepts of the cleansing of the heavenly sanctuary and the "investigative judgment" of God's people. The book of Hebrews does sound a judgment theme, mainly in its hortatory sections.[31] But it does not pull together the concept of 9:23—the necessity of purifying the heavenly things—with this theme. The two ideas are referred to separately.

The minimal theological idea in such a view is this: Heaven and earth are interconnected. What happens on earth has cosmic ramifications,

---

30 Arndt and Gingrich, p. 124.
31 Heb 2:2-3; 3:12, 17-19; 4:1, 11-13; 6:7-8; 10:26-31; 12:25-29; 13:17.

ramifications that touch even heaven itself. Gone is any Platonic separation of the realm of God from the realm of humanity. Rather, the working out of the sin problem—as God Himself undertakes the resolution of the human dilemma—extends to the very heart of the universe.

Such a conception is foreign to many Christians, but not to Adventists. With our understanding of the great controversy between Christ and Satan we all along have seen the salvation of humanity in a cosmic setting. Our pioneers saw in Hebrews 9:23 support for this view. We affirm that their basic insight was correct.

Time of Christ's Purifying Work

We must now address this issue: Does Hebrews teach that Christ *completed* His work of purification at Calvary? The question arises naturally out of the topic of this study. Our interpretation of 9:23 given above drives it home with compelling force. That is, Does 9:23 tell us that already, at His ascension, Christ had cleansed the heavenly sanctuary?

The statement in the book's introduction is unequivocal: "When he had made purification for sins." The Aorist Middle form employed (in the Greek text) indicates beyond a doubt a completed work. That understanding is confirmed by the elaboration provided in 9:1–10:18.

We need to be clear on the author's concept, however, lest we read into his words more than he intended to convey. As we have seen, his argument in 9:1–10:18 takes up Israel (in a corporate understanding) and proceeds more by way of contrast than comparison. In particular, he contrasts the repeated, inadequate sacrifices of the OT cultus with Christ's single, sufficient Sacrifice.

In terms of worshipers, this contrast is also one of benefits, expressed by access to God and extent of purification. Access: Christians have access by faith to the "real" sanctuary where the true high priest ministers (10:19-22; 12:18-24). Extent: Whereas the OT cultus provided ceremonial purity (*sarx*—the "flesh"), the new cultus in Christ provides purification of the *suneidēsis* ("consciousness/conscience." See 9:9, 13-14; 10:1-4).

That is, the argument concerning purification is framed in terms of relative *efficacy of sacrifices*—the many, ultimately inadequate sacrifices and the single all-sufficient Sacrifice that provides the means of purging human defilement.[32]

But existentially this presentation does not suggest that Christians face

---

32 See Heb 10:14; but contrast 2:11.

no more danger from sin. Although they now are a holy people ("sanc-tified"!), they remain pilgrims and confront the perils of neglect, even overt rejection of the faith, as we have shown elsewhere.[33] Christ's having made purification for sins means that He provided the great means for its removal, now and eternally—not that sin *has been* fully removed.

Nor does 9:23 necessarily imply that "the heavenly things" were purified at Calvary. As we noticed, the idea is not elaborated in Hebrews. The time frame of the verse is unclear, the simple point of the *necessity* of heavenly purification being made.

Indeed, the reasoning of the author concerning the heavenly ministry of Christ would point in a direction away from a work completed at Calvary.[34] While he gives very few details concerning the nature of that high priestly function, he clearly holds to an actual ministry being carried out.

He tells us Christ "always lives to make intercession" for us (7:25); that He is "a minister in the sanctuary and the true tent" (8:2); that He is the mediator of a new covenant (9:15); that He appears in the presence of God on our behalf (9:24); that this "appearing" involves the putting away of sin by the sacrifice of Himself (9:26). It is manifest that the purification for sins at the cross in no wise negates ongoing heavenly activity for the plan of salvation.

Thus, 9:23 remains a significant verse in Seventh-day Adventist under-standing of the sanctuary doctrine. While, bearing in mind that the argu-ment of Hebrews looks *back* to Calvary rather than forward to our times, we may not press this one verse unduly, we nevertheless may call upon it for support for the fundamental idea of the need of a purification of the heavenly things.

Furthermore, discerning that the overall theological argument of Hebrews proceeds in terms of sacrifice—all OT sacrifices and Christ's one sacrifice—we should not permit the book to be wrested to address ques-tions foreign to its purpose. To be precise: Hebrews teaches that the great Sacrifice, Jesus, provides what all animals could not—a solution to the sin problem, a sacrifice that is able to purify decisively. It does *not* address the time when the heavenly sanctuary is to be cleansed.

---

33 See William G. Johnsson, "The Pilgrimage Motif in the Book of Hebrews," *JBL*, vol. 97, No. 2 (1978), pp. 239-51.

34 Semantics are important in discussions of this matter. In affirming Christ's ongoing work as heavenly high priest, we nonetheless underscore the all-sufficiency of the sacrifice of Calvary. That sacrifice provides the basis for this priestly work.

Role of Blood in the Argument

We have seen in this chapter that "blood" is the chief theme of the sustained theological argument of 9:1–10:18. The *better blood* of Christ, more efficacious than all sacrifices, able to provide thoroughgoing cleansing and access to the very presence of God—this is the author's leading point.

It is important to discern this critical role of blood in the reasoning, lest undue emphasis be placed on the Day of Atonement. There are three indisputable references to the latter in these chapters (9:7, 25; 10:3),[35] but they are part of the larger ongoing argument concerning sacrifice. Thus, we find also mentioned daily sacrifices (9:9-10), the sacrifice of the red heifer (9:13), the sacrifices at the inauguration of the covenant with Israel (9:18-20), and the generalized "sacrifices and offerings and burnt offerings and sin offerings" (10:8, 11).[36]

We emphasize: The intent of the author is *not* to show that Calvary is the antitype of the Day of Atonement of the OT, but rather that Calvary is the antitype of all the sacrifices of the OT. We must not confuse considerations of *function* (of sacrifice) with those of time.

This issue is important in current discussions among Adventists, inasmuch as some have sought to inject (in our judgment, unwarrantedly) time aspects into the interpretation of Hebrews. In Hebrews time enters the argument only in this respect—that at Calvary God provided the single, all-sufficient Answer to sin. But Hebrews does not take up the *time* of the cleansing of the heavenly sanctuary and the judgment (Heb 9:23).[37]

"Perfection" in the Book of Hebrews

The question of perfection long has been a source of discussion and debate among Seventh-day Adventists. In Hebrews we find the vocabulary of "perfection" associated with the argumentation concerning defilement and purification.

The author of Hebrews discusses perfection in two respects: of Christ and of the people. The references to Christ are found in the context of His preparation for His high priestly office. They are not associated with the defilement-purification complex of ideas.

---

35 Some expositors see many more allusions to the Day of Atonement in the book of Hebrews, but the evidence for them is subject to dispute.

36 Outside chapters 9 and 10, we find other references to sacrifice: 5:1-3, "gifts and sacrifices for sins"; 7:27, daily sacrifices for sins; 10:29, "the blood of the covenant"; 11:4, Abel's sacrifice; 11:28, the blood of the Passover; and 12:24, the blood of the new covenant.

37 We have summarized here. For a more detailed discussion see William G. Johnsson, "Day of Atonement Allusions," chap. 6 in this volume.

Concerning Jesus, we read:

2:10   "For it was fitting that he, for whom and by whom all things exist, in bringing many sons to glory, should *make* the pioneer of their salvation *perfect* [*teleioun*] through suffering."

5:9   "And being *made perfect* [*teleioun*] he became the source of eternal salvation to all who obey him."

7:28   "Indeed, the law appoints men in their weakness as high priests, but the word of the oath, which came later than the law, appoints a Son who has been *made perfect* [*teleioun*] for ever."

What is the nature of the Son's perfecting? We may discount at once two possible interpretations.

First, it does not mean an adoptionistic Christology, that is, that God raised Jesus to the level of a divine status that He did not have before. The apostle's words deny such a view. For example, we remember the "being" of 1:2-3 ("He reflects the glory of God" [RSV] = in the Greek text "who *being* the brightness of the glory," not *"became"*). Passages 5:7-9 and 7:28, which speak of His perfecting, call Him "Son" *during* the perfecting. That is, He is not a man or superior being who, because of His earthly perfecting, becomes qualified to be Son. Rather, it is the Son, while Son, who is perfected.

Second, the perfecting does not signify a work of purifying the Son's humanity. The author does not set forth Jesus' experience "in the days of his flesh" (Heb 5:7) as a progressive overcoming of sins in Himself. Rather, the sermon[38] unequivocally contrasts the sinfulness of common man with His undefiled person:

4:15   Though tested in every way, He remained "without sin."

5:3, 9 The moral weakness of the Aaronic priests finds no counterpart in Him.

7:26   He is termed "holy, blameless, unstained."

7:27   He had no need to offer up sacrifices on His own behalf, as did the Aaronic priests.

9:14   He offered Himself as a sacrifice "without blemish" to God.

---

38 See my article in this volume, "Hebrews: An Overview," chap. 2.

The context gives us the clue for grasping the nature of the Son's "perfecting." We note that both 2:10 and 5:8-9 speak of His perfecting through suffering, and three passages relate the perfecting work to His role as high priest (see 2:17-18; 5:9-10; 7:27-28). The "perfecting" describes the successive experiences of the incarnate Son, experiences that led Him into new levels of dependence on God and so qualified Him to be our high priest. The "perfecting" of the Son, then, indicates a learning process. Jesus learned, not as we often do, by falling and rising up to overcome the next time, but by continual submission to the will of God. He was ever learning anew the meaning of conformity to the divine will as the experiences of life unfolded. It was as that will challenged Him to act that submission brought suffering. But He went forward, constantly working out in Himself the divine plan, never turning from it no matter what its cost. The final test was the ultimate one. In the garden He cried out with loud shouts and tears. But even there He went forward—forward to the cross!

As a man He *became*—became a sufferer, became a suppliant, became a dependent, became a learner. So, by what He went through—because He went through—He was "perfected." His human experiences—intense, real, genuine—made Him complete for the heavenly work of high priest that the divine plan had ordained.[39]

The references to the perfecting of God's people occur in quite a different setting, namely, the cultus:

> 7:11 "Now if *perfection* [*teleiosis*] had been attainable through the Levitical priesthood. . . ."

> 7:19 "(For the law made nothing *perfect* [*teleioun*]); on the other hand, a better hope is introduced, through which we draw near to God."

> 9:9 "According to this arrangement, gifts and sacrifices are offered which cannot *perfect* [*teleioun*] the conscience of the worshiper."

> 10:1 "For since the law has but a shadow of the good things to come instead of the true form of these realities, it can never, by the same sacrifices which are continually offered year after year, *make perfect* [*teleioun*] those who draw near."

---

39 This understanding of Jesus' high priestly office is especially supported by Hebrews 2:17, which in turn must be understood as resting on the argument of chapters 1 and 2. At times students of Scripture have argued on other grounds that Jesus already was high priest during the period of the Incarnation; the book of Hebrews runs counter to this idea, however.

10:14   "For by a single offering he *has perfected* [*teleioun*] for all time those who are sanctified."

A study of these references in context suggests a twofold understanding of "perfection" with regard to the people of God:

First, "perfection" is associated with access to God "(for the law made nothing perfect); on the other hand, a better hope is introduced, through which we draw near to God" (7:19).

Second, "perfection" is associated with the purified *suneidēsis,* the consciousness of sin. We note the parallel between 9:9-10 and 9:13-14. Whereas under the old cultus the gifts and sacrifices could not "perfect the conscience of the worshiper," Christ's offering is able to "purify your conscience." Likewise in 10:1-2. The yearly sacrifices could not "perfect" those who drew near each year, because there was a continuing "consciousness (*suneidēsis*) of sin."

Thus, "perfection" in Hebrews (in terms of the people of God) signifies *the benefits of the new cultus.* It does not indicate a growth in character or a goal for Christians to strive toward. It has a corporate sense, comprehending the people of God under the new cultus.[40] "Perfection" means that the age-old problem of defilement has been met by a Sacrifice that provides thoroughgoing purification, throwing wide open the doors to the presence of God and bringing to an end all other sacrifices and human effort to find cleansing.

Thus, in Hebrews "perfection" is used in two quite different, although related, senses. It is affirmed in the individual context of Jesus when the author of Hebrews describes those human experiences that qualified the Son to be designated high priest. It is also used in a corporate context to sum up the finality of the sacrifice of Christ in removing all the barriers to God thrown up by the sin problem.

Conclusion

The study of the motifs of defilement and purification in the book of Hebrews is one that may be of great value to all who seek to unlock the close-knit reasoning of this document. All Christians who place priority on the cross of Christ will find much here that enhances His sacrifice.

---

40 The vocabulary of "perfection" in the letter to the Hebrews has attracted considerable scholarly attention. Among the many contributions to the discussion that might be mentioned we note just two: P. J. du Plessis, *Teleios: The Idea of Perfection in the New Testament* (Kampen, 1959); and Allen Wikgren, "Patterns of Perfection in the Epistle to the Hebrews," *NTS* 6 (1959-1960): 159-67.

Adventists, however, with our insights into the sanctuary truth and the Great Controversy, find all this and much more. For we see exposed the terrible dilemma of humanity under the reign of sin—defiled, seeking cleansing, shedding blood, but finding no final answer. We see God's Answer, the Son who came to provide purification through His own blood, to become high priest in the heavenly courts with a sacrifice all-sufficient, eternal in quality and provision. And we see the benefits that flow from God's gracious provision for our salvation: full, unhindered access to the heavenly sanctuary; an end to sacrifices and human efforts to provide cleansing; purification on a cosmic scale so that the universe at length will be totally and finally free of the pollution of sin.

> "For us he would provide a bath
> Wherein to cleanse from sin,
> And drown the bitterness of death
> In His own blood and wounds,
> And so create new life."
> —Martin Luther,
> "Epiphany Hymn"

Chapter VI

Day of Atonement Allusions

William G. Johnsson

Editorial Synopsis. How are we to understand the Day of Atonement allusions in the book of Hebrews? Does the Epistle point to the cross as the antitype of the Day of Atonement ritual, as some assert? If so, how can we look for the commencement of the antitypical day of atonement event—the preadvent judgment—in 1844? These are serious questions inasmuch as they touch on the very roots of the Seventh-day Adventist Church. Unfortunately, over the years some ministers and members have found their "theological Waterloo" in Hebrews and have lost their way.

The concept of Christ's two-phased priestly ministry in the heavenly sanctuary was the "key" that resolved the bitter disappointment our pioneers experienced in 1844. From the book of Hebrews they learned that neither the earth nor the church was the sanctuary of the Bible. Instead, they perceived that Christ ministered in their behalf in a heavenly sanctuary of which the Israelite tabernacle/temple was a type. And from the earthly type they grasped the significance of the two divisions of His work.

Thus, our pioneers came to understand that in 1844—the close of Daniel's 2300 year prophecy—Christ entered the Most Holy Place to begin the second phase of His priestly ministry as foreshadowed by the Day of Atonement ritual. At the completion of this additional ministry, He will return the second time for His people. From this beginning our pioneers went on to discover a whole series of interlocking truths and the prophetic reasons for the rise and mission of a remnant people in the end of time.

Why then has the book of Hebrews led some Adventists to leave the church over the sanctuary doctrine when insights from the same book enabled our pioneers originally to explain the Disappointment? The

Reprint of "The Significance of the Day of Atonement Allusions in the Epistle to the Hebrews," in Arnold V. Wallenkampf and W. Richard Lesher, eds., *The Sanctuary and the Atonement* (Biblical Research Institute: Washington, DC, 1981), pp. 380-93.

105

answer seems to lie—at least in part—in a failure to grasp the main argumentation of the Epistle. Albion F. Ballenger (1861-1921), a minister who left the church in 1905 over the sanctuary doctrine, may be taken as an example. The main argument he advanced from Hebrews for seeing the cross as the antitypical day of atonement was the expression "within the veil" (Heb 6:19-20). From this expression he inferred that upon His ascension, Christ began His ministry "within the veil," that is, in the Most Holy Place of the heavenly sanctuary.

The present writer agrees that the linguistic data (Hebrew OT, and the Greek Septuagint translation of the OT) appear in general to support Ballenger's contention that the phrase "within the veil" refers to the Most Holy place. However, he argues that Ballenger's isolated exegesis of 6:19-20 caused him to distort the actual message of Hebrews and to draw wrong conclusions. Says the writer, "He failed to study sufficiently *the book of Hebrews itself.* The first principle of exegesis calls upon the student to consider the context." Such an examination of the context might have led him to consider the purpose for which the Day of Atonement allusions were employed. The author's *purpose* for employing such allusions is crucial to a correct understanding of his message.

In the book of Hebrews three passages unambiguously set the work of Christ on Calvary against the imagery of the Day of Atonement services (Heb 9:6-7, 24-25; 10:1-4). It is inconclusive whether eight other suggested passages contain such an allusion. But while conceding that the author does allude to the Day of Atonement, the important question is to determine how the allusions are to be understood. Perhaps it should be stated at this point what is obviously axiomatic: all ritual sacrifices—whether daily or yearly, public or private—pointed forward to the cross and met their *sacrificial aspect* in the death of Christ. However, other features of these could find their total fulfillment only in connection with Christ's priestly ministry subsequent to Calvary.

It is evident that the Day of Atonement allusions are not central to the discussion in Hebrews. The sacrificial argument (8:1–10:18) is not the Day of Atonement, but the *better blood of Christ.* Animal blood—whether in the form of a daily, private, or yearly sacrifice—could not actually cleanse from sin (10:4). *Even at its highest point*—the Day of Atonement ritual— the Levitical rites were inadequate.

The good news, says the author of Hebrews, is that all that the old system—including the Day of Atonement—failed to do because of its inherent insufficiencies, has now been done by Christ on Calvary. Instead of repeated sacrifices, He made one, once for all time. And thus by that one act, all barriers between Deity and man have been abolished so that we now may come boldly into the presence of God.

"The day of atonement references of Hebrews, therefore, are *not* designed to show that the antitypical day of atonement began at the ascension (contra Ballenger), nor to suggest a brief entry into the most holy for its inauguration (contra Andross), nor to set forth the first fulfillment of the OT high point, the complete fulfillment commencing in 1844 (and not addressed by Hebrews). Rather, the argument swings on the *relative value of sacrifice,* contrasting the apex of the OT cultus with the surpassing achievement of Jesus Christ on Calvary." The comparison and contrast centers on the efficacy of Christ's sacrifice and the free, direct access it provides into the presence of God.

Thus, the author's use of Day of Atonement imagery heightened the fact that Christ's death accomplished permanent purification for sin and access to God—accomplishments that the ritual, even at its most intense point, did not do. It was, therefore, not within his purview to provide a detailed exposition on the significance of either the daily or yearly ritual beyond this aspect. Such matters have tremendous significance for us, but they did not come within his pastoral concern at the point of his writing.

Chapter Outline

    I. Introduction
    II. Ballenger's Treatment of "Within the Veil"
    III. The Day of Atonement Allusions in Hebrews
    IV. Interpretations of the Day of Atonement Allusions

* * * * * * *

Seventh-day Adventists early held the book of Hebrews as a source of our unique understanding of the heavenly sanctuary and ministry. As I have argued in an earlier chapter, interpretation of the cultic language of Hebrews is fraught with heavy consequences for SDA theology. If we take the position that the heavenly temple, sacrifice, and ministry are meant to be merely figurative, our sanctuary teaching will need to be reordered.[1]

This chapter presupposes the results of that earlier presentation. That

---

1 William G. Johnsson, "The Heavenly Sanctuary—Figurative or Real?" chap. 3 in this volume.

is, we hold that the cultic language of Hebrews comports with the model of apocalyptic Judaism, rather than with Philo's model, and points to an *actual* heavenly temple and ministry of Christ. But thereby a new issue arises as to how we are to understand the Day of Atonement allusions in the book of Hebrews. Given an actual heavenly sanctuary, does Hebrews then point to the cross as the antitype of the OT Day of Atonement?

The importance of the issue is obvious. If Calvary is set forth as the NT day of atonement, what becomes of our emphasis upon 1844 as the commencement of the antitypical day of atonement? Then the book of Hebrews, to which Adventists have so often made appeal for our most distinctive doctrine, would prove to be our theological Waterloo.

Not surprisingly, the history of SDA thought is strewn with controversy over this issue.[2] The most famous effort is Albion Foss Ballenger's *Cast Out for the Cross of Christ*.[3] As early as 1846, however, O.R.L. Crosier felt the force of the problem,[4] and in 1877 Uriah Smith[5] gave consideration to it. Also, D. M. Canright[6] argued that Jesus entered the Most Holy Place at His ascension, 1800 years before 1844. An Australian leader of the Seventh-day Adventist Church, W. W. Fletcher, listed this matter as one of the principal reasons for his defection.[7] Other contributors to the debate include E. E. Andross, whose book, *A More Excellent Ministry*,[8] sought to reply to Ballenger's work, W. H. Branson,[9] C. H. Watson,[10] and W. E. Howell.[11]

The issue has been met with strong convictions and painful results on occasion as some brethren of experience and stature have come to a parting of the ways with the church because of this controversy. Thus particular care is called for in our day as we seek to understand the thought of Hebrews.

We do not intend to take up all of Ballenger's arguments here.[12] Our

---

2 In writing this paragraph I have drawn upon material by Norman Young in an unpublished article entitled "The Checkered History of the Phrase 'Within the Veil.' "

3 Published by the author, Tropico, CA, n.d.

4 "The Law of Moses," *The Day Star* (February 7, 1846), p. 41.

5 *The Sanctuary and the Twenty-Three Hundred Days of Daniel VIII* 14 (Battle Creek, MI, 1877): 221ff.

6 *Seventh-day Adventism Renounced* (New York, 1899), p. 122.

7 *The Reasons for My Faith* (Sydney, 1932), p. 11.

8 Mountain View, CA, 1912.

9 *Reply to Canright* (Washington, DC, 1933), pp. 222-23.

10 *The Atoning Work of Christ* (Washington, D.C., 1934), pp. 181-91.

11 "The Meaning of the Veil," *The Ministry* 13/11 (1940): 13ff.

12 For a more detailed study see, Arnold V. Wallenkampf, "A Brief Review of Some of the Internal and External Challengers to the Seventh-day Adventist Teachings on the Sanctuary and the

focus in this chapter is on the Day of Atonement allusions in Hebrews and their interpretation. Accordingly, we shall confine our critique of the Ballenger thesis to his treatment of the phrase "within the veil," which is the main argument he advances from Hebrews for seeing the cross as the antitypical day of atonement. Then we shall turn to Hebrews itself to examine its allusions to the Day of Atonement. Finally, we shall attempt to interpret these allusions.

Ballenger's Treatment of "Within the Veil"

Hebrews 6:19-20 is the crucial verse in Ballenger's argument: "Which hope we have as an anchor of the soul, both sure and stedfast, and which entereth into that within the veil; whither the forerunner is for us entered, even Jesus, made an high priest for ever after the order of Melchisedec" (KJV).

Note how his argumentation builds on the lack of specification in the phrase "within the veil": "Now, if the Scripture in Hebrews 6:19 had said that Christ had entered the 'first veil,' then the question would be settled; but he simply says that Christ has entered 'within the veil.' Now, inasmuch as he uses the term without explaining it, taking it for granted that his readers understand to what place he refers, the all-important question arises: To which place—within the first veil, or within the second veil—would the reader understand the term 'within the veil' to apply? If the term 'within the veil' applies to the first apartment, then we would expect that it had been thus applied so universally in the Old Testament Scriptures, that the reader would not hesitate in applying it to the first apartment. But when I came to study the matter carefully I found that the term, 'within the veil,' in the Old Testament never applied to the place within the door of the tabernacle, or the first apartment, but always to the Holy of Holies, within the veil which separated the holy from the Most Holy. I found that the Hebrew Scriptures never call the curtain at the door of the tabernacle a 'veil,' much less 'the veil.' On the other hand, the term 'veil' is applied to the curtain separating the holy from the Most Holy; and the term 'within the veil' applies only to the Holy of Holies."[13]

Accordingly, we notice the following points developed in order by Ballenger.

Atonement," *The Sanctuary and the Atonement,* eds., Arnold V. Wllenkampf and W. Richard Lesher (Washington, DC, 1981), pp. 582-603; reprinted in Frank B. Holbrook, ed., *Doctrine of the Sanctuary: A Historical Survey* (Washington, DC, 1988), Appendix B.

13 Ballenger, pp. 20-21.

The Hebrew Term for Veil (*Pārōket*)

In every case the Hebrew term *pārōket* applies to the second curtain, the one that separates the holy from the Most Holy. By contrast, the first curtain throughout the OT is called the "door of the tabernacle."[14] Ballenger quotes the 23 references to *pārōket* in support (Exod 26:31, 33, 35; 27:21; 30:6; 35:12; 36:35; 38:27; 39:34; 40:3, 21-22, 26; Lev 4:6, 17; 16:2, 12, 15; 21:23; 24:3; Num 4:5; 18:7; 2 Chr 3:14).

When we examine these passages, we find in almost every case the reference is clearly to the second veil. In two places, however, the meaning is open to question: (1) "But he shall not come near the veil or approach the altar, because he has a blemish, that he may not profane my sanctuaries; for I am the Lord who sanctify them" (Lev 21:23); and (2) "You and your sons with you shall attend to your priesthood for all that concerns the altar and that is within the veil; and you shall serve. I give your priesthood as a gift, and any one else who comes near shall be put to death" (Num 18:7).

Further, we should note that the second veil is not always designated simply as "the veil," that is, by *pārōket* without amplification: "the veil which is before the testimony" (Exod 27:21), "the veil that is by the ark of the testimony" (Exod 30:6), "the veil of the screen" (Exod 35:12), "the veil of the screen" (Exod 39:34), "the veil of the screen" (Exod 40:21), "the veil of the sanctuary" (Lev 4:6), "the veil of the testimony" (Lev 24:3), and "the veil of the screen" (Num 4:5). Thus, although the data of the OT support Ballenger's point here, he has overstated his case by arguing that "the Lord invariably applies the term ['veil'] to the curtain separating the holy from the Most Holy. Never has he called the first curtain 'the veil' in the Hebrew Scriptures . . . the Lord was careful, in naming the two curtains, to give the first one the name of 'the *door* of the tabernacle,' and the second one the name of 'the veil.' "[15]

The LXX Term for "Veil" (*Katapetasma*)

Ballenger now turns to the Septuagint: "Never in the Septuagent [*sic*] is the first curtain called a veil except in the directions for the *making* and *moving* of the tabernacle, and then only when the connection plainly shows to which curtain it is applied."[16] The Greek word in question is *katapetasma*. It is true that this word, which is used also in Hebrews 6:19 for

14 Ibid., pp. 21-27.
15 Ibid., p. 27.
16 Ibid.

"veil," is regularly used for the veil of the Second Apartment. As with *pārōket*, however, it occurs both with and without qualifications, as in Exodus 27:21: "the veil that is before the ark of the covenant"; and in Exodus 30:6: "the veil that is over the ark of the testimonies."

In at least one place, contrary to Ballenger, the unqualified use refers to the first veil, as a careful study of Exodus 26:31-37 reveals. In verses 31-35 the second veil is shown with four posts, gold tops, and silver sockets (cf. Exod 37:3-4 where the second veil has four posts and silver sockets). In verse 37 the *katapetasma*, which is quite unqualified, has five posts, tops of gold, and sockets of brass (cf. Exod 37:5-6 where the first veil has five posts and sockets of brass). Clearly, the reference in verse 37 is to the first veil; Ballenger's assertion that "whenever the term veil appears in the Septuagent [*sic*] *without qualification* it refers to the veil separating the holy from the Most Holy"[17] is incorrect in at least this one case.

Apart from this flaw in Ballenger's research, his argument on the use of *katapetasma* is not so strong as the one on the occurrences of *pārōket*. This is because *katapetasma* is used in the LXX to translate *pārōket* as well as *māsāk*, and so can be used for the hanging at the gate of the courtyard, the first veil, and also the second veil.[18]

The Terms "Within the Veil" and "Without the Veil"

As a third argument Ballenger studies the usages of "within the veil" and "without the veil" in the OT. He finds that the five occurrences of the former phrase (Exod 26:33; Lev 16:2, 12, 15; Num 18:7), "*in the mind* of the student of the Hebrew Scriptures, meant in the *holy of holies,* and *not* in the first apartment."[19] He then looks at the places where "without the veil" or "before the veil" occurs (Exod 26:35; 27:20-21; 40:22, 26; Lev 4:6, 17; 24:1-3), and concludes that both expressions "*invariably apply* to the *holy place,* or *first apartment.*"[20] The argument, although strong, is overstated. We have already pointed out that the reference in Numbers 18:7 is ambiguous but that "veil" is further amplified in Exodus 27:21; 40:21; and Leviticus 4:6; 24:3.

It is not clear in this section whether Ballenger is reasoning from the MT or the LXX. He could have strengthened his case by appeal to the

---

17 Ibid., pp. 27-28. I am indebted to an Andrews University doctoral student, Lloyd A. Willis, for bringing this point to notice.
18 See Exodus 38:18; 39:40; Numbers 3:26; 4:32; see also Appendix B in this volume.
19 Ballenger, p. 29.
20 Ibid., p. 30 (italics supplied).

LXX for the phrase *to esōteron tou katapetasmatos* ("the inner of the veil"). This expression, which is found in Hebrews 6:19, occurs in the LXX only in Exodus 26:33 and Leviticus 16:2, 12, 15; and in each case it refers to the inner veil. It is interesting to note in Numbers 18:7 that the LXX has *to endothen tou katapetasmatos.*

New Testament Usage of the Term "the Veil"

Ballenger's final appeal is to the NT itself.[21] He quotes from the three synoptic accounts of the rending of "the veil" at the death of Jesus (Matt 27:50-52; Mark 15:37-38; Luke 23:44-45). Of course, in each of these references we find "the veil of the temple" rather than simply "the veil." The passages probably refer to the second veil; however, this section does not significantly advance the argument. The final three references to *katapetasma* in the NT come from the book of Hebrews itself (6:19-20; 9:3; 10:19-20).

Ballenger's Position Summarized

We may summarize our assessment of Ballenger's treatment of the phrase "within the veil" as follows: (1) The word used for veil in Hebrews 6:19-20, *katapetasma,* cannot decide the issue as to which veil is intended; (2) The actual phrase "within the veil" (*to esōteron tou katapetasmatos*) used in Hebrews 6:19 occurs only four times in the LXX and refers to the second veil; and (3) although in general the linguistic data examined by Ballenger support his thesis, he has overstated his case.

So far we have followed Ballenger as he has searched through the OT to find the interpretation of Hebrews 6:19-20. Our chief criticism is in terms of what he *failed* to do rather than what he presented in discussing the phrase "within the veil," namely, he failed to study sufficiently *the book of Hebrews itself.* The first principle of exegesis calls upon the student to consider the context. In this case, Ballenger should not merely have exegeted Hebrews 6:19-20 in its own right; he should have taken up the Day of Atonement allusions in the book of Hebrews. To this we now turn.

The Day of Atonement Allusions in Hebrews

We shall first notice unambiguous references to the Day of Atonement in Hebrews, of which there are three, and then list other possible allusions in the document.

---

21 Ibid., pp. 30-34.

Unambiguous References to the Day of Atonement

1. Hebrews 9:6-7. "These preparations having thus been made, the priests go continually into the outer tent, performing their ritual duties; but into the second only the high priest goes, and he but once a year, and not without taking blood which he offers for himself and for the errors of the people." These verses focus the concerns of the chapter to this point. Apparently the thumbnail sketch of the OT sanctuary with its two apartments—a sketch that is concluded quite abruptly in verse 5 ("Of these things we cannot now speak in detail.")—was provided to underscore the two types of service, which are stated in verses 6-7. The contrast between the two apartments and their accompanying ministries is obvious:

First Tent	Second Tent
continually	once a year
the priests	the high priests
(many priests)	only the high priests
ritual duties	bloody offering

The reference to the OT Day of Atonement is unambiguous.

2. Hebrews 9:24-25. "For Christ has entered, not into a sanctuary made with hands, a copy of the true one, but into heaven itself, now to appear in the presence of God on our behalf. Nor was it to offer himself repeatedly, as the high priest enters the holy place yearly with blood not his own." The RSV translation here is obviously faulty. The Greek *ta hagia* must be translated "sanctuary" or "holy places" in both verse 24 and verse 25! (The RSV switches from "sanctuary" [vs. 24] to "holy place" [vs. 25]). The translation "holy place" is especially faulty, because the context points clearly to a Day of Atonement allusion (high priest . . . yearly . . . blood [cf. 9:7]).

3. Hebrews 10:1-4. "For since the law has but a shadow of the good things to come instead of the true form of these realities, it can never, by the same sacrifices which are continually offered year after year, make perfect those who draw near. Otherwise, would they not have ceased to be offered? If the worshipers had once been cleansed, they would no longer have any consciousness of sin. But in these sacrifices there is a reminder of sin year after year. For it is impossible that the blood of bulls and goats should take away sins." The specifications of "year after year" and "blood of bulls and goats" again indicate a Day of Atonement setting.

In these three passages Hebrews presents the sacrifice of Christ against the backdrop of the OT Yom Kippur (Day of Atonement). The second passage contains this comparison in itself. In the first passage, the block 9:1-10, outlining the old sanctuary and its services, is followed by the contrasting block 9:11-14, portraying the sacrifice of Christ. Likewise in the third passage, the account of the old sacrifices in block 10:1-4 is set against the accomplishment of Christ in block 10:5-18. The significance of these data must be our concern shortly; first, however, we will list other possible allusions to the Day of Atonement in Hebrews.

Possible Allusions to the Day of Atonement

1. Hebrews 4:16. The "throne of grace" here is said to be the antitype of the mercy seat of the old cultus. It was before the mercy seat that the blood was sprinkled on the Day of Atonement; therefore, it may be argued, the allusion here is to the antitypical work of Christ.

2. Hebrews 5:3. The requirement of the high priest, to offer sacrifices for himself as well as for the people, was a specific injunction for the Day of Atonement.

3. Hebrews 7:26-27. Again, the need of the earthly high priests to offer sacrifices for themselves is indicated. The inclusion of *daily*, however, destroys the passage as a Day of Atonement allusion, even as it seriously weakens the case for the preceding one.

4. Hebrews 9:5. The mention of "mercy seat" recalls the services of the Day of Atonement. But it is *not* clear that the description of the furniture in verses 1-4 is presented in such a manner as to suggest the Day of Atonement ritual, so the point is not convincing.

5. Hebrews 9:8. We have discussed this passage elsewhere. It is argued that the teaching here points to the first or outer apartment as symbolic of the age of the OT, with the second pointing to the era of the NT. This would equate the entire period since Calvary with the Day of Atonement. As we suggested, however, the "first tent" here probably points to the entire sanctuary of the old cultus, in contrast to the genuine or "true tent" of the heavenly sanctuary (Heb 8:1-2). That is, the contrast is between the two sanctuaries rather than the two eras.

6. Hebrews 9:13. Maimonides indicates that the high priest was sprinkled with the ashes of a heifer twice during the seven days of isolation preceding the Day of Atonement.[22] There is no suggestion of any connection between the red heifer ceremony and the Day of Atonement in the OT, however.

---

22 See F. F. Bruce, *The Epistle to the Hebrews* (Grand Rapids, 1971), pp. 203-4.

7. Hebrews 9:27-28. As the Israelites anciently waited for the reappearance of the high priest on the Day of Atonement, so, it may be argued, Christians await the return of their Lord from the Most Holy, into which He entered at His ascension. This idea, however, is clearly not the prime intent of the passage, and is a questionable extension of it.

8. Hebrews 13:10-11. On the Day of Atonement the carcasses of the bullock and Lord's goat were burned outside the camp (Lev 16:27). But the point is not clear-cut because this procedure was also followed for some sin offerings, apart from the Day of Atonement (Exod 29:14; Lev 4:12; 8:17; 9:11).

On examination, therefore, we find at least three passages in Hebrews where the work of Christ on Calvary is set against the Day of Atonement services of the OT. It is not sure that other passages suggested as Day of Atonement allusions are in fact to be so interpreted.

We turn now to consider the meaning of the unquestioned allusions of Hebrews to the Day of Atonement.

Interpretation of the Day of Atonement Allusions

There are at least two ways of understanding the Day of Atonement references in Hebrews.

Under the Principle of Double Fulfillment

It may be held that the Levitical Day of Atonement does have an initial fulfillment at the cross, which in no way lessens its future application to the cleansing of the heavenly sanctuary which began in 1844. This would be in keeping with the "already-not yet" tension that runs throughout the NT.[23] Several statements of Ellen White appear to support this interpretation. Although she unambiguously applies the antitypical day of atonement to the events that began in 1844,[24] in some places she seems to see a fulfillment at the cross: "The great sacrifice has been made. The way to the holiest is laid open. A new and living way is prepared for all. No longer need sinful, sorrowing humanity await the coming of the high priest. Henceforth the Saviour was to officiate as priest and advocate in the heaven of heavens."[25]

---

23 The NT writers balance the hope of the Parousia and final fulfillment of the plan of redemption with what has been realized or inaugurated by the First Advent and the cross, e.g., the "kingdom" motif.

24 See *Early Writings*, pp. 244, 251-54; *The Great Controversy*, pp. 352, 400, 421-22, 433, 480, etc.

25 *The Desire of Ages*, p. 757.

"The mercy seat, upon which the glory of God rested in the holiest of all, is opened to all who accept Christ as the propitiation for sin, and through its medium, they are brought into fellowship with God. The veil is rent, the partition walls broken down, the handwriting of ordinances canceled. By virtue of His blood the enmity is abolished. Through faith in Christ Jew and Gentile may partake of the living bread."[26]

"A new and living Way, before which there hangs no veil, is offered to all. No longer need sinful, sorrowing humanity await the coming of the high priest."[27]

The question must be raised whether these statements are not a new form of the Ballenger teaching. Ellen White, it will be remembered, wrote thus concerning his views: "Elder Ballenger's proofs are not reliable. If received they would destroy the faith of God's people in the truth that has made us what we are. We must be decided upon this subject; for the points he is trying to prove by Scripture, are not sound."[28]

Did Ellen White intend to condemn every aspect of Ballenger's interpretation? Unfortunately, we do not have a specific discussion of his teachings from her pen.[29] Ballenger's views covered a wide gamut, however, and included the following: (1) The ministry of the heavenly sanctuary is operative from the Fall of man to the Parousia;[30] (2) The ministry in the first apartment began at the Fall and ended with the crucifixion;[31]

---

26 *The SDA Bible Commentary,* vol. 5, p. 1109.
27 Ibid.
28 Letter No. 329, 1905.
29 Ellen White gave pointed warnings against A. F. Ballenger's teachings, without indicating which particular areas were at fault. The following statements are representative: "There is not truth in the explanations of Scripture that Elder Ballenger and those associated with him are presenting. The words are right but misapplied to vindicate error. We must not give countenance to his reasoning. He is not led of God. . . . 'I am instructed to say to Elder B., Your theories, which have multitudes of fine threads, and need so many explanations, are not truth, and are not to be brought to the flock of God.' " —MS Release 737 (May 20, 1905). "If the theories that Brother B presents were received, they would lead many to depart from the faith. They would counterwork the truths upon which the people of God have stood for the past fifty years. I am bidden to say in the name of the Lord that Elder B. is following a false light. The Lord has not given him the message that he is bearing regarding the sanctuary service." —MS 62, 1905 (May 24, 1905). "Elder B. thinks that he has new light, and is burdened to give it to the people; but the Lord has instructed me that he has misapplied texts of Scripture, and given them a wrong application. 'Repent of the inclination to distinguish yourself as a man that has great light. Your supposed light is shown to me to be darkness, which will lead into strange paths.' " —MS 145, 1905. "So you see it is impossible for us to have any agreement with the positions taken by Brother A. F. Ballenger; for no lie is of the truth. His proofs do not belong where he places them, and although he may lead minds to believe his theory in regard to the sanctuary, there is no evidence that his theory is true." —Letter 50 (January 30, 1906).
30 Ballenger, p. 45.
31 Ibid., p. 56.

(3) Christ did not become a high priest until after His incarnation—the first apartment ministry was conducted by Melchizedek and the angels;[32] (4) Because Christ agreed to bear man's sin at the time of the Fall, He was physically separated from His Father for 4000 years until the ascension;[33] (5) The ministry in the Second Apartment was initiated with the ascension of Christ and ends at the Second Coming;[34] (6) The blood of the daily offerings of the OT represented only the sinner's confession and prayer for pardon whereas only the blood sprinkled before the mercy seat represented the sinner's substitute.[35]

The double fulfillment, it must be obvious, differs from the Ballenger view. Apart from some of the quaint points that we listed above, it denies that the Day of Atonement was *completely* fulfilled at the Cross, as Ballenger proposed. It bears some similarity to the interpretation of Andross, who saw a limited work of Christ upon His ascension as He entered to inaugurate or anoint the Most Holy.[36]

In my judgment, this view misplaces the role and emphasis of the Day of Atonement allusions in Hebrews. To see these allusions in the light of the overall theological development of the document is to interpret them differently, namely, in terms of the efficacy of sacrifice.

The Efficacy of Sacrifice

We must first locate the place of the Day of Atonement allusions in Hebrews and then proceed to understand their function.

1. The role of the Day of Atonement allusions. The Day of Atonement motif is not the central one in the argumentation of Hebrews concerning sacrifice. Although it is important in the three passages that we have already noticed, it is by no means the exclusive emphasis. Rather, it is part of a complex of references to the cultus: 5:1-3, "gifts and sacrifices for sins"; 7:27, the high priest offered *daily* sacrifices for his own sins and those of the people; 9:9-10, "gifts and sacrifices . . . food . . . drink . . . various ablutions"; 9:12, "the blood of goats and *calves*"; 9:13, "blood of goats and bulls . . . the ashes of a heifer"; 9:18-21, ratification of the first covenant by the blood of goats and calves; 10:8, sacrifices, offerings, burnt offerings, sin offerings; 10:11, the daily services of the old sanctuary; 10:29, "the

---

32 Ibid., p. 83.
33 Ibid., pp. 45-46.
34 Ibid., p. 56.
35 Ibid., pp. 40-41.
36 Andross, p. 53.

blood of the covenant"; 11:4, the sacrifice offered by Abel; 11:28, the blood of the Passover; and 12:24, the blood of the new covenant.

The Day of Atonement motif of Hebrews must be placed within this larger cultic context. In my judgment, the first interpretation raises the motif to a place of undue prominence. As I have argued in my dissertation,[37] the leitmotif of the sacrificial argument of Hebrews (8:1–10:18) is the *better blood* rather than the Day of Atonement. As the apostle has presented previously, the better speech, the Son better than angels, the better priesthood, the better covenant, the better high priest, and the better tabernacle, so here he develops the *better blood.* It is the motif of *haima* ("blood") that links together the various references to daily sacrifices: heifer, inauguration of covenant and Yom Kippur. We notice this in the three ringing affimations "not without blood" (9:7, 18, 22), in the logic of 9:13-14 (if the blood of goats and bulls . . . *how much more* the blood of Christ), and in the fundamental axiom of the passage, the "blood rule" of 9:22—without *haimatekchusia* ("blood shedding"), no *aphesis* ("forgiveness"). This leitmotif of blood is not to be subsumed or superseded—it gathers up all talk of sacrifice, offering, and Day of Atonement; it alone can bring cleansing from the basic human problem of defilement that the book of Hebrews sets forth.

2. The function of the Day of Atonement allusions. Why then does the Day of Atonement enter the argument? Because it was the high point of the old cultus. It was the *one* day when man (although only one) entered the Most Holy; it was *the* day for the removal of Israel's sins. The argumentation of 8:1–10:18 is shaped to bring out the superiority of the blood of Christ. Its force is that, whatever value the OT sacrifices might have had, they could not in themselves provide final putting away of sins: "For it is impossible that the blood of bulls and goats should take away sins" (10:4). So the argument is that the OT services, *even at their high point,* were inadequate. They provided woefully limited access to God (one man alone) and their very repetition showed their failure: "Otherwise, would they not have ceased to be offered?" (10:2). So even the annual Day of Atonement hammered home Israel's need: limited access, no finality in purging sins.

So at length the entire old cultus is to be set aside in the divine plan ("until the time of reformation," 9:10). If the sacrificial system falls short

---

37 William G. Johnsson, *Defilement and Purgation in the Book of Hebrews* (Unpublished Ph.D. dissertation, Vanderbilt University, 1973), chap. 4.

at its high point, the complete structure must be branded inadequate. But, says Hebrews, the good news is that of *better blood*! All that the old system failed to do because of its inherent insufficiencies, all that the repeated days of atonement could not accomplish, has now been done by Calvary. Instead of many repeated sacrifices, there is one sacrifice once for all. By that one act, all barriers between God and man have been abolished so that we may come boldly into the presence of God. At last a sacrifice has been made that is able to provide thoroughgoing purification of sins.

The Day of Atonement references of Hebrews, therefore, are *not* designed to show that the antitypical day of atonement began at the Ascension (contra Ballenger), nor to suggest a brief entry into the Most Holy for its inauguration (contra Andross), nor to set forth the first fulfillment of the OT high point, the complete fulfillment commencing in 1844 (and not addressed by Hebrews). Rather, the argument swings on the *relative value of sacrifice,* contrasting the apex of the OT cultus with the surpassing achievement of Jesus Christ on Calvary. As I see it, the *time* element is not at all in view here (9:1-5 should already have put us off the track of trying to reason from type to antitype in this section). The comparison and contrast, as clearly set out in 9:13-14, centers on *efficacy of sacrifice.*

As we noticed under the first interpretation of the Day of Atonement allusions, Ellen White at times employs the language of Hebrews of "the new and living way" and "the veil." When she does so, she shares the conceptions of Hebrews—a Sacrifice that has provided total purification of sin and unimpeded access to God.

Conclusion

It is the larger context—the ebb and flow of the argument—that Ballenger failed to grasp in his struggle to understand the book of Hebrews. One gains the impression that the phrase "within the veil" came to occupy an all-consuming place in his thinking until it prevented his perception of the development of the reasoning of this carefully wrought document. Likewise, he sought to inject questions of typology and events in time, which are foreign to the concerns of the apostle here.

The reasoning of 8:1–10:18 would have solved his dilemma if he had dwelt sufficiently long on it. He might have seen that the total cultic argumentation, with its references to sacrifices, sanctuaries, and Day of Atonement, is shaped to portray the magnificence of Christianity—Jesus

Christ, our High Priest, with a once-for-all, all-sufficient sacrifice. Then "within the veil" would have been viewed in perspective—as setting forth in elliptical form the accomplishment of Christ that has dissolved all barriers between God and man.

Chapter VII

Typology in the Book of Hebrews

Richard M. Davidson

The Nature of Biblical Typology

Editorial Synopsis. Seventh-day Adventists affirm that passages such as Hebrews 8:5 and 9:24 (in context) teach that the Israelite sanctuary functioned as a "copy" or shadow-type pointing to the greater reality, the true sanctuary in heaven (8:2). Consequently, the earthly sanctuary with its two apartments (and the distinctive ministries related to each) is instructive for Christians and provides important insights into the nature of Christ's priestly ministration in the heavenly sanctuary.

It is argued by some, however, that biblical types may not be used to establish doctrine and that the book of Hebrews itself is the final norm for the interpretation of sanctuary types. It is asserted that the writer of Hebrews has emphasized the disparity between the type and antitype to such a degree that he has collapsed their fundamental continuity. Therefore, the argument concludes that it is not sound to trace basic relationships between the earthly and heavenly sanctuaries.

Naturally, such a stance must deny the truth of Christ's two divisions of priestly activity in succeeding ministrations (corresponding to the ministrations of the two apartment earthly sanctuary). It must also reject the onset of Christ's Second Apartment ministry in 1844, the pioneer's key to explain the Millerite disappointment.

In order to test the validity of these challenges the writer of this chapter explores the subject of biblical typology. In this section he describes the characteristics of typology as it occurs in the NT writings (apart from the book of Hebrews). In a later section he compares general typology with the typology found in Hebrews. Finally, he will apply the results of these studies to the allegations.

The English word, "type," is derived from the Greek word, *"tupos."*

121

Tupos and its related forms appear 20 times in the NT. Analysis of the passages, where the NT writer employs these terms to interpret the OT, indicates that five characteristics or "structures" are inherent in biblical types.

1. The historical structure. Types are rooted in history. Historical persons (Adam, etc.), events (Exodus, Flood), or institutions (sanctuary) are used as prefigurations. Their antitypes in the NT are likewise historical realities.

2. The eschatalogical structure. Types have a final-age quality. For example, Israel and her experience in the wilderness is a type of the later Christian communion "upon whom the end of the ages has come" (1 Cor 10:6, 11).

3. The Christological-soteriological structure. OT types find their fulfillment in Christ or in some aspect of His saving work. For example, Adam is viewed as a type of Christ (Rom 5:14).

4. The ecclesiological structure. Types may have also a congregational aspect to them. For example, the salvation of Noah and his family "through water" has its antitype in the ordinance of baptism which saves the Christian congregation through the resurrection of Jesus Christ (1 Pet 3:20-21).

5. The prophetic structure. OT types pointed forward. They may be seen as prefigurations of the corresponding NT reality. As noted above, Adam as a type carries a Christological emphasis. But he has also a prophetic aspect as well, for Adam is seen as a "type of the one who *was to come*" (Rom 5:14).

The post-critical view of typology recently being advocated by noted scholars within the Biblical Theology Movement does not view the historicity of a type as being essential. It rejects the concept that a type is a designed, prospective foreshadowing. Rather, this school of thought is content to see only analogies and general parallel situations within God's similar modes of activity.

On the contrary the five "structures" or characteristics that emerge from the biblical data reaffirm the more traditional view: that biblical typology is built upon the historical reality of both the type and antitype and that it consists of a divinely-designed, prophetic prefiguration involving at times detailed correspondences between OT and NT realities as well as between general, similar situations.

Section Outline

I. Introduction
II. Resurgence of Interest
III. Structures of Typology

* * * * * * *

Introduction

Modern scholarly studies of the Epistle to the Hebrews generally agree that typology plays a crucial role in the argument, particularly in the author's treatment of the sanctuary and its services. At the same time current literature reveals sharp divergences of opinion on issues connected with the nature and function of typology in the Epistle. These issues may be divided into four major areas, each of which will be the focus of a separate section of this chapter.

The first and broadest category pertains to the nature of biblical typology in general. Two modern views of typology—the "traditional" and the "post-critical"—currently claim to represent the fundamental biblical perspective. Since these modern assessments differ so widely and at such critical points, it is imperative that we give some attention to the nature of typology in the Scriptures as a whole.

The first section of this study, therefore, outlines the major differences between the current views of biblical typology. We will then provide a brief summary of my previously published analysis of the characteristics or "structures" of typology as they emerge from Scripture.[1]

The second major area concerns the relationship between the typology of Hebrews and the typological perspective found elsewhere in Scripture. A number of recent studies have argued that the vertical (earthly/heavenly) typology in Hebrews is a vestige of mythic or dualistic thought forms that are alien to the Bible. Many discussions of typology build upon this distinction between the vertical typology in Hebrews and the horizontal (historical) typology used by other Bible writers. The conclusion is then drawn that only horizontal typology is acceptable within the modern world view.

In the second major section of this study we will seek to analyze the conceptual structures of typology in Hebrews and will determine how they

---

1 Richard M. Davidson, *Typology In Scripture* (Berrien Springs, MI, 1981).

compare or contrast with those found in representative typological passages outside of Hebrews.

A third major concern relates to the OT *basis* for sanctuary typology in Hebrews. The author of Hebrews (8:5) substantiates his vertical (earthly/heavenly) sanctuary typology by citing Exodus 25:40. But it has been argued recently that, contrary to the claim in Hebrews, the passage in Exodus does not support the idea of a vertical correspondence between earthly and heavenly sanctuaries. Consequently, in this third section we will take an excursus from Hebrews to examine whether Exodus 25:40 (in context) indicates a vertical sanctuary typology.

The fourth major cluster of issues revolves around the question of the relationship between type and antitype in Hebrews. This area is of particular significance in the light of Seventh-day Adventist discussion of the doctrine of the sanctuary.

Seventh-day Adventists have understood from such passages as Hebrews 8:5 and 9:24 (in their contexts) that the OT earthly sanctuary is a copy or model of the heavenly sanctuary. It is held, therefore, that a basic continuity exists between the essential contours of "type" and "antitype." The author of Hebrews recognizes that the earthly is a "shadow" pointing to the greater reality, the "true" sanctuary in heaven. Nonetheless, he still maintains the fundamental continuity between the "type" and "antitype." The earthly sanctuary, with its apartments and services, is regarded as instructive in clarifying the basic contours of the NT heavenly sanctuary.

Recently, however, it has been argued that in the book of Hebrews there is a "tremendous disparity" between types and antitypes, a frequent setting aside of earthly sanctuary "specifics" because of their "weakness and uselessness." It is maintained that the author's "repeated deviations" from the OT sanctuary types in order to explain the NT heavenly reality, and his "laboring to modify the type to Christian beliefs," has collapsed the fundamental continuity between type and antitype. Based on or closely related to this general argument are several additional assertions regarding the interpretation of typology in Hebrews:

1. Typology may not be used to establish doctrine, but only to illustrate that which is taught elsewhere in clear didactic, non-symbolic language.

2. Argument may not proceed from OT type to NT antitype, but only the other way around—from heavenly to earthly.

3. The author of Hebrews has no concern for the details of the OT type. He often alters the type to fit the NT fulfillment and makes blunders in discussing those details that he does mention.

4. The book of Hebrews is the ultimate norm for interpreting the OT sanctuary types since only in this book do we find NT interpretation of the first and Second Apartment ministries.

Such issues concerning the relationship of type and antitype in Hebrews call for careful consideration. We will explore these in the final section of this chapter. Though this study makes no attempt to provide the "last word" on the nature of typology in Hebrews, it is hoped that progress will be made toward identifying principles of typological interpretation that emerge from, and are faithful to, the infallible norm of Scripture.

Resurgence of Interest

In recent decades a number of prominent biblical scholars have given a strikingly positive assessment of the role of typology in Scripture. For example, Leonard Goppelt, who produced the first comprehensive survey of NT typology from a modern historical perspective,[2] has in later articles continued to emphasize that typology "is the central and distinctive NT way of understanding Scripture." Properly understood, "it is the decisive interpretation of Jesus, the Gospel, and the Church. . . . According to its NT *core* . . . typology is theologically constitutive for an understanding of the Gospel."[3]

Other similar statements may be noted. G. Ernest Wright asserts that "the one word which perhaps better than any other describes the early Church's method of interpreting the Old Testament is 'typology.' "[4] R. M. Grant concurs, "The New Testament method of interpreting the Old was generally that of typology."[5] E. Earle Ellis (following W. G. Kümmel) maintains that "typological interpretation expresses most clearly 'the basic attitude of primitive Christianity toward the Old Testament.' "[6]

These recent affirmations of the centrality and importance of biblical typology appear remarkable in view of the prevailing negative evaluation by critical scholars in previous decades. The triumph of historical criticism

2 Leonard Goppelt, *Typos: Die typologische Deutung des Alten Testaments im Neuen* (Gütersloh, 1939; reprint ed., Darmstadt, 1966); Eng. tr., *Typos: The Typological Interpretation of the Old Testament in the New* (Grand Rapids, 1982).

3 Leonard Goppelt, *"tupos, antitupos, tupikos, hupotupōsis," TDNT,* 8:255-56.

4 George E. Wright, "God Who Acts: Biblical Theology as Recital," SBT, No. 8 (London, 1952), p. 61.

5 Robert M. Grant, *A Short History of the Interpretation of the Bible,* rev. ed. (New York, 1963), pp. 54-55.

6 E. Earle Ellis, *Prophecy and Hermeneutic in Early Christianity* (Tübingen, 1978), p. 165, cited Werner G. Kümmel, "Schriftauslegung," Religion in Geschichte und Gegenwart, 3rd ed., vol. 5, p. 1519.

within liberal scholarship had virtually eliminated any serious interest in the subject throughout the nineteenth and early twentieth centuries. Except in certain conservative circles, typology was merely "an historical curiosity, of little importance or significance for the modern reader."[7]

After World War II strong advocates of the historical-critical method—which had dealt the deathblow to nineteenth century traditional typology—exuberantly embraced a "post-critical neo-typology."[8] Thus, in recent decades a host of scholars have participated in the discussion of biblical typology.[9] New interest has occurred not only within biblical studies but also among such related disciplines as dogmatic and systematic theology, church history, art and architecture, and literary criticism.

Major Trends

A survey of significant participants and issues in the modern discussion reveals two major views on the nature of biblical typology.[10] The "traditional" understanding is that typology refers to the study of divinely ordained, detailed OT predictive prefigurations of Jesus Christ and gospel realities brought about by Him.[11]

The "post-critical"[12] view of typology, advocated by noted scholars within the Biblical Theology Movement, makes significant departures from the traditional understanding. It is founded on a different view of history and revelation which has little room for the predictive element. Typology is viewed as a common human way of analogical thinking. Typological interpretation involves the retrospective recognition of general correspondences within the consistent divine "revelation in history."[13]

---

7 Geoffrey W. H. Lampe, "The Reasonableness of Typology," in Geoffrey W. H. Lampe and Kenneth J. Woollcombe, "Essays on Typology," SBT, No. 22 (Naperville, IL, 1957), p. 16.

8 This phrase is coined by Gilbert F. Cope, *Symbolism in the Bible and the Church* (New York, 1959), p. 20.

9 For a survey of the major participants, views, and issues in this discussion, see my dissertation, *Typology in Scripture: A Study of Hermeneutical Typos Structures*, Andrews University Seminary Doctoral Dissertation Series 2 (Berrien Springs, MI, 1981): 15-114.

10 For a discussion of the two major views, see especially ibid., pp. 46-75.

11 Three main "traditional" modes may be distinguished. The Cocceian mode (named after Johannes Cocceius—see ibid., pp. 33-36, 46, for discussion) operates with little or no hermeneutical controls and tends to posit typological correspondences where there is even the slightest resemblance between OT and NT realities. At the other extreme, the Marshian mode (named after Bishop Herbert Marsh—see ibid., pp. 36-37, 46-48, for discussion) maintains that the only true types are those explicitly confirmed in the NT. A mediating position, represented in the classical nineteenth century work of Patrick Fairbairn (see ibid., pp. 38-42, for discussion), espouses a typology controlled by carefully delineated hermeneutical principles.

12 For an overview of major advocates of the "post-critical" view of typology, see ibid., pp. 51-88.

13 Two main emphases within this postcritical neotypology may be distinguished. An English tradition represented by G.W.H. Lampe and K. J. Woollcombe, stresses the "recurring rhythm" of

The major elements of difference between these two views of the nature of typology may be summarized as follows:

"Traditional"	"Post-Critical"
1. Rooted in historical realities (historicity essential)	1. Historicity not essential
2. Divinely-designed prefigurations	2. Analogies/correspondences within God's similar modes of activity
3. Prospective/predictive	3. Retrospective (little or no predictive element)
4. Prefigurations extend to specific details	4. Involves only general "parallel situations"
5. Includes vertical (sanctuary) typology	5. Rejects vertical as alien to biblical perspective (Hebrews = mythic/dualistic)
6. Involves consistent principles of interpretation	6. No system or order—freedom of Spirit

The question immediately arises, How does one decide what is the *biblical* perspective on typology? This leads us to important aspects of methodology.

Methods of Approach

A comprehensive review of the prodigious amount of literature on the subject of biblical typology reveals a surprising deficiency with regard to method. Although definitions and lists of characteristics have been forthcoming, none of these studies has really allowed the structures—the conceptual elements—of typology to emerge from within Scripture.

Instead, a preconceived understanding of typology—based on little or no exegetical evidence—is projected upon the Scriptures. The biblical material is then examined from the perspective of this a priori understanding. In the haste to "get on" with the search for typological correspondences, previous studies have neglected the painstaking but unavoidable task of laying a solid linguistic-exegetical foundation for understanding what biblical typology really is.

God's saving activity, while a German emphasis, represented by Gerhard von Rad, conceives of an unlimited number of "structural analogies within tradition history." For discussion of these two emphases, see ibid., pp. 59-65, 68-69.

In fairness to these previous studies, we should point out the difficulty in defining typology by Scripture itself without imposing preconceived ideas from the outside. For example, if we do *not* define typology before coming to Scripture, how shall we recognize where it is present? But if we do define it in advance, then we bring our a priori understanding of its nature to Scripture rather than letting it emerge *from* Scripture! What is the way out of the impasse? How do we enter the "hermeneutical circle" and recognize the *existence* of typology in biblical passages without already defining its *nature* in advance?

In the present writer's dissertation a method is articulated which attempts to penetrate the impasse that has just been described.[14] This approach may be sketched as follows: One may certainly define typology as "the study of types." This step imposes no previous understanding of types upon the Scriptures. But this simple process leads us to a word bridge into the "hermeneutical circle," because the English word "type" is the equivalent of the Greek word *tupos*.

A study of the usage of *tupos* (and its cognates) in the NT reveals that in six occurrences *tupos* (or cognate) is employed as a technical hermeneutical term to describe the NT author's interpretation of the OT. Therefore, in these passages *tupos* (or cognate) clearly provides an indicator of the presence of "typology." We do not have to decide in advance the NT author's hermeneutical approach. We can be certain that it involves typology—the study of types—because the Bible writer has designated this by the use of the word *tupos* (or cognate).

Thus, we may proceed with a detailed exegesis of the NT "hermeneutical *tupos* passages." From such an analysis these should emerge at least a preliminary delineation of the fundamental conceptual structures of biblical typology. Along with the exegetical analysis, a detailed word study of *tupos* (and cognates) in both biblical and extrabiblical literature would be expected to provide additional insights on the nature of typology in Scripture.

The succeeding pages will provide a brief summary of the results of the attempt to apply this method suggested above. For substantiation and more detailed discussion of the conclusions set forth in this section, the reader is encouraged to consult the writer's published dissertation.[15]

---

14 For a detailed description and defense of this method, see ibid., pp. 4-14.
15 See ibid., pp. 115-336.

Structures of Typology

The word *tupos* (or cognate) appears 20 times in the NT. As we have already noted, six of these occurrences appear in a hermeneutical context, that is, in a setting where the NT author is engaged in the interpretation of the OT. The word *tupos* is found in three passages (Rom 5:14; 1 Cor 10:6; Heb 8:5 = Exod 25:40); *antitupos* occurs twice (Heb 9:24; 1 Pet 3:21); and *tupikos* appears once (1 Cor 10:11). In this section we will limit our examination to those passages (and their immediate contexts) which lie outside of Hebrews.

Five typological structures consistently emerge from a detailed analysis of the non-Hebrews passages (Rom 5:12-21; 1 Cor 10:1-13; 1 Pet 3:18-22). The first conceptual element may be termed the *historical* structure. The remaining four are theological: the *eschatological* structure, the *Christological-soteriological* structure, the *ecclesiological* structure, and the *prophetic* structure.

1. The historical structure. The presence of this conceptual element underscores the fact that typology is rooted in history. This is in contradistinction to allegory. Allegory is not concerned primarily (if at all) about the literal historical sense but with the figurative or spiritual "kernel" hidden under the historical "husk."

In typology the historical structure involves three crucial aspects. First, the OT type is assumed to be a *historical reality*. For example, the historical realities may be persons (Adam, Rom 5), events (the Exodus, 1 Cor 10), or institutions (the sanctuary, Heb 8, 9—see next section). The historicity of these realities is assumed. In fact, the typological arguments in Romans 5, 1 Corinthians 10, and 1 Peter 3 depend upon the historicity of Adam, the Exodus, and the Flood and would collapse if their historical reality was not accepted.

The second aspect is that of a *historical correspondence* between the OT type and the NT antitype. Thus, Adam is a type *(tupos)* of Christ (Rom 5); the Exodus events occurred as types *(tupoi)* corresponding to the experience of the Christian church (1 Cor 10); and the Flood corresponds to its antitype *(antitupos)*, Christian baptism (1 Pet 3).

The content of the correspondences extends even to details connected with the type. But apparently the links are to those details already invested with redemptive significance in the OT. The correspondence can involve aspects of antithesis as well as comparison, for example, between Adam and Christ in Romans 5.

But even when there is only a comparison of similarities, a third aspect of the historical structure is present, that of intensification. The type and antitype are never on the same plane. The NT antitype invariably involves an absolute escalation or intensification of the OT type. So, for example, Israel's food and drink in the wilderness are intensified in the antitype as the Christian Lord's Supper (1 Cor 10). Again, the physical deliverance through the Flood waters is escalated in the antitypical spiritual deliverance through the waters of baptism (1 Pet 3). Or to borrow an example outside our hermeneutical *tupos* passages, in Jesus the Antitype "*something greater* than the temple is here" (Matt 12:6); "*something greater* than Jonah is here" (Matt 12:41); "*something greater* than Solomon is here" (Matt 12:42).

2. The eschatological structure. This element further clarifies the nature of the historical correspondence and intensification described above. The OT (*tupoi*) are not linked to just *any* similar reality. Rather, certain OT persons/events/institutions find their fulfillment in the *eschatological* realities of the NT. (We use the word "fulfillment" because of the prophetic structure described below.)

In 1 Corinthians 10 the experiences of Israel in the wilderness are types (*tupoi*) of the eschatological "us"—"upon whom the end of the ages has come" (vs. 11). In Romans 5 the first representative man, Adam, is a type (*tupos*) of "the one to come"—the second Adam whose coming brought about the eschatological New Age. In 1 Peter 3 the salvation of Noah and his family through the Flood finds its antitype (*antitupos*) in the sacramental salvation (baptism) of the eschatological "now [*nun*]" (vs. 21).

It should be noted that the eschatological fulfillment of the *tupos* passages involves three perspectives. (1) The first advent of Christ brought about an *inauguration* of the eschatological fulfillment in the kingdom of grace. (2) The church now lives in the time of *appropriation,* the time of eschatological *tension* between the "already" and the "not yet." (3) The Second Advent will usher in the eschatological *consummation* in the kingdom of glory.[16] The various *tupos* passages focus upon one or more of these aspects of eschatological fulfillment.

3. The Christological-soteriological structure. This structure is significant in its determination of the content of the type and antitype. The OT types find their fulfillment in Christ. Sometimes there is a direct

---

16 For convenience we may call these three aspects of fulfillment the Christological, Ecclesiological, and Apocalyptic. For further discussion, see ibid., pp. 388-97.

correspondence between an OT reality and the person of Christ, as in Romans 5. Adam is equivalent to Christ. At other times the primary fulfillment of the OT type is viewed as occurring in various realities of the new covenant related to and brought about by Christ. For example, in 1 Corinthians 10 and 1 Peter 3, ancient Israel and Noah and his family are equivalent to the Christian church—individually, corporately, and sacramentally.

A further aspect of the Christological determination is brought to the fore in 1 Corinthians 10. Here Christ is presented as the ultimate orientation point of the OT types and their NT fulfillments. The types and their NT correspondents are *Christocentrically* determined. They may carry a positive or negative moral "charge" depending on whether they are *for* or *against* Christ. Thus, in 1 Corinthians 10 the "most" of ancient Israel who persisted in disobedience are types of those in the Christian church who similarly orient themselves against Christ.

Closely bound up with the Christological is the *soteriological* component of this structure. The correspondence of the type-antitype is not between "bare" or "neutral" historical events, persons, or institutions, but between ones that are salvation oriented. The OT types are *redemptive* realities, and they find their fulfillment in the saving work of Christ and in the new covenant realities issuing from Christ. This soteriological or saving dimension is thoroughly *Christocentric,* that is, either positive (redemptive for those responding to Christ's grace) or negative (retributive for those who spurn His mercy).

4. The ecclesiological structure. This fourth element in biblical typology includes three aspects: the individual worshipers, the corporate community, and the ordinances of the church. In 1 Corinthians 10 all three are emphasized. The experiences of ancient Israel in the wilderness happened typologically (*tupikos*), as types (*tupoi*) of the end-time congregation (vss. 6, 11), the Christian church. This involved the sacraments (vss. 2-4) and a personal decision whether to be faithful or disobedient (vss. 5-10).

In Romans 5 there is a correspondence between "the many" in Adam (vs. 15) and "the many" ("those who receive," vs. 17) in Christ. This theme is developed in terms of baptism in the following chapter. In 1 Peter 3 the salvation of Noah and his family "through water" (vs. 20) has its eschatological antitype (*antitupos*), in which the ordinances of baptism saves the Christian congregation (the "you" who have been baptized, vs. 21) through the resurrection of Jesus Christ.

5. The prophetic structure. This last conceptual element also involves three aspects. First, the OT type points forward—it is an *advance presentation* or *prefiguration* of the corresponding NT reality or realities. In 1 Corinthians 10 the experience of ancient Israel in the wilderness is shown to be an advance presentation of the experience of the Christian church. In Romans 5 the first man, Adam, is seen to prefigure the second Adam, Jesus Christ. In 1 Peter 3 the divine salvation of Noah and his family through water was revealed as pre-presenting the salvation of Christians in the sacrament of baptism (through the resurrection of Jesus Christ).

Second, in each of these instances there is revealed a *divine design*. The OT realities were superintended by God so as to be prefigurations of the NT realities. The divine design includes specific details as well as the general soteriological contours. However, God's design does not interfere with the freedom of the individuals involved nor detract from the historical redemptive significance of the OT realities in themselves.

Third, the divinely designed advance-presentations involve a "must needs be" quality giving the OT types the force of *prospective-predictive foreshadowings* of their NT fulfillments. In 1 Corinthians 10 Paul builds up the typological relationship between ancient and eschatological Israel. His purpose is to show that what happened to disobedient Israel in the wilderness "must needs be" what will come upon the Corinthians who persist in disobedience. In Romans 5 Paul is able to argue from the Adam-all-men solidarity to the Christ-all-men solidarity, because he posits a "must needs be" relationship between them. In 1 Peter 3 the apostle assures the readers that as Noah and his family experienced divine salvation through water, so it "must needs be" that the antitypical baptism now saves them through the resurrection of Jesus Christ.

Tupos As a Hermeneutical Term

A word study of the Greek *tupos* and NT cognates up to and including NT times reveals a wealth of dictionary data.[17] Of particular interest at this point is the early use of *tupos* to mean "form," that is, a "hollow form" or "mold." The term *tupos* in its original (and continued) signification of hollow mold is strikingly suited to encompass the dynamics involved in the typological structures we have just described.

A hollow mold involves five basic spatial and linear dynamics: (1) It is a concrete reality. (2) It has been formed from some proto-type which exists previously (either concretely or in the mind of the designer). (3) It

---

17 Ibid., pp. 115-90.

functions as a matrix for shaping the end product. (4) The end product invariably conforms to the basic contours of the mold. (5) But it transcends the mold in that it fulfills the purpose for which the mold was designed.

As with the *tupos* as "hollow mold," so with the *tupos* as a hermeneutical term for the biblical type. The type (*tupos*) is (1) a concrete (historical) reality that (2) has been "shaped" according to the previous (divine) design and (3) functions as a "mold" to "shape" the end (eschatological) product (the NT antitype), which end product (4) invariably ("must needs be") corresponds to the basic contours of the (OT) type, but (5) transcends the type in that it fulfills the ultimate (Christological-soteriological/ecclesiological) purpose for which the (OT) type was intended.

Implications for the Current Debate

In light of the preceding synthesis it is apparent that the typological structures emerging from *tupos* passages (at least outside of Hebrews) generally coincide with the traditional and not the post-critical understanding of typology. We may summarize these by noting that according to the NT writers:

1. Typology necessarily presupposes and builds upon the historical reality of both type and antitype (versus the post-critical view that historicity of the type/antitype are unessential).

2. Typology consists of divinely-designed prefigurations (versus the post-critical view that it simply reflects the analogies or correspondences within the recurring rhythm of God's divine activity in history).

3. Typology is basically prospective/predictive (versus the post-critical view that it is retrospective with little or no predictive element).

4. Typology involves detailed correspondences between OT and NT realities as well as general "similar situations" (versus the postcritical view that it relates only to general "parallel situations").

We have thus far dealt with the typological structures of Scripture outside the book of Hebrews. We may now move to the second major area outlined in the introduction, that is, the nature of typology in the Epistle to the Hebrews. To what degree do the typological structures of Hebrews—as they become apparent in the cultic typology surrounding the *typos* passages of Hebrews 8:5 and 9:24—coincide with the typological structures inherent in other NT *tupos* passages? This question leads us to our next section.

Typology in Hebrews

Editorial Synopsis. Hebrews 8:5 and 9:24 are important passages for determining the characteristics of the typology employed in the book of Hebrews. The first contains the Greek word *tupos* ("type," "pattern," RSV); the latter uses the related word *antitype* ("copy," RSV). The two passages appear in the context of the central discussion of the sanctuary cultus (7:1–10:18). The use of the *tupos/antitupos* word-indicators alerts us to the presence of typology in this portion of the author's argument; the context will disclose its distinguishing marks.

Biblical types may be classified as horizontal or vertical according to their directional orientation. Horizontal types prefigure future antitypes on the continuum of historical time. The movement is horizontal, as it were, from the type (person, event, or institution) to a later antitype. The Adam/Christ correspondence (Rom 5:14) is an example of horizontal typology. Vertical typology on the other hand has an earth/heaven alignment. The classic example of vertical typology is the earthly/heavenly sanctuary correspondence. Both horizontal and vertical typologies occur and intersect in the book of Hebrews.

Modern scholars generally reject the earth/heaven typology in Hebrews. They argue that it reflects the philosophical views of Plato and Philo or else it is a carryover from "the mythic cosmic analogy of antiquity." But neither inference is in harmony with the scriptural facts. In this section the present writer demonstrates that the vertical typology in Hebrews is drawn from the OT's own understanding of the earthly/heavenly sanctuary dimension.

The question addressed in this section is, Does the typology of Hebrews have the same five characteristics found in biblical typology elsewhere? The answer is, Yes—for both horizontal and vertical typologies. On the horizontal line major historical correspondences are drawn between the old and new covenants, between the Levitical sacrifices and Christ's once-for-all-time sacrifice, and between the Levitical priesthood and Christ's priesthood. At times the correspondence involves specific details. Intensification occurs in the antitype as movement is made from the limited, ineffective OT cultus to the effective, all-sufficient sacrifice and priesthood of Christ.

The other structures (surveyed in the first section) are also present in the horizontal types. There is a strong emphasis on eschatology. The Christological-soteriological structure is central to the book's main theme:

defilement/purgation. The only solution to man's problem of defilement is purification—not by animal blood (type)—but by the cleansing blood of Christ (antitype). The ecclesiological structure is reflected in the fact that sinners purified by the blood of Christ are drawn into the fellowship of the new covenant community. The prophetic element appears as the old cultus reveals its ineffectiveness and provisional nature. Its limited function provided an advance-presentation of the essential contours of a coming eschatological fulfillment: the coming Saviour, His atoning death and priestly ministry in a better sanctuary.

A strong vertical typology pervades Hebrews. The earth/heaven axis intersects the horizontal time-continuum. The book draws correspondences between the earthly priests and the heavenly high priest, between the earthly sanctuary and the heavenly sanctuary, and between the earthly ritual and its heavenly counterpart. Likewise the same eschatological, Christological-soteriological, and prophetic characteristics are present in the vertical typology as in the horizontal perspective.

Thus, a unique blending of the two kinds of typology takes place in the book. The vertical dimension provides the believer with an understanding of the link that exists between heaven and earth as God unfolds the plan of salvation horizontally, as it were, on the earth.

We commonly refer to the OT person, event, or institution as the "type" (*tupos*) and its respective NT fulfillment as the "antitype" (*antitupos*). However, in Hebrews this terminology is reversed. The heavenly sanctuary is referred to as the "type" and the earthly sanctuary as the "antitype." This appears to be due to the fact that the heavenly sanctuary *existed prior* to the OT sanctuary and was the basis for the origin of the latter. Hence, the apostolic author designates the heavenly reality as the *tupos* (8:5) and the earthly sanctuary as the *antitupos* (9:24)—"that which corresponds to"—the heavenly. However, since the *functional* movement of the typology in Hebrews is from OT reality to NT fulfillment, it is convenient and consistent to speak of the earthly sanctuary as "type" and the heavenly sanctuary as its "antitype."

The presence in the book of Hebrews of the five structures common to typology suggests that other typological motifs may be found in the book outside the central section that was analyzed. It is evident from this study that the typology found in Hebrews is similar to the typology found elsewhere in Scripture. Furthermore, we may affirm that the vertical typology (earth/heaven correspondences), underscored so forcefully in Hebrews, finds its roots not in pagan thought, but in Israel's Scriptures.

Section Outline

* * * * * * *

Introduction

Among the numerous recent exegetical studies there is "very wide agreement that Hebrews contains typology."[18] This consensus applies also to Hebrews 8:5 and 9:24.[19] However, until 1980 there existed no substantive analysis of the cultic context of these *tupos* passages which would lay bare their inherent typological structures. This analysis was undertaken in the present author's dissertation,[20] and is set forth in a less technical format in the pages that follow in this section. Built upon previous studies, augmented by further analysis of significant unresolved structural issues, our investigation seeks to synthesize the horizontal and vertical typological structures that emerge from these *tupos* passages and their larger cultic setting within the Epistle.

Preliminary Considerations

Various questions of introduction for the Epistle to the Hebrews (such as authorship, readers, circumstances of writings, etc.) have been widely

---

18 Jerome Smith, *A Priest Forever: A Study of Typology and Eschatology in Hebrews* (London, 1969), p. 10; cf. p. 30: "It is agreed by all commentators there are types."

19 See, e.g., Goppelt, *TDNT,* 8:256-59; Frederick F. Bruce, *The Epistle to the Hebrews,* NICNT (Grand Rapids, 1964), pp. 1-11, 166, 220; George W. Buchanan, *To the Hebrews,* AB (Garden City, NY, 1972), pp. xxiv-xxv, 153-54, 250-51; Andrew B. Davidson, *The Epistle to the Hebrews,* Handbooks for Bible Classes (Edinburgh, 1882), pp. 158-59, 186; Delitzsch, *Hebrews,* 2:126-27; Thomas Hewitt, *The Epistle to the Hebrews: An Introduction and Commentary,* TNTC (Grand Rapids, 1960), p. 144; Philip E. Hughes, *A Commentary on the Epistle to the Hebrews* (Grand Rapids, 1977), p. 382; Richard C. H. Lenski, *The Interpretation of the Epistle to the Hebrews* (Columbus, OH, 1946), p. 315; Floyd V. Filson, " 'Yesterday': A Study of Hebrews in the Light of Chapter 13," SBT, 2nd ser., No. 4 (Naperville, IL, 1967), p. 83; Aelred Cody, *Heavenly Sanctuary and Liturgy in the Epistle to the Hebrews* (St. Meinrad, IN, 1960), p. 46; Sidney G. Sowers, *The Hermeneutics of Philo and Hebrews: A Comparison of the Old Testament in Philo Judaeus and the Epistle to the Hebrews;* Basel, *Studies of Theology,* No. 1 (Richard: John Knox, 1965), pp. 89-97.

20 See Davidson, *Typology in Structure,* pp. 336-67.

discussed. William G. Johnsson has aptly observed, "Despite the torrents of ink that have flowed regarding the writer and his readers, the 'assured results' are practically nil."[21] Fortunately, our analysis of inherent *tupos* structures in the cultic context of Hebrews 8:5 and 9:24 is not dependent upon the identity of the author, his readers, or the date of writing.[22] There are, however, certain philosophical-hermeneutical and contextual issues that call for special consideration. To these we now turn our attention.

Philosophical-Hermeneutical Considerations

While it is generally agreed that typology exists in the cultic context of Hebrews 8:5 and 9:24, there is debate over the origin and nature of the concepts and terms used. It has often been asserted (and sometimes vigorously defended) that Platonic-Philonic philosophical ideas and expressions lie behind the earth-heaven correspondence presented in Hebrews.[23] On the other hand various recent studies have denied the

---

21 William G. Johnsson, "Defilement and Purgation in the Book of Hebrews," (Ph.D. dissertation, Vanderbilt University, 1973), p. 23. For the host of suggestions regarding these questions, consult the standard NT introductions.

22 Naturally, a clear determination of the date and author of the Epistle would be helpful, especially for the purpose of placing Hebrews 8:5 and 9:24 in proper historical sequence with other hermeneutical tupos passages by the same or different author so that possible shifts or development in usage might become apparent. Certain evidence appears to favor a date in the period of imminent crisis just prior to the destruction of Jerusalem in A.D. 70 (see, e.g., R. K. Harrison, *Introduction to the Old Testament* [Grand Rapids, 1969], p. 380). The traditional view of the essential Pauline authorship of the Epistle (with perhaps a literary transcriber who strongly colored the final literary form) does not appear to be as untenable as is usually argued in recent literature (cf., i.e., *The SDA Bible Commentary*, 7:387-89). But regardless of the date and author of this Epistle, since we are considering Hebrews 8:5 and 9:24 under a separate subheading (because of its vertical as well as horizontal *tupos* structures), the order of treatment of hermeneutical *tupos* passages remains unchanged.

23 For the early champions of a Platonic-Philonic influence in Hebrews, see the bibliography in Bruce, *Hebrews*, p. lvii. The most vigorous modern proponent of direct influence is Ceslaus Spicq, "Le philonisme de l'Épître aux Hébreux," *RB* 56 (1949): 542-72; 57 (1950): 212-42. This same material is also found in Spicq's *L'Épître aux Hébreux*, 2 vols. (Paris, 1952-53), 1:39-91; cf. Bultmann, "Ursprung und Sinn," p. 210; James Moffatt, "A Critical and Exegetical Commentary on the Epistle to the Hebrews," ICC (Edinburgh, 1924), pp. xxxi-xxxiv, 106-7; Wilbert F. Howard, *The Fourth Gospel in Recent Criticism and Interpretation*, 3rd ed. (London, 1945), p. 115; William Manson, *The Epistle to the Hebrews* (London, 1951), pp. 124-26; Jean Héring, "Eschatologie biblique et idéalisme platonicien," in *The Background of the New Testament and Its Eschatology*, ed. W. D. Davies and Daube (Cambridge, 1956), pp. 444-63; id., *The Epistle to the Hebrews*, tr. A. W. Heathcote and P. J. Allcock (London, 1970), p. 66; Goppelt, *Tupos*, p. 62; C.F.D. Moule, "Sanctuary and Sacrifice in the Church of the New Testament," *JTS* 1 (1950): 37. Varying degrees of dependence are recognized; for a survey of the positions and quotations from representative proponents up to 1970, see Ronald Williamson, *Philo and the Epistle to the Hebrews* (Leiden, 1970), pp. 1-10. More recent advocates of a Platonic-Philonic model include especially the following: Theodore G. Stylianopoulous "Shadow and Reality: Reflections in Hebrews 10:1-18," *Greek Orthodox Theological Review* 17 (Holy Cross Orthodox School of Theology, 1972): 217; James W. Thompson, "That Which Abides: Some Metaphysical Assumptions in the Epistle to

existence of Platonic-Philonic thought-forms in the Epistle.[24]

A careful treatment of the Platonic-Philonic issue has already been undertaken by Ronald Williamson.[25] We are in agreement with the essentials of his prodigious research that has "pronounced a negative verdict on the Philonic school."[26]

Williamson deals extensively with the linguistic evidence, themes, and ideas and the use of Scripture in Philo and Hebrews. He demonstrates major divergencies of thought between Philo and the author of Hebrews. We list the points most crucial to an understanding of *tupos/antitupos* in Hebrews 8 and 9:

1. The author of Hebrews does not use the allegedly Platonic terminology in true Platonic fashion.

2. The heavenly world of Ideas in Plato and Philo—which could not be entered except by pure intellect—has no room at all for the historical person of Jesus as described by the writer of Hebrews.

3. The temporal-historical sequence of movement in Hebrews is totally incompatible with Platonic eternal/timeless principles of ethics and metaphysics.[27]

---

the Hebrews" (Ph.D. dissertation, Vanderbilt University, 1974); Lala K. K. Dey, *The Intermediary World and Patterns of Perfection in Philo and Hebrews,* SBL Dissertation Series, No. 25 (Missoula, MT, 1975); and George W. MacRae, "Heavenly Temple and Eschatology in the Letter to the Hebrews," *Semeia* 12 (1978): 179-99.

24 E.g., Charles K. Barrett, "The Eschatology of the Epistle to the Hebrews," in *The Background of the New Testament and Its Eschatology,* ed. W. D. Davies and David Daube (Cambridge, 1956), pp. 363-93; Bruce, Hebrews, pp. 229-30; Buchanan, pp. xxv, 134-35; Sowers, passim; Woollcombe, pp. 67-68. The most detailed elucidation of this position is Williamson, *Philo and Hebrews.* More recently, see especially Allan J. McNicol, "The Relationship of the Image of the Highest Angel to the High Priest Concept in Hebrews" (Ph.D. dissertation, Vanderbilt Univ., 1974); Otfried Hofius, *Der Vorhang vor dem Thron Gottes: Eine exegetisch-religionsgeschichtliche Untersuchung zu Hebräer 6.9f. und 10, 19b,* Wissenschaftliche Untersuchungen zum Neuen Testament, No. 14 (Tübingen, 1972); Ronald H. Nash, "The Notion of Mediator in Alexandrian Judaism and the Epistle to the Hebrews," *WTJ* 40 (1977): 105-115; and L. D. Hurst, "How Platonic are Heb vii.5 and ix.23f.?" *JTS* 34 (1983): 156-68. These studies allow for (possible) verbal similarities between Philo and Hebrews, but insist on the absence of the conceptual structures of Platonic-Philonic idealism.

25 Williamson's monograph was originally his Ph.D. thesis presented to the University of Leeds. It is difficult to understand how major proponents since 1870 of a Philonic-Platonic model for the Epistle to the Hebrews—notably Dey and Thompson—make no mention at all of Williamson's study. The works produced since 1970 appear to have set forth no evidence nor argumentation that has not already been anticipated and effectively dealt with by Williamson.

26 William G. Johnsson, "The Cultus of Hebrews in Twentieth-Century Scholarship," *ExpTim* 89 (1978): 105.

27 See Barrett, "Eschatology of Hebrews," for the distinction in regard to eschatology. For a summary of these first three arguments with particular attention to Hebrews 8:1-5, see Ronald Williamson's earlier article, "Platonism and Hebrews," *SJT* 16 (1963): 418-19; cf. the similar arguments in Buchanan, pp. xxv, 134-35.

4. There is allegory, not typology, in Philo; and typology, not allegory, in Hebrews.[28]

5. There is no appreciable Messianism in Philo's works, as opposed to the dominant Christological theme of Hebrews.[29]

Williamson analyzes Hebrews 8:5 in detail for Platonic-Philonic influence.[30] He substantiates his contention that "although something like the language of Philonic Platonism may be found in 8:5, there is no trace in that verse, or indeed anywhere else in the Epistle, of the fundamental attitudes or convictions which constitute Platonism either in its original or in its Philonic form."[31] Williamson's research is persuasive. He locates the background of thought-forms (including those regarding the sanctuary) within the "dramatic, historical metaphysics of Jewish-Christian theology,"[32] not Platonic idealism.[33]

This is not to rule out the possibility of Philonisms in the vocabulary of the author of Hebrews. Those who deny the existence of Platonic-Philonic thought-forms in the Epistle still generally allow for possible employment of Philonic terminology. Even Williamson admits the possibility that the Epistle to the Hebrews contains certain Philonisms.[34]

On the other hand whatever quasi-Philonic vocabulary may be found, such terms appear to have been modified by the author. The fundamental conceptual structures of Platonic-Philonic idealism seem to have been replaced by thought-forms from Judeo-Christian apocalyptic theology. In

---

28 Sowers, p. 91: "Typological exegesis is totally absent from Philo's writings." R. Hanson, *Allegory and Event*, p. 49: "Philo exhibits no typology whatever"; cf. also ibid., p. 86, and Sowers, p. 137, for discussion of lack of allegory in Hebrews.

29 Williamson, *Philo and Hebrews*, pp. 23-31, 423-24, where the two possible messianic references are shown to be totally different from those in Hebrews.

30 Ibid., pp. 557-70.

31 Ibid., p. 557.

32 Ibid.

33 So Barrett, "Eschatology of Hebrews," p. 389: "The heavenly tabernacle in Hebrews is not the product of Platonic idealism, but the eschatological temple of apocalyptic Judaism." F. F. Bruce, " 'To the Hebrews' or 'To the Essenes'?" *NTS* 9 (1963): 229-30, concurs: "His [the author of Hebrews] portrayal of the earthly sanctuary as a copy of the 'real' one in heaven is strongly reminiscent of Platonism; but, when we come to look at it more closely, it is evident that he draws primarily on the instruction to Moses in Exod. xxv. 40 . . . [quoted] — and he develops this idea in much the same way as apocalyptic writers do, including the NT Apocalyptist, who has not generally been regarded as influenced by Plato." More recently, Nash, pp. 105-115, has shown that the nature of Christ and His mediatorial work in Hebrews is totally different from the Logos Christology/heavenly mediator conceptions of Philo. In Hebrews, as opposed to Philo, there is (1) not a metaphysical abstraction but a historical person, (2) not platonic dualism, but incarnation, (3) not disparagement of emotions, but expression of emotion, and (4) the ability in Christ to suffer, be tempted, and die, as Philo could never allow.

34 Williamson, *Philo and Hebrews*, p. 579.

the course of our analysis of conceptual structures in the cultic context of Hebrews 8:5 and 9:24, we will have further occasion to elucidate the difference in thought-forms between Platonic-Philonic philosophy and the book of Hebrews.

An analysis of the use of *tupos* and the underlying Hebrew term *tabnît* ("model") in Exodus 25:40 (LXX and MT)—the passage cited in Hebrews 8:5 as proof of an earthly/heavenly sanctuary correspondence—will be reviewed in the next section. We may say here, however, that it appears to support the conclusion that "the writer of Hebrews derived this mode of thinking [earthly/heavenly sanctuary correspondence] from the OT itself, and not from Alexandrian philosophy."[35]

It will become apparent that the Hebrew term *tabnît* ("model")—like the Greek word *tupos* in its basic meaning as "(hollow) mold"—can denote both "copy" (that which *is formed*) and "pattern" or "prototype" (that which *forms*) simultaneously. In Exodus 25:40 it seems probable that *tabnît* (*tupos,* LXX) refers to a miniature model or copy *of* the heavenly sanctuary and/or the heavenly sanctuary itself (with an implied mediating miniature model). But the *tabnît* ("copy/mold") also functions as a prototype or pattern *for* the construction of the earthly sanctuary.

Tupos Passages in Context

The literary structure of Hebrews has been analyzed in detail by Albert Vanhoye.[36] As Johnsson has rightly observed, Vanhoye has shown that the section 7:1–10:18, which deals with the cultus, "is not only central in location but one which is almost certainly central to the overall plan of the work."[37] Chapters 8-9 belong together as part of the same cultic argument (7:1–10:18): the efficacious sacrifice of the High Priest Jesus Christ in contrast with the inadequacy and ineffectiveness of the old worship.[38]

---

35 Charles T. Fritsch, *"To Antitypon,"* in *Studia Biblica et Semitica* (Wageningen, 1966), p. 103. That is to say, the earthly/heavenly sanctuary correspondence was already at home in the OT and need not have been borrowed from Platonic-Philonic thought. This of course does not rule out the possibility that the *auctor ad Hebraeos* recognizes the OT vertical dynamics of *tupos* (*tabnît*) as it is made explicit by Philo, even though for the latter it is transcendent ideas and not material heavenly realities (as in Exodus 25:40 and parallel OT passages) that are in view.

36 Albert Vanhoye, *La structure littéraire de l'épître aux Hébreux* (Paris, 1963); id., *A Structured Translation to the Epistle to the Hebrews,* tr., James Swetnam (Rome, 1964).

37 Johnsson, "The Cultus of Hebrews," p. 104; cf. Vanhoye, *La structure,* pp. 137-71; id., *A Structured Translation,* pp. 17-25.

38 See Michel Gourgues, "Remarques sur la 'structure centrale' de l'épître aux Hébreux. A l'occasion d'une réédition," *RB* 84 (1977): 31-32, where chap. 8, in Gourgues' structure, states the main point regarding Christ as high priest (vss. 1-5) and mediator of the new covenant (vss. 6-13), and chap. 9 forms the first development of this main point. Similarly with Vanhoye (*La structure,* pp.

Thus, we will deal with 8:5 and 9:24 together in their larger cultic setting in the elucidation of conceptual structures.

Let us note briefly the context of these passages. The first seven chapters of the homily to the Hebrews reveal Christ's superiority to the angels (1:4–2:18), Moses and Joshua (3:1–4:13), and the Aaronic priesthood (4:14–7:28).

In Hebrews 8:1, 2 the author summarizes the main point of his preceding discussion: "We have such a high priest, one who is seated at the right hand of the throne of the Majesty in heaven, a minister in the sanctuary and the true tent which is set up not by man but by the Lord." In verses 3-6 it is shown how Christ is high priest of a "better sanctuary," the true "heavenly sanctuary" (vs. 5). This is supported by the citation from Exodus 25:40. In verse 6 the author underscores the superior ministry of Christ and launches into a discussion of the better promises and superiority of the new covenant over the old covenant (vss. 7-13).

The "better sacrifice" of the new covenant is the focus of Hebrews 9:1–10:18. Hebrews 9:1-5 briefly describes the earthly (OT) sanctuary. Then the author points out the limitations of the OT sanctuary services (vss. 6-10) in comparison with the eternal heavenly sacrifice of Christ (vss. 11-14). In verses 15-22 Christ is presented as the mediator of the new covenant, offering "better blood" (vss. 12-14).

The cultic axiom presented in verse 22, "without the shedding of blood there is no forgiveness [aphesis] of sins," is in verse 23 applied to the cleansing of the "heavenly things themselves." In verse 24 the relationship between the earthly and heavenly sanctuary is reiterated. The earthly "sanctuary made with hands" (cheiropoiēta hagia) is a "copy" (antitupa) of the true. Christ entered into the true sanctuary, "into heaven itself, now to appear in the presence of God in our behalf."

Christ does not offer Himself repeatedly as the high priest offered blood from year to year in the Day of Atonement services. Rather, Christ appeared "once for all at the end of the age to put away sin by the sacrifice of himself" (vss. 25-26). And He will appear a second time, not to deal again with sin, but to bring salvation to those who expect Him (vss. 27-28). The superiority, efficacy, and finality of Christ's sacrifice in contrast to the inadequacy and ineffectiveness of the OT animal sacrifices is the emphasis of Hebrews 10:1-18.

137-71; *A Structured Translation*, pp. 17-25), where 8:1 — 9:10 points up the inadequacy of the old worship, and 9:11-28 shows the efficacy and adequacy of Christ's sacrifice.

Horizontal Typological Structures

Biblical types may be classified according to their directional orientation: horizontal or vertical. Horizontal types prefigure future antitypes on the continuum of historical time. Vertical types on the other hand have an earthly/heavenly alignment.

In the *tupos* passages now under consideration we find horizontal typological structures intersecting with vertical structures. In order to clarify these structures, however, we will examine the horizontal and vertical dimensions separately. Then we will attempt to ascertain the relationship between the two. We turn first to the horizontal structures.

Historical Structure

We have seen how the arguments and descriptions of the author are structured in a temporal-historical sequence of movement. He takes for granted the *historical reality* of the OT persons, events, and institutions mentioned in the Epistle. The same is true with regard to the NT counterparts. As Johnsson expresses it, "His (the author of Hebrews) concern throughout the sermon is to ground Christian confidence in objective *facts.* . . . *Real* deity, *real* humanity, *real* priesthood—and we may add, a *real* ministry in a *real* sanctuary."[39]

In Hebrews 8 the overriding *historical correspondence* is between the old and new covenants. In Hebrews 9 this motif continues, but the focus shifts to the historical correspondence between the temporary Levitical sacrifices and the once-for-all-time sacrifice of Christ. Both chapters continue the previous correspondence between the Levitical priesthood and Christ's Melchizedek (high) priesthood.

The correspondence between the OT and NT cultus involves specific, crucial *details.* For example, as the earthly priests offered sacrifices, so must Jesus (8:3). Again, as the carcasses of those sacrifices whose blood was brought into the sanctuary were burned "outside the camp," so Jesus "suffered outside the gate" (13:11-13).

The historical correspondence involves an absolute *escalation* or *intensification* from the OT to the NT reality. There is an escalation from the inadequate, ineffective, temporary OT cultus to a superior and permanent priesthood (4:14–7:28) with a "more excellent ministry" (8:6), to a "better covenant" based on "better promises" (that is, the effective dealing with

---

39 William G. Johnsson, *In Absolute Confidence: The Book of Hebrews Speaks to Our Day* (Nashville, 1979), p. 91, italics his.

the sin problem, 8:6-13), to the "better sacrifice" (9:23) with better blood (9:13, 14). In other words, the type meets its historical fulfillment in a once-for-all-time, all-sufficient and efficacious Sacrifice (9:25–10:18).

Theological Structures

The various theological structures also function horizontally in the typology of Hebrews 8, 9.

1. The eschatological structure is prominent in the Epistle. Charles K. Barrett's analysis, including the section containing 8:5 and 9:24, convinces him "that the thought of Hebrews is consistent, and that in it the eschatological is the determining element."[40] Or, to express it differently, he asserts that ". . . the framework of thought in Hebrews is eschatological."[41]

For Barrett the eschatology of Hebrews is essentially the same as that which is characteristic of NT Christianity in general: "The common pattern of NT eschatology is in Hebrews made uncommonly clear. God has begun to fulfill his ancient promises: the dawn of the new age has broken, though the full day has not yet come. The church lives in the last days, but before the last day."[42] "The characteristically Christian conviction . . . that eschatological events have already taken place (though others remain in the future as objects of hope) is found as clearly in Hebrews as in any part of the NT."[43]

Others have recognized this strong eschatological tension between the "already" and the "not yet" in Hebrews. Cora Brady demonstrates the movement in Hebrews along a "temporal ascending line."[44] It runs from yesterday (the once-for-all-time act of Christ in the past, 10:10), through today (Christ reigns, 1:3; 2:9; but victory is not complete, 2:8; 10:13), to the future (the future hope, centered in the Second Coming, 9:28; 10:25, 37; involving forever, 13:8). Bertold Klappert lays bare the structure of the "already" and the "not yet."[45] Jerome Smith speaks of the "thoroughgoing eschatology of the structure of thought in Hebrews."[46] Floyd Filson's work rests on the recognition of a temporal eschatological structure.[47]

---

40 Barrett, "Eschatology of Hebrews," p. 366; cf. Hans Windisch, "Der Hebräerbrief," Handbuch zum Neuen Testament, 2nd ed. (Tübingen, 1931), p. 86; Otto Michel, "Der Brief an die Hebräer," Kritisch-Exegetischer Kommentar (Göttingen, 1966), p. 17; J. Smith, p. 172.
41 Barrett, "Eschatology of Hebrews," p. 391.
42 Ibid.
43 Ibid., p. 364.
44 Brady, p. 330; cf. pp. 329-39.
45 Bertold Klappert, Die Eschatologie des Hebräerbriefs (Munich, 1969), pp. 54-58.
46 J. Smith, p. 172.
47 Filson, "Yesterday."

This eschatological time-continuum has been emphasized especially in regard to the non-cultic parts of the book. For instance Johnsson schematically illustrates how the pilgrimage motif has three stages parallel to the eschatological pattern of the book:[48]

Then   (past)   separation   (baptism, persecution)

Now   (present)   transition   (journeying, proleptic participation)

Not yet (future)   incorporation (attainment of city, see God)

This horizontal-temporal eschatology can be seen also in the immediate context of our passages (chaps. 8, 9). For example, in 8:6 and onward the historical correspondence is between the old and new covenants, which Barrett analyzes in terms of the common "eschatological faith of the primitive church."[49] In 9:25 and onward the author of Hebrews makes clear the temporal movement from Christ's historical, once-for-all-time sacrifice "at the end of the age" (9:26) to His appearance "a second time, not to deal with sin but to save those who are eagerly waiting for him" (9:28).

2. The *Christological-soteriological* structure of typology immediately comes into view as one examines the cultic context of Hebrews 8, 9.[50] The crucial point of the author's argument concerns the efficacy and all-sufficiency of Christ's sacrifice and high priestly ministry to purify the conscience. A defilement-purgation motif is dominant, not the legal guilt-forgiveness theme.[51]

Johnsson has summarized the cultic issues in his review of modern investigation on the cultus of Hebrews[52] and has made a careful exegesis of Hebrews 9-10.[53] His conclusions highlight the central structures of Christology and soteriology in the argument of the Epistle: The solution

---

48 William G. Johnsson, "The Pilgrimage Motif in the Book of Hebrews," *JBL* 97 (1978): 246; cf. the basic study of the pilgrim motif, Ernst Käsemann, *Das wandernde Gottesvolk: Eine Untersuchung zum Hebräerbrief*, 4th ed. (Göttingen, 1961).

49 Barrett, "Eschatology in Hebrews," p. 366.

50 For a detailed discussion of the issues in Christology in Hebrews, see, e.g., Erich Grässer, *Der Glaube im Hebräerbrief*, Marburger theologische Studien 2 (Marburg, 1965): 214-23; Anthony Snell, *New and Living Way: An Explanation of the Epistle to the Hebrews* (London, 1959), pp. 40-45; for soteriology, see Stephen S. Smalley, "Atonement in the Epistle to the Hebrews," *EvQ* 33 (1961): 36-43.

51 Johnsson, "Defilement and Purgation," p. 39.

52 Ibid., pp. 27-96; cf. his synthesis and update in "The Cultus of Hebrews," pp. 104-8.

53 Johnsson, "Defilement and Purgation," pp. 206-379.

to man's problem of "defilement" is "purgation" through the application of Christ's blood.[54]

3. Already the *ecclesiological* structure of typology has become evident in our reference to the pilgrim motif. This motif parallels the eschatological tension of the Epistle and may be viewed as "the organizing idea of Hebrews."[55] Johnsson provides a persuasive analysis of how the author "uses Christianity as a pilgrimage for his ruling conception."[56]

The elements of pilgrimage—separation, journey to a sacred place, fixed purpose, and hardship—converge in the Epistle. The eschatological people of God have left home, separated from the world (11:13-16; 13:14). The way is beset with hardship (3:12-18; 5:11–6:12; 10:23-26; 12:4), but the pilgrims are journeying with a fixed purpose to the heavenly city of God (11:10, 16; 13:14).

The ecclesiological structure is basic to the cultic argument of 7:1–10:18. While the "defilement-purgation" motif concerns Christology and soteriology, it obviously involves people who are defiled and purified. Though the dominant horizontal correspondence is drawn between the old and new cultic institution, yet the underlying reason and purpose for the cultus must not be overlooked.

Man is defiled by sin, and the sin problem needs to be dealt with. The sacrifice of Christ "perfects" or "purifies" the "conscience" (9:9, 14; 10:2, 14, 22) of the individual worshiper. Furthermore, under the new covenant the believers are also united into an eschatological community (10:8-13; cf. 10:21; 12:22-24). Thus the ecclesiological structure in its individual and corporate dimensions emerges from the immediate context of Hebrews 8:5 and 9:24. It should be noted, however, that there is apparently no allusion to the sacraments of the Christian church in the context of Hebrews 8:5 and 9:24.

4. The *prophetic structure* of typology is clearly evident within the argument of Hebrews. In fact, as George B. Caird rightly observes, the author of Hebrews "regarded the whole of the OT as a prophetic work, both because God spoke in it to his people and because in it he everywhere directed their attention to the eschatological future."[57] Caird demonstrates how the whole argument of Hebrews hinges on the "self-confessed

---

54 See his summary of conclusions in chap. 6 of "Defilement and Purgation," esp. pp. 429-35.

55 Johnsson, *Absolute Confidence,* p. 152.

56 Ibid.; see his analysis of pp. 152-60; cf. id., "Pilgrim Motif," pp. 239-51; id., "Defilement and Purgation," pp. 380-424.

57 George G. Caird, "The Exegetical Method of the Epistle to the Hebrews," *CJT* 5 (1959): 47.

inadequacy of the order,"[58] illustrated in Hebrews by an exegesis of Psalms 8, 95, 110, and Jeremiah 31.[59] The OT pointed forward to an eschatological intensification. As the old revealed its own ineffectiveness and provisional nature, it also provided a *prefiguration* of the essential contours of the eschatological fulfillment.

Of particular interest to us (in the context of Hebrews 8, 9) are the OT cultic *institutions* (priesthood, sanctuary service, sacrifices, etc.). In their very ineffectiveness they presented an anticipation of the realities in Jesus and His work. For example, in Hebrews 8:3, 4 the author argues from the sacrifices of the high priests in the old covenant to the *necessity* of a sacrifice offered by Christ. The prophetic "must needs be" nature of the historical correspondence is thus revealed.

Furthermore, it is by *divine design* that the sacrificial law of the old covenant constitutes a "shadow of the good things to come" (10:1). The institution of the old covenant was *ordained by God* (9:1), served its temporary function (9:10), but pointed forward as a shadow (10:1) to the realities of the new covenant to be effected by Jesus.

Vertical Typological Structures

We have surveyed the horizontal structures of typology inherent in Hebrews. But along with the historical-temporal sequence of movement there is also a strong vertical (earthly/heavenly) dimension. As Johnsson describes it, "the time-continuum of Hebrews is crossed by a vertical, earthly/heavenly mode."[60] Thus, Hebrews 8:5 marshals Exodus 25:40 as evidence that the earthly sanctuary is a copy (*hupodeigma*), a shadow (*skia*), of the heavenly sanctuary.[61]

Throughout chapters 7-10 the historical correspondences are inter-woven with crucial complexes of earth-heaven correspondences. There are the correspondences between the earthly priests and the heavenly High Priest, between the earthly sanctuary and the heavenly sanctuary, and between the earthly ritual and its heavenly counterpart. This vertical dimension involves the same structures that have emerged from our survey of the horizontal dimension.

---

58 Ibid.

59 Caird argues that in each instance the use of the OT passages (Pss 8, 95, 110, Jer 31) by the author of Hebrews is "a perfectly sound piece of exegesis" (p. 47; cf. pp. 47-49).

60 Johnsson, "Pilgrimage Motif," p. 247.

61 For further discussion see below, pp. 151-64.

Historical Structure

The earthly sanctuary and its services are assumed to be a *historical reality*. Likewise, in the description of the heavenly sanctuary and liturgy the author of Hebrews "holds to their reality."[62] The *correspondence* between earthly and heavenly sanctuary involves an absolute *intensification* or *escalation* from "copy and shadow" (8:5) to the "true" (9:24).

Theological Structures

Christ's ministry in the heavenly sanctuary is conditioned by the *eschatological structure* involving the tension of the "already" and "not yet." Christ has already inaugurated His kingdom by His once-for-all-time sacrifice and entry upon His high priestly ministry (9:24-26). He now continues His intercession in the heavenly sanctuary (7:25). He will soon consummate His dealing with sin and appear a second time to save those who are waiting for Him (9:27, 28).

The vertical sanctuary typology is inextricably bound up with a *Christological-soteriological structure*. Even Christ's sacrifice may be inferred as taking place on an altar that is in the (earthly) court of the heavenly sanctuary.[63] Christ's high priestly ministry in the heavenly sanctuary is clearly soteriological, that is, for the purpose of saving penitent believers who come to God (Heb 7:25; 9:12-14, 24-26). His appearing the "second time" is also "to save those who are eagerly waiting for him" (9:28).

Likewise, the *ecclesiological structure* is a component of the vertical dimension. The beneficiaries of Christ's sacrifice and heavenly mediation are the individual worshipers who, under the new covenant, form an eschatological community. The vertical movement is especially evident in Hebrews 12:22-24, which describes believers approaching (by faith) to the heavenly Jerusalem, to "the assembly of the first-born," and to the heavenly Mediator.

Finally, the *prophetic structure* functions in the vertical as well as the

---

62 Johnsson, *Absolute Confidence*, p. 91.

63 This seems to be implied already in Hebrews 8:1-5. As the priests of the earthly sanctuary offered sacrifices, so Jesus the high priest of the heavenly sanctuary must also offer a sacrifice. This He did in the offering up of Himself (Heb 7:27; 9:14; 10:12; etc.). But it was on earth that the antitypical sacrifice was slain. This corresponds to the court of the Levitical sanctuary—the place where the priests slew the victims whose blood was to be taken into the holy or Most Holy Place. Hebrews 13:10 seems to make clear that the *auctor ad Hebraeos* considers the cross of Calvary to be the antitypical altar (in the court of the heavenly sanctuary). For further discussion see, i.e., Edwin W. Reiner, *The Atonement* (Nashville, 1971), pp. 88-92; *The SDA Bible Commentary*, 7:492.

horizontal dimension. In Hebrews 9:23, for example, the author argues from the cleansing of the earthly sanctuary to the necessity ("must needs be") of a cleansing of the heavenly sanctuary. By *divine design,* the earthly sanctuary, modeled after the heavenly original, with all its cultic functions becomes a prefiguration or *advance-presentation* of the realities connected with Christ's ministry in the heavenly sanctuary (8:5).

The existence of two modes of typological thought in the book of Hebrews—the horizontal and vertical—has been long recognized. But the usual interpretation by modern commentators, based on the tendency to equate the vertical thinking with Platonic-Philonic dualism, has been to posit a theological dichotomy between the two. James Moffatt, for example, is convinced that in Hebrews the Platonic idea of two worlds (eternal and material) is present. This "deeper thought" he argues cannot be reconciled with the author's eschatological thought-forms.[64]

Other scholars believe the author of Hebrews has reinterpreted one mode of thought so as to make it serve the other. Thus J. Cambier argues that the horizontal ("eschatological") thought-forms are reinterpreted by the author of Hebrews into an Alexandrian-Hellenistic mode.[65] Klappert, on the other hand, concludes that the function of the vertical (Alexandrian-Hellenistic) correspondence is to provide a basis for the radical grounding of the horizontal future-apocalyptic hope.[66]

Even Goppelt, who does not find in Hebrews a direct dependence on Philonic vocabulary or development, still relegates vertical thinking to "the mythic cosmic analogy of antiquity"[67] which is in Hebrews "merely an aid to the presentation and characterization of the horizontal."[68]

However, Williamson's study has indicated[69] that the source of the vertical thinking is not Plato or Philo. Our study of the vertical correspondence in Exodus 25:40 and throughout the OT[70] leads to the conclusion that it is not a foreign vestige of "mythic cosmic analogy." Rather, it is an integral part of Israel's understanding of the relationship between earthly and heavenly sanctuaries within the unfolding linear-historical plan of God.

---

64 Moffatt, *Hebrews,* pp. liv, xxxii, xxxiv.
65 J. Cambier, "Eschatologie ou hellénisme dans l'Épître aux Hébreux: Une étude sur menein et l'exhortation finale de l'Épître," Salesianum 11 (1949): 62-96.
66 Klappert, pp. 50, 59.
67 Goppelt, *TDNT,* 8:259.
68 Ibid., p. 258.
69 See above, pp. 133-34.
70 See below, pp. 151-64.

Thus, there is no inconsistency between the vertical and horizontal correspondences. They are descriptions of the same reality from two perspectives. "The heavenly tabernacle and its ministration are from one point of view eternal archetypes, from another they are eschatological events."[71]

A holistic approach to the book of Hebrews must recognize that the horizontal and vertical typologies harmonize and blend with each other in the book of Hebrews. Both are essential to the understanding of eschatology. The horizontal correspondence provides the linear dimension of God's saving activity. That activity reaches its basic eschatological fulfillment in the historical work of Christ, extends ecclesiologically as the church appropriates Christ's work, and reaches its consummation at the Second Coming.

The horizontal is inextricably tied to the vertical dimension in eschatology, Christology-soteriology, and ecclesiology. The vertical dimension provides an understanding of the link between heaven and earth in the unfolding of God's plan of salvation. Throughout the OT this vertical alignment is maintained, and the heavenly is presented as the ultimate source of meaning for the earthly.

In Hebrews the vertical "makes the typological intensification unmistakably plain both materially and linguistically."[72] The sacrifice of Christ on earth is viewed as taking place on an altar that is in the (earthly) court of the heavenly sanctuary. Christian worshipers have salvation in Christ as they by faith relate to Him in the heavenly sanctuary (10:19-22), where He intercedes continually on their behalf (7:25). From the heavenly sanctuary Christ will come the second time, having dealt fully with sin, to bring the consummation of salvation (9:28).

Although an indivisible connection exists between the horizontal and vertical correspondences, it is true (as Klappert[73] and Goppelt[74] maintain) that the horizontal seems to take precedence in terms of the author's ultimate emphasis. But this does not involve the subordinating of an alien "Alexandrian-Hellenistic" (Klappert) or "mythic-cosmic" (Goppelt) vertical dimension to an indigenous Judeo-Christian, eschatological-historical dimension. On the contrary, the vertical dimension is already at home in the Christian tradition. It is employed here in a uniquely cultic argument to explain the *nature* of the historical fulfillment of salvation, inaugurated

---

71 Barrett, "Eschatology of Hebrews," p. 385.
72 Goppelt, *TDNT,* 8:258.
73 Klappert, p. 50.
74 Goppelt, *TDNT,* 8:258.

by Christ in His once-for-all-time sacrifice, available to the church by a spiritual/heavenly relationship to Him as high priest, and soon to be consummated at the completion of His priestly ministry.

The importance of grasping the relationship between the vertical and horizontal structures in the argument of Hebrews 8, 9 becomes more apparent as we investigate the use of *tupos* and *antitupos* in 8:5 and 9:24 respectively. To this we now turn our attention.

Tupos/Antitupos As Hermeneutical Terms

As one examines the usage of *tupos* and *antitupos* in Hebrews 8:5 and 9:24 respectively, a surprising departure from NT usage becomes immediately evident. In the *tupos* passages outside of Hebrews (1 Cor 10; Rom 5; 1 Pet 3) the *tupos* ("type") refers to the OT reality and the *antitupos* ("antitype") to the NT reality. In the book of Hebrews, however, the *antitupos* denotes the OT reality (the earthly sanctuary), and the *tupos* refers (directly or indirectly) to the NT reality (the heavenly sanctuary). Because of this apparent reversal in the application of typological terminology, it is necessary to examine in some detail the usage of *tupos* and *antitupos* in the book of Hebrews.

In Hebrews 8:5 the author affirms that the earthly sanctuary was "a copy (*hupodeigma*) and shadow (*skia*) of the heavenly sanctuary." He supports this assertion by citing Exodus 25:40 (LXX). He writes:

> For when Moses was about to erect the tent,
> he was instructed by God, saying "See that you
> make everything according to the pattern (*tupos*)
> which was shown you on the mountain."

In the third section of this chapter it is concluded that *tupos* (LXX)/ *tabnît* (MT) in this passage refers either to the heavenly sanctuary itself (with a mediating miniature model assumed), or to a miniature (three-dimensional) representation of the heavenly sanctuary, or to both.

If our analysis of Exodus 25:40 is correct, then the author of Hebrews is justified in marshaling this OT passage as evidence for the existence of a heavenly sanctuary of which the earthly was a copy and shadow. But just as Exodus 25:40 could refer either to the heavenly sanctuary or its mediating miniature model, so Hebrews 8:5 is equivocal at this point. The author affirms the earthly/heavenly sanctuary correspondence on the basis of Exodus 25:40, but he does not state explicitly that the *tupos* is the heavenly sanctuary.

150

It is possible that he conceives of the *tupos* as a miniature model of the heavenly sanctuary but not primarily the heavenly sanctuary itself.[75] This possibility finds further support if *tupos* (along with *hupodeigma* and *skia*) is seen to be part of the Philonic vocabulary employed by the author, as is often suggested. It is true that Philo conceived of the *tupos* in Exodus 25:40 as simultaneously a copy of the heavenly archetype and a pattern for the earthly sanctuary.[76] If the author of Hebrews utilizes Philonisms here, even though the terminology is filled with new apocalyptic content, the same vertical dynamics still are seen to function.

It is not certain, however, that the author of Hebrews employs *tupos* with the same vertical dynamics as Philo. He does not introduce the accompanying characteristic Philonic terms (*archetupos* and *mimēma*) to describe the archetype and earthly copy, respectively. Moreover, it seems that the primary concern of this passage is to establish the correspondence between the earthly and heavenly sanctuary, not to deal with a mediating miniature model.

We must tentatively conclude, therefore, that any of the three options we have posited with regard to *tupos* in Exodus 25:40 (LXX) is possible in this passage: (1) *Tupos* may apply to the miniature model *of* the heavenly sanctuary, designed for the purpose of constructing the earthly sanctuary. (2) It may refer directly to the heavenly sanctuary (as most modern commentators suggest).[77] (3) Or, perhaps, both the miniature model and the heavenly sanctuary are in the mind of the author. But regardless of which option is correct, it is clear that a vertical (earthly/heavenly) sanctuary correspondence is affirmed.

The term *tupos* in this passage encompasses the same *linear* dynamics as we have seen in 1 Corinthians 10 and Romans 5. The *tupos* is a prototype of, or pattern for, a later copy. If *tupos* refers primarily to the miniature model of the heavenly sanctuary, then the same *qualitative* dynamics are also retained. As with a "hollow mold," which derives from an original and is secondary to the final product that it molds, so the *tupos* (miniature model) derives from an original (the heavenly sanctuary). It serves a secondary role to "shape" a reality of a higher order, the earthly sanctuary. If, however, *tupos* refers primarily to the heavenly sanctuary itself (which

---

75 See esp. Samuel T. Lowrie, *An Explanation of the Epistle to the Hebrews* (New York, 1884), p. 275, following Alford, vol. 4, p. 150.

76 Philo *Legum allegoriae*, 3.102; De vita Mosis 2.74ff.; De Somniis 1.206. See the discussion in Davidson, pp. 130-32.

77 E.g., Moffatt, *Hebrews*, p. 132; Bruce, *Hebrews*, pp. 220-21; McGaughey, p. 61.

may be more in harmony with the author's argument), then the qualitative dynamics are reversed. The *tupos* is the original and functions as the prototype of a "lower," secondary order (the earthly sanctuary).[78]

The use of *antitupos* in Hebrews 9:24 appears to be controlled by the meaning of *tupos* in 8:5.[79] The word *antitupos,* as Moffatt correctly notes, is "literally 'answering to the type' which was shown to Moses in the mount."[80] Selwyn rightly points out that the term *antitupos* "is itself a neutral word which may either . . . 'depreciate relatively,' or 'extol relatively.' The meaning, therefore, must be determined by the context: in itself it means 'corresponding' or 'the corresponding thing.' "[81]

In Hebrews 8:5 the citation of Exodus 25:40 has committed the author of Hebrews to a usage of *tupos* that (directly and/or indirectly) refers to the heavenly sanctuary. Thus in Hebrews 9:24 he remains consistent to that usage and allows *antitupos* to have the meaning "counterpart, corresponding to" with the connotation of "copy."[82]

This usage of *antitupos* virtually renders it a synonym of the other words such as *skia* ("shadow") and *hupodeigma* ("copy") which point the reader from the earthly copy/shadow to the heavenly reality. In so doing, the author maintains the same *linear* sequence as we have seen in other *tupos* passages: pattern/prototype (*tupos*) followed by a later copy (*antitupos*). The prior original (or miniature model of the original) heavenly sanctuary is the pattern for the later earthly sanctuary.

The usage of *antitupos* in Hebrews 9:24 is unique, however, in that the *tupos* (directly or indirectly the heavenly sanctuary), which is *prior* to the

---

78 If in Hebrews 8:5 the author understands *tupos* to refer to both the miniature model of the heavenly sanctuary and the heavenly sanctuary itself, the context of the passage seems to indicate that the ultimate concern is with the heavenly sanctuary (whether directly or indirectly). Thus the qualitative dynamics (higher [heavenly] = lower [earthly]) would still be reversed from those in the noncultic hermeneutical *tupos* passages.

79 It is significant to note at this juncture that Philo never employs this word in his hermeneutical endeavors. If the *auctor ad Hebraeos* does employ Philonisms in his Epistle, he departs from Philonic vocabulary at this crucial point.

80 Moffatt, *Hebrews,* p. 132.

81 Edward G. Selwyn, *The First Epistle of St. Peter* (London, 1946), p. 299.

82 If the *tupos* (8:5) refers primarily to the miniature model of the heavenly sanctuary, then the *antitupos* would be that which corresponds to (is a copy of) the miniature model (of the heavenly sanctuary). This is the way Lowrie, p. 323, interprets it: "The Apostle calls it [the earthly sanctuary] an antitype of the true Holies, meaning that it was the correlative of the type of the true, as that type was shown to Moses in the mount." If on the other hand the *tupos* refers also or primarily to the heavenly sanctuary—which may be more consonant with the context of 8:5 and 9:24—then the *antitupos* would be that which corresponds to (is a copy of) the heavenly sanctuary. In this case, the *antitupos* would "depreciate relatively" in contrast to its usage in 1 Peter 3:21 (where it is employed to "extol relatively").

earthly in *existence,* succeeds the earthly in soteriological *function.* The *antitupos* "corresponds" to the preceding *tupos* but also points forward to the eschatological inauguration of its services. Thus the normal typological application of the terms *tupos* and *antitupos* is reversed. The *antitupos* ("antitype") denotes the OT reality, and the *tupos* ("type") denotes the NT heavenly reality which the OT institution foreshadowed.

As we have already noted, this reversal in terms occurred because the author has committed himself in Hebrews 8:5 to the usage of *tupos* as it is found in Exodus 25:40 (LXX). In that reference *tupos* already refers to the heavenly sanctuary and/or the miniature model of the heavenly sanctuary. Therefore, in Hebrews 9:24 he remains consistent with the usage of *tupos* in Hebrews 8:5 and employs *antitupos* in the common Greek sense of "that which corresponds to the *tupos,* " that is, the earthly copy.

Summary

Findings

The structural components of typology that have emerged from our study of the *tupos* passages in Hebrews may be summarized under the same headings as we have employed for the other *tupos* passages in the first section of this chapter.

There is first the historical structure. This involves a historical correspondence between the OT realities and the NT eschatological fulfillment. In the *tupos* passages of Hebrews it is primarily cultic institutions and not specific historical events or persons which form the content of the OT realities.

The correspondence, as in other *tupos* passages, is seen in crucial details as well as general contours. And the correspondence involves an absolute intensification in its eschatological fulfillment. In the Epistle to the Hebrews the eschatological intensification is highlighted by a vertical correspondence that intersects the horizontal correspondence and overarches all historical saving activity.

Theological structures in the *tupos* passages of Hebrews include the eschatological, Christological-soteriological, ecclesiological, and prophetic. These structures are intersected by intertwining horizontal and vertical typological correspondences.

The eschatology of Hebrews reveals what we have found in other *tupos* passages: a tension between what is already fulfilled in Jesus Christ and what is not yet consummated. But in Hebrews the Christian's certainty of the future consummation is grounded more in the vertical earth-heaven correspondence.

The immediate context of Hebrews 8:5 and 9:24 moves more freely in the realm of cultic soteriology and Christology than in other *tupos* passages. The ecclesiology is likewise cultically determined in 7:1–10:18. The sacramental aspect of this ecclesiological structure does not appear. The argument of this section, and in particular the *tupos-antitupos* terms themselves, clearly reveals the prophetic aspects of advance-presentation, predictive prefiguration, and divine design.

Both *tupos* and *antitupos* are seen to function as technical terms. Thus they may be regarded as word indicators of the presence of typology in these passages. The use of *tupos/antitupos* follows the linear sequence (prototype = copy) as in other *tupos* passages. However, since *tupos* (in the citation of Exodus 25:40) refers (directly and/or indirectly) to the heavenly sanctuary, the *antitupos* denotes what "corresponds" to the preceding *tupos,* that is, the OT earthly sanctuary. Thus the usual application of the terms is reversed in Hebrews. The *antitupos* is the OT earthly reality and the *tupos* is (directly and/or indirectly) the NT heavenly sanctuary (which predated the earthly in *existence* but began officially to *function* only after the ratification of the new covenant with the death of Jesus).

Implications

From this analysis of typological structures in the *tupos* passages of Hebrews, certain significant implications appear to follow.

1. First, our study has indicated that the typology in Hebrews is comprised of the same basic conceptual structures found in the typology of the rest of Scripture. In the *tupos* passages the correspondence is broadened to include the sanctuary institution as well as persons and events. Also a vertical (earthly/heavenly) correspondence is presented along with the usual horizontal (historical) alignment. However, the basic structures of typology remain unchanged.

The inclusion of the sanctuary simply serves to expand the scope of typological realities to encompass three categories: persons, events, and institutions. Likewise the introduction of the vertical dimension actually serves to reinforce the element of escalation or intensification which forms part of the historical structure.

2. Reference to the vertical dimension leads us to a second important implication. On the basis of our analysis of Hebrews 8:5 and 9:24 in their

cultic contexts, it is inappropriate to consider vertical typology as a vestige of ancient Near Eastern mythical thinking or a component of Platonic-Philonic dualism. Such perspectives are alien to the eschatological-historical dimension of Judeo-Christian thought.

On the contrary we have found that the vertical (earthly/heavenly) sanctuary correspondence is already at home in the OT (compare Exodus 25:40 and many other passages). In the Epistle to the Hebrews the vertical sanctuary correspondence harmonizes and blends with the intersecting horizontal structures. Thus vertical as well as horizontal *tupos* structures appear to be indigenous to biblical typology, even though both are not employed in every *tupos* passage. This implication stands in opposition to the views of major advocates of postcritical neotypology who depreciate vertical typology and accept only horizontal typology as truly representing the biblical perspective.

3. A third implication from this study has to do with the use of the most appropriate terminology to describe the corresponding OT and NT realities in biblical typology. We have noted that in general Scripture the word *tupos* ("type") refers to the OT reality and *antitupos* ("antitype") to the NT fulfillment. In Hebrews the reverse is true. The word *antitupos* refers to the OT earthly sanctuary, and *tupos* indicates (directly or indirectly) the heavenly sanctuary.

As we have seen, the difference in Hebrews arises because the NT reality (the heavenly sanctuary) *existed prior to* the OT reality (the earthly sanctuary); consequently, the earthly is in Hebrews the *antitupos* of ("that which corresponds to") the heavenly.

Strictly speaking, in the book of Hebrews, the word "antitype" should be used to indicate the OT earthly sanctuary, and "type" should have reference to the heavenly sanctuary (and/or its miniature model shown to Moses). However, the *functional* movement of the typology in Hebrews (from OT reality to NT fulfillment) is the same as in other *tupos* passages. Therefore, it does not violate the basic thrust in Hebrews if, for the sake of convenience and consistency, the common usage of the terms "type" and "antitype" are employed to refer to the OT reality and NT fulfillment respectively.

4. A final implication stemming from our analysis of *tupos* structures in Hebrews concerns the scope of typology in the Epistle. Following the methodology that has been outlined in the preceding section, we have focused upon the central cultic section where the occurrence of *tupos* and *antitupos* have provided word indicators of the presence of typology. Thus,

it has been possible to allow the structures of typology to arise from Scripture without imposing an a priori understanding upon the biblical text.

We have seen that the characteristics of the *tupos* passages in Hebrews coincide with the typological structures encountered in 1 Corinthians 10, Romans 5, and 1 Peter 3. It is now possible to look for typology in other passages of Hebrews where these same structures appear but the word *tupos* (or "cognate") is not present. It is not our purpose here to move beyond a discussion of the *nature* of typology into a comprehensive investigation of the *scope* of typology in Hebrews. However, even a cursory survey indicates that the Epistle is rich in typological motifs in passages outside the central cultic section. As examples, we note that typological structures appear to function in references to Moses (3:1-5), Joshua (4:1-10), Melchizedek (7:1-28), Mt. Zion (12:22), and the whole motif of pilgrimage to the Promised Land (which pervades the noncultic sections of the Epistle). These and other possible typological motifs call for further study. Any statement of the nature of typology in Hebrews must remain open to further amplification that may appear from case studies of these other typological motifs.

Old Testament Basis for Sanctuary Typology in Hebrews

Editorial Synopsis. In order to demonstrate a vertical relationship between the earthly and heavenly sanctuaries, the writer of Hebrews cites God's instructions to Moses in Exodus 25:40. " 'See that you make everything according to the *pattern* [Greek, *tupos*; Hebrew, *tabnît*] which was shown you in the mountain' " (Heb 8:5).

The citation is drawn from the Greek Septuagint (LXX), a translation of the Hebrew Bible made in the third/second centuries B.C. The translators employed the Greek word *tupos* to render the Hebrew word *tabnît*.

In this section the author explores the question whether *tabnît* itself (in the Exodus 25 context) implies a vertical (earthly/heavenly) sanctuary correspondence.

Tabnît, a noun derived from the verb *bānāh* ("to build"), occurs 20 times in the OT. According to its given context *tabnît* may denote one of three basic concepts. The term may mean (1) a *copy of* something, (2) a *model/ pattern for* constructing something, or (3) a copy of something and a model/pattern for constructing something—both at the same time. These shades of meaning are also found in the Greek *tupos.*

Seven lines of evidence are cited to indicate that the use of *tabnît* in Exodus 25:40 reflects the idea that the earthly sanctuary was viewed as the counterpart of the heavenly dwelling of the Deity. Consequently, in this passage *tabnît* is best understood to mean a miniature model *of* the heavenly sanctuary (copy of the original) that was shown to Moses as a pattern *for* (model/pattern for) the purpose of constructing the earthly sanctuary.

Such a meaning for *tabnît,* therefore, clearly emphasizes a vertical (earthly/heavenly) sanctuary correspondence which the writer of Hebrews recognized and employed in his argument and which the LXX translators appropriately rendered with *tupos.*

Section Outline

I. Introduction
II. Meaning of *Tabnît*
III. *Tabnît/Tupos* Structures
IV. Summary and Implications

* * * * * * *

Introduction

In Hebrews 8:5 the apostolic writer cites Exodus 25:40 from the Greek Septuagint (LXX) to prove that the earthly sanctuary was a copy and shadow of the heavenly sanctuary.

> For when Moses was about to erect the tent, he was instructed by God, saying, "See that you make everything according to the *pattern* [Greek, *tupos*] which was shown you on the mountain."

The Hebrew word, translated by the Greek *tupos* in this passage, is *tabnît. Tabnît* also appears twice in the statements of verse 9 which parallel the statement made in our cited verse. It is important, therefore, to investigate the Hebrew term (*tabnît*) to determine whether it implies a vertical (earth-heaven) correspondence.[83]

Exodus 25 begins the section of the book dealing with the construction of the sanctuary. First the Lord lists the materials for the people to bring (vss. 1-7). He next expresses the divine purpose: "And let them make me a sanctuary, that I may dwell in their midst" (vs. 8).

Moses is then cautioned to make the sanctuary according to what he is shown, that is, according to the pattern (*tabnît*) of the tabernacle and its furniture. After detailing the specifications for the ark (vss. 10-22), the table (vss. 23-30), and the lampstand (vss. 31-39), God repeats His admonition to Moses to "make them after the pattern (*tabnît*) for them, which is being shown you on the mountain" (vs. 40).

Meaning of Tabnît

Does this section of Scripture refer to the heavenly sanctuary, as Hebrews 8:5 asserts? The answer to this question depends largely on the meaning of the Hebrew term *tabnît* in this context.[84] This Hebrew word is used three times in verses 9 and 40, and is translated by most English versions as "pattern." We must examine the word lexicographically and contextually in order to ascertain its semantic range in Scripture.

Tabnît is a noun derived from the verb *bānāh*, "to build."[85] *Bānāh* appears in the OT at least 370 times,[86] and the substantive *tabnît* occurs 20 times.[87] Lexicographers Brown, Driver, and Briggs define the basic meaning of *tabnît* as "construction," "pattern," "figure"[88] and divide the usages of *tabnît* very neatly into these three categories:[89]

1. "Construction," "structure" (apparently original usage)

Examples: The tribes of Ruben and Gad made an altar, an actual construction (though a copy of the original at the tabernacle), Joshua 22:28.

Daughters are compared to pillars cut from the "structure" of a palace, Psalm 144:12.

---

83 The material in this section is adapted from Davidson, *Typology in Scripture,* pp. 367-88.
84 This is correctly pointed out by Cody, p. 16.
85 Siegfried Wagner, "*bānāh,*" *TDOT,* 2:179.
86 BDB, p. 124, notes 373 times. A. R. Hulst, *THAT,* 1:325, has 376 times. *HAL,* p. 133, lists 370 times. Our own count from Solomon Mandelkern, *Veteris Testamenti Concorcantiae Hebraicae atque Chaldaicae,* 3rd ed. (Tel Aviv, 1978), pp. 204-6, is 373 times.
87 Mandelkern, p. 225.
88 BDB, p. 125.
89 Ibid.

2. "Pattern" (according to which anything is to be constructed)

Examples: The tabernacle was built according to a "pattern," Exodus 25:9.

Its utensils were made according to a "pattern," Exodus 25:9, 40.

Ahaz sends a "pattern" of an altar he has seen at Damascus back to Israel to be copied, 2 Kings 16:10.

The "pattern" of the temple and its furnishings are given by David to Solomon, 1 Chronicles 28:11, 12, 19.

3. "Figure, image, form"

Examples: Idols made in the "form, image" of animals, Deuteronomy 4:16, 17 (2x), 18 (2x).

Israelites exchanged their glory for the "image" of an ox, Psalm 106:20.

Idol shaped into the "figure" of a man, Isaiah 44:13.

The "form" of a hand, Ezekiel 8:3.

Every "form" portrayed on the wall, Ezekiel 8:10.

The cherubim appeared to have the "form" of a human hand, Ezekiel 10:8.

Lexicographers Ludwig Koehler and Walter Baumgartner divide the usages somewhat differently:[90]

1. "Original," "proto-type" *Urbild,* Exodus 25:9, 40.

2. "Copy," "duplicate" (*Abbild*), Deuteronomy 4:10-18; Joshua 22:28.

3. "Model" (*Modell*), 2 Kings 16:10; Psalm 144:12; 1 Chronicles 28:11, 12, 18.

4. "Image" (*Bild*), Isaiah 44:13; Ezekiel 8:10; Psalm 106:20.

5. "Something like" (*etwas wie*), Ezekiel 8:3; 10:8.

6. "Architect's plan" (*Bauplan*), 1 Chronicles 28:19.

If we analyze the above usages of the Hebrew word *tabnît,* we find they are similar to the Greek word *tupos* which was used to translate *tabnît* in the Greek Septuagint (LXX) in Exodus 25:40. Like *tupos,* the Hebrew *tabnît* can carry three meanings: a "copy (*of*)," (2) a "model/pattern (*for*)," or (3) a "copy (*of*)" and a "model/pattern (*for*)" at the same time.

In at least 12 of the 20 uses there is an explicit reference to the *tabnît* as a *copy of* an original. We find copies of an altar (Josh 22:28), animals (Deut 4:16, 17, 18; Ps 106:20; Ezek 8:10), humans (Isa 44:13), or of human hands (Ezek 8:3; 10:8).

---

90 Ludwig Koehler and Walter Baumgartner, *Lexicon in Veteris Testamenti Libros,* 2nd ed. (Leiden, 1958), p. 1018.

At least eight times *tabnît* has the character of *model/pattern for.*[91] We find patterns/models for the sanctuary and utensils (Exod 25:9, 40), the Solomonic temple and furnishings (1 Chr 28:11, 12, 19), and the golden chariot of the cherubim (1 Chr 28:18).

In at least one of the 20 references *tabnît* signifies a *model/pattern for* and a *copy of* simultaneously (2 Kgs 16:10-11). It is recorded that Ahaz saw an original altar in Damascus and sent back a *copy* (*tabnît*) of it, which then became a *model/pattern for* another altar constructed by Uriah the priest. Here it is explicitly stated that *tabnît* is both a *copy of an original* as well as a *model/pattern for* constructing another object. Such a double meaning for *tabnît* may be implied in Exodus 25:9, 40 if it can be ascertained that it is patterned after a heavenly original.

Thus we have in the term *tabnît* a wide semantic range, focusing on three basic meanings and including various nuances.

Tabnît/Tupos Structures

Scholars have applied different combinations of basic meanings and semantic nuances to the three appearances of *tabnît* in Exodus 25:9, 40, with six resultant possibilities. We may schematically diagram the suggested concepts as follows:

1. A miniature 3-D model for the earthly sanctuary:[92]

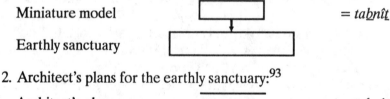

Miniature model = *tabnît*

Earthly sanctuary

2. Architect's plans for the earthly sanctuary:[93]

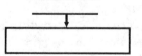

Architect's plans = *tabnît*

Earthly sanctuary

91 Or a *norma normans,* to use Franz Delitzsch's designation. Franz Delitzsch, *Commentary on the Epistle to the Hebrews,* tr. James Martin (Grand Rapids, 1952), p. 32.

92 Cody, p. 16; R. Alan Cole, *Exodus: An Introduction and Commentary, TOTC* (Downers Grove, IL, 1973), p. 190.

93 Johannes H. A. Ebrard, *Biblical Commentary on the Epistle to the Hebrews,* tr. John Fulton, Clark's Foreign Theological Library, 32 (Edinburgh, 1853), pp. 248-50; Joseph M'Caul, *The Epistle to the Hebrews* (London, 1871), p. 98.

3. *A copy of* the heavenly sanctuary which functions as a *model/pattern for* the earthly sanctuary (in the form of a miniature model):[94]

Heavenly sanctuary

Miniature model   = *tabnît*

Earthly sanctuary

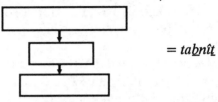

4. *A copy of* the heavenly sanctuary which functions as a *model/pattern for* the earthly sanctuary (in the form of architect's plans):[95]

Heavenly sanctuary

Architect's plans   = *tabnît*

Earthly sanctuary

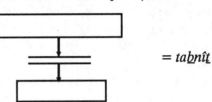

5. The heavenly sanctuary itself as the *model/pattern for* the earthly sanctuary:[96]

Heavenly sanctuary   = *tabnît*

Earthly sanctuary

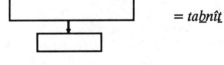
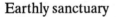

6. Subjective inspiration (with no communication or propositional facts) as the *model/pattern for* the earthly sanctuary:[97]

Subjective encounter   ?   = *tabnît*

Earthly sanctuary

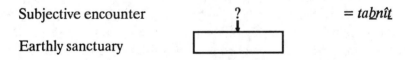

94 Bruce, *Hebrews*, pp. 165-66; John H. Davies, *A Letter to Hebrews*, Cambridge Bible Commentary (Cambridge, 1967), p. 201.

95 Henry Alford, *The Greek Testament: With a Critically Revised Text, a Digest of Various Readings, Marginal References to Verbal and Idiomatic Usage, Prolegomena, and a Critical and Exegetical Commentary*, 4 vols. (London, 1864-1868), 4:150; cf. earlier commentators (Faber Stapulensis, Bleek, Schlichting, and Storr) mentioned and/or quoted by Alford (Ibid.) as propounding a similar position. Cf. also the discussion of these commentators (plus Rivet) by Ebrard, pp. 249-50, n. 1.

96 Umberto Cassuto, *A Commentary on the Book of Exodus*, tr. Israel Abrahams (Jerusalem, 1967), p. 322. Goppelt, *TDNT*, 8:256; David N. Freedman, "Early Israelite History in the Light of Early Israel Poetry," in *Unity and Diversity*, ed. H. Goendicke and J.M.M. Roberts (Baltimore and London, 1975), p. 26.

97 George A. Chadwick, *The Book of Exodus* (New York, 1908), p. 25.

Since there are proponents for each of these suggestions, how does one decide which is correct? William G. Moorehead flatly answers, "We cannot tell."[98] We acknowledge that there is some ambiguity with regard to the term *tabnît*, but a number of considerations point toward probable conclusions.

It is generally agreed that the prepositional prefixes k^e ("according to") before "all" (*kol* in Exodus 25:9) and b^e ("by/after")[99] before "pattern" (*tabnît*, Exod 25:40) indicate that *tabnît* is (at least) a *model/pattern for* the earthly sanctuary. But what is the nature of this *tabnît*? Is it a miniature model (Nos. 1 or 3 above), or an architect's plan (Nos. 2 or 4), the heavenly sanctuary itself (No. 5), or simply further reflections after a subjective "divine encounter" (No. 6)?

Position No. 6 may be rejected as an option. It stands in tension with Exodus 25:9 where it is affirmed that Moses was "caused to see" (Hiphil participle of *rā'āh*). The text indicates that there was a visible reality made known to Moses. Numbers 8:4 uses the word *appearance, view, vision* (*mar'eh*) to describe the same event. Other parallel passages support the conclusion that Moses beheld a visible reality.[100]

Does the *tabnît* involve a solid construction or architect's blueprint? In 12 of the 20 usages of *tabnît* in the OT there is explicit reference to a solid structure or form. Leaving Exodus 25 out of consideration, we have seen how Koehler and Baumgartner categorize a number of the 20 references under the meaning "model,"[101] which seems to imply a solid structure. Numerous scholars have argued forcefully for this same meaning of "model" in Exodus 25:9, 40.[102]

If Moses had been shown merely architect's plans, it would seem that these would have been made available to him on the mountain. But the record maintains that he brought down only the two tables of stone (Exod 32:15). It would seem more consonant with the context that Moses was provided in vision with a view of something constructed, relating in vivid reality to how the sanctuary was going to look. In the light of a quantitative analysis of the uses of *tabnît* and the sense of the immediate context of Exodus 25:9, 40, the conclusion as stated by David N. Freedman seems

---

98 William G. Moorehead, *Studies in the Mosaic Institutions: The Tabernacle, the Priesthood, the Sacrifices, the Feasts of Ancient Israel* (Dayton, OH, 1896), p. 16.

99 BDB, p. 90 (III, 8).

100 See Exod 26:30; 27:8.

101 See above, p. 154.

102 Besides the references listed above, see the bibliography in R. G. Hamerton-Kelly, "The Temple and the Origins of Jewish Apocalyptic," *VT* 20 (1970): 6, n. 1.

preferable: "Moses was shown something constructed, rather than a blue-print."[103]

If *tabnît* refers to something constructed, what is the nature of its construction? Is it a miniature model by which to construct the earthly sanctuary, or a miniature model *of* the heavenly sanctuary *for* the building of the earthly (that is, both a copy of and a *model/pattern for*)? Or, is it the heavenly sanctuary itself (that is, the original)? Or, did Moses first see the heavenly sanctuary itself and then a three-dimensional model of the heavenly, according to which he was to pattern the construction of the earthly?

Vertical Earthly/Heavenly Sanctuary Correspondence

The basic question that must first be addressed is whether a vertical earthly/heavenly sanctuary correspondence emerges from this passage. Exodus 25:9, 40 does not explicitly state that Moses saw the heavenly sanctuary[104] Yet the weight of evidence favors an implied earthly/heavenly sanctuary correspondence in the passage and its context.

1. We have seen how the semantic range of the word *tabnît* allows for, and even leans toward, a heavenly original and/or miniature model of a heavenly original. In Psalm 144:12 *tabnît* seems to refer to an original temple structure. This usage would tend to support the idea of a heavenly original in Exodus 25:9, 40.

In 2 Kings 16:10, 11 *tabnît* refers to a copy of an original which serves as a model for the construction of another copy. In at least 11 other OT occurrences, the *tabnît* is likewise a copy founded on some previously existing idea or object.[105] These usages would support the idea of a miniature model of a previously existing sanctuary in heaven.

2. The immediate theophanic, visionary context of this passage appears to suggest heavenly sanctuary connotations.[106] In the preceding chapter Moses and other representatives of Israel "saw the God of Israel; and there was under his feet as it were a pavement of sapphire stone" (Exod 24:10). This is suggestive of the throne vision in Ezekiel 1—in the context of the heavenly temple—where the throne was "in appearance like sapphire" (vs. 26).

It seems likely that in the narrative of Exodus 24 Moses and the elders

---

103 Freedman, p. 26.
104 So argues Cody, pp. 17, 20, and is content to leave it at that. He finds in Wisdom 9:8 the explicit reference that he believes to be the ultimate source of Hebrews 8:5.
105 See C. F. Keil, *Biblical Commentary on Exodus,* tr. James Martin (Grand Rapids, 1952), p. 165.
106 See Wagner, *TDOT,* 2:179.

glimpsed the heavenly sanctuary itself as God's heavenly dwelling place. If then in the very next chapter Moses is told to build an earthly dwelling place for God (Exod 25:8), it would appear probable that the earthly dwelling place is in some sense a replica of God's heavenly dwelling place.[107]

3. This contextual probability is strengthened by a third consideration, namely, the common ancient Near Eastern belief that an earthly temple is built as a copy of a heavenly original.[108] A few examples of this widespread notion may be noted. In the Babylonian *Enuma elish* we find a heavenly court of assembly (*Ubshukkinna*) corresponding to an earthly temple.[109] According to the Code of Hammurabi the Ebabbar temple in Sippar was "like the heavenly dwelling."[110] The famous neo-Sumerian cylinder texts portraying the exploits of Gudea of Lagash provide the oldest and clearest example.[111] King Gudea tells how he was guided in the building of temples,[112] and recounts on one occasion his vision of the goddess Nina, her brother Nigirsu, and her sister Nindub. Nina orders him to build a temple, Ningirsu shows him the heavenly temple that he is to copy,[113] and Nindub

---

107 Bruce, *Hebrews*, p. 166, effectively argues that since the idea of the earthly tabernacle as a dwelling place of God is emphasized in Exodus 25:8, in Exodus 25:9, 40, "it would be completely in keeping with current practice that such earthly dwelling place should be a replica of God's heavenly dwelling place." This argument combines the contextual indicators that we have just considered with the current ancient Near Eastern parallels, which are discussed in our next point.

108 Numerous scholars have recognized the emphasis upon an earth/heaven (vertical) correspondence within ancient Near Eastern literature, particularly in regard to a heavenly temple/sanctuary as the divine original of the earthly one. Hans Bietenhard, *Die himmlische Welt in Urchristentum und Spätjudentum*, Wissenschaftliche Untersuchungen zum Neuen Testament 2 (Tübingen, 1951): 13; F. J. Schierse, *Verheissung und Heilsvollendung: Zur theologischen Grundfrage des Hebräerbriefes* (Munich, 1955), p. 15; J. Coert Rylaarsdam, "The Book of Exodus: Introduction and Exegesis," *IB*, 1:1021, summarizes thus: "The notion of a heavenly model for temples, cult objects, and laws is universal in the ancient Near East." Hugh Montefoire, *A Commentary on the Epistle to the Hebrews*, Harpers New Testament Commentaries (New York and Evanston, 1964), p. 135, remarks that "the idea of a heavenly temple, with an earthly temple as its counterpart, is very ancient indeed. It can be traced right back to Babylonia...." Finally, Mircea Eliade, the prolific writer in the area of phenomenology of religion, states regarding ancient Near Eastern beliefs in his book *Cosmos and History* (New York, 1954), p. 7: "The temple in particular — preeminently the sacred place — had a celestial prototype."

109 *Enuma elish* 3.61, 119, 131 (*ANET*, p. 65); cf. Bruce, *Hebrews*, p. 166.

110 *ANET*, p. 164; cf. Montefiore, p. 135.

111 See, Hammerton-Kelly, p. 7; Cody, p. 17; Robert W. Rogers, *A History of Babylonia and Assyria*, 2 vols. (London, 1902), 1:369; Driver, *Exodus*, p. 267; Menahem Haran, "Shiloh and Jerusalem: The Origin of the Priestly tradition in the Pentateuch," *JBL* 81 (1962): 21; Henri Frankfort, *Kingship and the Gods: A Study of Ancient Near Eastern Religion as the Integration of Society and Nature* (Chicago, 1948), pp. 255-56.

112 Cylinder A. For the text (transliteration and translation), see George A. Barton, *The Royal Inscriptions of Sumer and Akkad* (New Haven, 1929), pp. 205-37; Francois Thureau-Dangin, ed., *Die sumerische und akkadische Königsinschriften* (Leipzig, 1907), pp. 89-123.

113 According to the analysis of Hamerton-Kelly, p. 7. The text at this point (A, 5.8-9) is not clear

gives him the "plan" (*gishar*)[114] of the temple by which he is to build.

The Semitic parallels must not be taken as a final determiner for the Israelite conception. Nevertheless, we may allow the parallel to have its full comparative weight and serve as one of several indicators that the people of Israel also knew of a heavenly-earthly correspondence.

4. A fourth strand of evidence in support of an earthly/heavenly sanctuary correspondence in Exodus 25:9, 40, is found in the various OT parallels. Allan J. McNicol correctly points out[115] that the idea of a vertical (earthly/heavenly) sanctuary correspondence is at home in the OT and not, as von Rad claims, "almost entirely foreign to ancient Israel."[116]

Helpful parallels are found already in the book of Genesis. With regard to Genesis 28:10-22, F. Jeremias argues effectively that Jacob saw at Bethel "the vision of the heavenly sanctuary."[117] The idea of a heavenly original/earthly counterpart is expressed by calling the earthly site of the vision the "house of God."[118] Tryggve N. D. Mettinger sees a further illustration in the analogy between *tabnît* and the *imago* concept of Genesis 1:27. Both are according to heavenly originals.[119]

In the Psalms and Prophets are found numerous explicit references to the heavenly sanctuary or temple in close parallelism or juxtaposition with the earthly sanctuary.[120] The thought of the biblical writers moves easily

---

(Thureau-Dangin, p. 95, does not attempt a complete translation). But elsewhere in Cylinder A it appears evident that the earthly temple was to be fashioned after a heavenly original. See, 11.16 (Barton, p. 227): "Like the great temple in heaven the whole [the earthly temple] rose." Note also 27.13 (Barton, p. 233): "its side, as the lofty temple of heaven filled with abundance." Cf. Cylinder B, 24:14 (Barton, p. 255): "At Eninnu, constructed in heaven and on earth."

114 Cylinder A, 5.4. Anton Deimel, ed., *Sumerisches Lexikon*, 3 vols. (Rome, 1925-1934; reprint ed., Graz, Austria, 1962), 2:797 (and 3:123), defines gishar as "Zeichnung; Bild; Emblem; Bestimmung . . . ; Plan." In the specific context of Cylinder A, 5.4, the Sumerian e2-a gis-har-bi is translated as a "Tempelriss." According to A. 4. 3-4 (Barton, p. 209), this "temple plan" was contained on a tablet of lapis lazuli.

115 McNicol, pp. 55-56.

116 Gerhard von Rad, "Typological Interpretation of the Old Testament," in *Essays on Old Testament Hermeneutics*, ed. Claus Westermann (Richmond, 1963), p. 19. Even von Rad points to a number of what he calls "vestiges" of the vertical correspondence in the OT (see von Rad, *TDNT*, 5:508). But he has not accounted for numerous examples of the earthly/heavenly sanctuary correspondences (especially in the Psalms and Prophets) nor the ease with which the thinking of the biblical writers moves from the earthly sanctuary to the heavenly.

117 F. Jeremias, "Das orientalische Heiligtum," *Angelos* 4 (1932): 56.

118 Ibid., pp. 56, 61-63.

119 Tryggve N. D. Mettinger, "Abbild oder Urbild? 'Imago Dei' in traditionsgeschichtlicher Sicht," *ZAW* 86 (1974): 410.

120 Note particularly the following six passages: Pss 11:4; 18:6(7 MT); 60:6(8) = 108:7(8); 63:2(3); 68:35(36); 96:9; 102:19(20); 150:1; Isa 6:1ff.; Ezek 1-10, 40-48; Jonah 2:7(8); Mic 1:2; Hab 2:20; Zech 3. For discussion of these and other texts, see my unpublished paper, "The Heavenly Sanctuary in the Old Testament" (Andrews University Seventh-day Adventist Theological Seminary, 1976); cf. Niels-Erik Andreasen, "The Heavenly Sanctuary in the Old Testament," in

from the earthly to the heavenly sanctuary, and liturgical aspects of the earthly sanctuary are frequently presented in vertical correspondence with heavenly sanctuary liturgy.[121]

5. Further strands of evidence for a vertical sanctuary correspondence in Exodus 25:9, 40 come from the literature of late Judaism. The Apocrypha and Pseudepigrapha give several indications of an earthly/heavenly correspondence of sanctuary/temple and liturgy.[122] Rabbinic sources frequently assert the existence of a full-blown original heavenly sanctuary corresponding to minute details of the Levitical sanctuary appointments and liturgy.[123] Many of the elaborations of the heavenly original are based on Exodus 25:9, 40 as a proof text.

The LXX use of the terms *tupos* and *paradeigma* may also indicate that the Hebrew (in Exodus 25:9, 40) was interpreted in terms of an earthly/ heavenly sanctuary correspondence.

Finally, as we have noted elsewhere,[124] Philo interprets what was shown to Moses as a *tupos of* the heavenly original *for* the earthly. Though Philo interprets the heavenly original in terms of transcendent, eternal ideas and not as material heavenly realities, nonetheless the same vertical (earth/ heaven) dynamics appear to be functioning as in the OT.

In sum, a grammatical analysis of *tabnît* in Exodus 25:40 allows for, and implies, a vertical earthly/heavenly sanctuary correspondence. This view is supported by (1) the immediate theophanic context, combined with the stated function of the sanctuary as a dwelling place for God; (2) ancient Near Eastern parallels; (3) OT parallels; (4) apocalyptic and pseudepigraphical literature; (5) Rabbinic sources; (6) the LXX translation; and (7) the interpretation of Philo. In light of this evidence, with Frank M. Cross, we would assert that "probably the conception of the *tabnith*, the 'model' (Exod 25:9), also goes back ultimately to the idea that the earthly sanctuary is the counterpart of the heavenly dwelling of a deity."[125]

The Sanctuary and the Atonement, ed. Arnold V. Wallenkampf and W. Richard Lesher (Washington, DC: Biblical Research Institute, 1981), pp. 67-86; and William H. Shea, *Selected Studies on Prophetic Interpretation* (Washington, DC: Biblical Research Institute, 1982), pp. 1-24.

121 See especially J. C. Matthews, "Die Psalmen und der Tempeldienst," *ZAW* 22 (1902): 65-82; Richard Preuss, "Die Gerichtspredigt der vorexilischen Propheten und der Versuch einer Steigerung der kultischen Leistung," *ZAW* 70 (1958): 181-84; Hans Strauss, "Zur Auslegung von Ps. 29," *ZAW* 82 (1970): 91-102.

122 See Wis 9:8; T. Levi, 3:508; 5:1; 2 *Apoc. Bar.*, 4:3-6; cf. the discussion in Cody, pp. 17-22.

123 For summaries of the evidence, see especially Raphael Patai, *Man and Temple in Ancient Jewish Myth and Ritual* (New York, 1967), pp. 130-33, 138-39; Strack and Billerbeck, 3:700-704; Bietenhard, pp. 125, 130, passim; Cody, pp. 22-25; Buchanan, p. 158.

124 See Davidson, *Typology in Scripture*, pp. 130-31.

125 Frank M. Cross, "The Tabernacle," *BA* 10 (1947), p. 62. See also Norman C. Habel, *Yahweh Versus*

If Exodus 25:9, 40 does indeed imply a vertical earthly/heavenly correspondence, it still remains to be determined precisely what Moses was shown.

We have noted that the theophanic context of Exodus 24 implies that Moses saw the heavenly sanctuary. But it does not appear likely that the *tabnît* refers exclusively to the heavenly sanctuary. If the heavenly sanctuary itself (unmediated by some miniature model presentation) were solely in view, this would not seem to coincide with other OT portrayals of the heavenly sanctuary.

Elsewhere in Scripture the heavenly sanctuary is described as a vast, majestic temple, accommodating countless angels.[126] If Moses had been able to take in such a display of majesty (unmediated by some kind of miniature model), it would not be necessary for God to tell him repeatedly to build it *according* to what he was shown (Exod 25:9, 40; 26:30; 27:8; Num 8:4). The emphasis of these latter passages rule out the view that Moses saw only the heavenly reality and then was left to translate it into earthly proportions.[127]

It seems more probable that Moses was first given a vision of the heavenly sanctuary and then was provided with a miniature model of it by which to construct the earthly.[128] If this was the case, there are still several possibilities as to the scope of *tabnît* in Exodus 25:9, 40.

The *tabnît* may refer primarily to the miniature model of the heavenly sanctuary (though not excluding an ultimate orientation to the heavenly sanctuary itself).[129] This suggestion is in harmony with the majority of usages of the term in which *tabnît* refers to a meaning other than "original." It particularly corresponds with the semantic range of *tabnît* made explicit in 2 Kings 16:10. Here the term refers to *a copy of the original* which is employed as a model for another copy. According to this suggestion the *tabnît* (in Exodus 25:9, 40) would refer to the miniature model of the original heavenly sanctuary which God instructed Moses to employ as a model/pattern for the earthly sanctuary.

On the other hand, in Exodus 25 *tabnît* may point primarily to the

---

Baal: A Conflict of Religious Cultures (New York, 1964), pp. 85-86.

126 Note Dan 7:9, 10.

127 See Delitzsch, *Hebrews,* 2:34.

128 Gray, p. 156, reminds us that it was not mutually exclusive in the minds of the ancient Semitic people to believe in an earthly/heavenly correspondence and at the same time have the concept of a model of the earthly. Habel, pp. 85-86, against this blended background of (earthly/heavenly and heavenly/earthly, sees Exodus 25:9, 40 as pointing ultimately to a heavenly original.

129 Suggestion No. 3 above.

heavenly sanctuary itself (though not excluding the necessity for a mediating miniature representation for Moses to follow).[130] This is in harmony with the usage of *tabnît* in Psalm 144:12. In this case the *tabnît* would signify *the original* which serves as a model for the earthly copy.

A third possibility is that both heavenly sanctuary *and* miniature model are in view. The *tabnît* would then involve the whole of what Moses was shown on the mountain—heavenly sanctuary original and miniature model—that was to serve as a pattern for the earthly sanctuary.[131]

It does not seem possible to decide with certainty from the available evidence whether the primary reference of *tabnît* is to a miniature model of the heavenly sanctuary, to the heavenly sanctuary itself (with a miniature model assumed), or to both. But whichever is primarily in view, both the heavenly sanctuary (the original) and miniature model (as copy and model/pattern for) appear still to be ultimately bound up with the term.

Drawing together the strands of argument and evidence for the nature of *tabnît* in Exodus 25:9, 40, we are in a position to conclude in favor of a vertical (earth/heaven) structure in this passage. The *tabnît* in verses 9 and 40 probably signifies a miniature model of the heavenly sanctuary and/or the heavenly sanctuary itself (with an implied mediating miniature model). This *tabnît* functions as a model/pattern for the construction of the earthly sanctuary.

What we have concluded concerning *tabnît* in Exodus 25:9, 40 (MT) appears also to be inherent in the LXX translation of this passage. The words *paradeigma* and *tupos,* which are used to translate *tabnît* in Exodus 25:9, 40 respectively, occur in Plato, Aristotle, and Greek thought of the third-second centuries B.C. to indicate an earthly/heavenly correspondence.[132]

The Greek *tupos* (like the Hebrew *tabnît*) has the potential for denoting both *copy of* and *model/pattern for* simultaneously. It is thus particularly appropriate as a word substitution for *tabnît*. Like the original Hebrew term, *tupos* can imply that Moses saw a copy (that is, a miniature model) of the heavenly sanctuary (or perhaps, the original, the heavenly sanctuary itself) that served as a model/pattern for the earthly sanctuary.[133]

---

130 Suggestion No. 5 above.

131 This view would encompass both suggestion Nos. 3 and 5 above.

132 See Hamerton-Kelly, p. 6. In Greek dualism, of course, this correspondence functions at a different level than in OT Scripture. It is transcendent ideas and not material heavenly realities that correspond to the earthly. Nevertheless similar vertical dynamics are functioning.

133 Since *tupos* and *paradeigma* were already employed in connection with a vertical correspondence in contemporary literature and earlier, the LXX translators may well have chosen these Greek

Summary and Implications

The Hebrew term *tabnît* appears to involve dynamics similar to those of the Greek *tupos*. It can denote a copy of, or a model/pattern for, or both together simultaneously. In Exodus 25:9, 40, it appears probable that *tabnît*—and *tupos* in verse 40 (LXX)—refers to a copy of an original (or the original itself) that serves as a model/pattern for another copy. It has in view the "pattern" *for* the earthly sanctuary that is simultaneously a miniature model *of* the heavenly sanctuary itself. Such a meaning is suggested by the use of *tabnît* elsewhere in the OT and supported by the immediate context and biblical, parabiblical, and extrabiblical parallels. A vertical (earth/heaven) sanctuary correspondence may, therefore, be regarded as present in Exodus 25:9, 40.

If Exodus 25:9, 40 does indeed imply a vertical correspondence between earthly and heavenly sanctuaries, then we may conclude that the author of Hebrews (Heb 8:5) has appropriately cited Exodus 25:40 to substantiate the existence of vertical sanctuary typology.

Relationship Between Type and Antitype in Hebrews

Editorial Synopsis. Seventh-day Adventists maintain that a basic continuity exists between the earthly sanctuary type and the heavenly sanctuary antitype. Thus, the priestly ministrations in the earthly sanctuary shed light on the nature of Christ's priestly ministry in the heavenly sanctuary.

This fundamental position is being challenged today. It is argued that contrary to the Adventist view the author of Hebrews makes a sharp discontinuity between type and antitype and repeatedly deviates from the OT type, altering it to fit NT fulfillments. Consequently, it is concluded that the type may never be used to explain the antitype, although the antitype may be used to illumine the type. Furthermore, it is contended

---

terms to indicate that they interpreted the Hebrew *tabnît* in terms of an earthly/heavenly correspondence (either in the OT sense of a material heavenly reality or in the Platonic sense of transcendent ideas). But regardless of their intentions, the word substitutions they chose for *tabnît* and in particular the word substitution of *tupos*, strikingly encompass the semantic dynamics inherent in the original.

that it is improper to employ typology to establish doctrine. Finally, it is held that Hebrews 9 is essentially the only norm for interpreting the OT sanctuary type.

In this section the present writer demonstrates that evidence in the book of Hebrews itself denies these charges. Major points may be summarized as follows:

1. The author of Hebrews himself establishes doctrine through typology. For example, he bases the doctrine of the cleansing of the heavenly sanctuary solely on typology (Heb 9:23). His argument is that the cleansing of the earthly sanctuary by animal blood points to a cleansing of the heavenly sanctuary by Christ's blood. There is no other discussion or presentation made. The doctrine is deducted strictly from the type.

2. The author of Hebrews likewise argues from the type to the antitype. This direction of thought is also illustrated by Hebrews 9:23. In this instance the argument moves from the cleansing of the earthly copy to the *necessity* for the cleansing of the heavenly sanctuary. In Hebrews 8:1-5 the argument moves from the sacrifices offered by earthly high priests (the type) to the *necessity* for a sacrifice to be offered by our heavenly High Priest (the antitype).

Actually, the correspondences between type and antitype function as a two-way street. This is particularly true of the relationships between the earthly and heavenly sanctuaries. While the heavenly reality does, indeed, shed great light on the earthly illustration, the earthly illustration also provides important insights into the function of the heavenly.

3. The author of Hebrews is fully aware that the earthly sanctuary is *not* an exact duplicate of the heavenly original. The earthly sanctuary is a "copy" of an original; a "shadow" of the real substance. Nevertheless his arguments testify that he recognizes a basic continuity between type and its antitype.

4. The author of Hebrews contrasts at certain points the antitype with the type (the charge is "deviation"). Specifically, he contrasts the priesthoods (Heb 7), the sacrifices (Heb 8, 10), the covenants (Heb 8), and the sanctuaries (Heb 8, 9). The question naturally arises: How can the author deviate from the type and yet, at the same time, maintain a fundamental continuity between the type and antitype? The answer is supplied by the book itself. According to the present writer, at each point of departure from the Levitical type, the author of Hebrews substantiates the change by referring to the OT which had earlier foretold these modifications.

For example, Christ's priesthood differs in essential features from the

170

Aaronic priesthood, but the author of Hebrews points out that these differences were already prophesied in Psalm 110. Christ's sacrifice differs from the animal sacrifices of the OT ritual, but this change from the type was already set forth in Psalm 40. The new covenant contains better promises than the old, but this was already pointed out in Jeremiah 31. The heavenly sanctuary is the "greater and more perfect tabernacle," but this too was already indicated in Exodus 25:40.

The author of Hebrews does not collapse the continuity between type and antitype. He regards this continuity so highly that wherever the NT antitype moves to an actual modification of the OT type, he is constrained to demonstrate that the alteration was already indicated in the OT.

5. Where no OT control texts are cited, the author of Hebrews consistently sees typological correspondences between the type and antitype.

6. The author of Hebrews gives no hint that his is the only inspired interpretation of the sanctuary ritual. As long as an essential continuity exists between the OT type and NT antitype and the type is understood as an illustration of the gospel (Heb 4:1-2), it is evident that the total witness of Scripture may be employed to explain the typology of the sanctuary. Its interpretation is not limited to Hebrews 9.

Section Outline

I. Survey of Issues
II. Analysis and Explanations
III. Conclusions

* * * * * * *

Survey of Issues

The most crucial cluster of issues regarding typology in Hebrews centers on the relationship between type and antitype in the Epistle. Seventh-day Adventists maintain that a basic continuity exists between Leviticus and Hebrews, between the essential contours of the OT sanctuary type and the NT sanctuary antitype. Therefore, the earthly sanctuary, with its apartments and services modeled after the heavenly original, may be regarded as instructive in clarifying the essential features of our Lord's priestly ministry in the heavenly sanctuary.

However, in recent years scholars both within and outside of Adventism have seriously challenged this position.[134] It is asserted that "there is a tremendous disparity between the types and their antitype."[135] This "tremendous disparity" is not simply due to the element of eschatological intensification (described in a previous section of our study). Rather, it is to be seen (so it is alleged) in the author's "repeated deviations from the Old Testament type" and in his "setting aside of earthly sanctuary 'specifics' because of their 'weakness and uselessness.' "[136]

Various passages in Hebrews are cited to illustrate the charge of "repeated deviations" of the antitype from the type.[137] But the greatest emphasis is placed upon the Day of Atonement motif in Hebrews 9. Here it is argued that the author consciously labors to modify the type to fit the antitype.[138] Several additional assertions frequently follow from this fundamental conviction of a stark discontinuity between type and antitype in Hebrews.

First, a presupposition is stated: Since there is disparity between the type and antitype, it is illegitimate to use typology in the establishment of doctrine. Typology may be used only to illustrate what is taught elsewhere in Scripture in clear, didactic (nonsymbolic, nontypological) language.[139]

A second, closely related point, follows: One can not legitimately argue from type to antitype, but only the other way around.[140] The heavenly antitype illuminates the earthly type, but the earthly sanctuary cannot function to illuminate one's understanding of the heavenly original. To support this second point, it is often suggested that Exodus 25:9, 40 does not imply a vertical correspondence between the earthly and heavenly sanctuaries.[141]

Third, since the author is regarded as frequently altering the type to fit the NT fulfillment, it is concluded that he had little concern for the details of the OT type. This point is underscored by identifying what are con-

---

134 The most recent protest within Adventism has been raised by Desmond Ford in his 1980 Glacier View manuscript, subsequently published under the title *Daniel 8:14: The Day of Atonement, and the Investigative Judgment* (Casselberry, FL, 1980). An array of writers both within and outside the Adventist Church who share similar convictions on typology are cited throughout, especially in chap. 3, and Appendix 9, "Quotations regarding the antithetical nature of the sanctuary types."

135 Ford, p. 133.

136 Ibid., p. 134.

137 See pp. 171-73 of the present study for listing and discussion of these passages.

138 See Ford, pp. 119, 142-44, for quotations from various biblical scholars to this effect.

139 So, ibid. p. 1: "Doctrine cannot be established by types or prophetic interpretation—these may only be used to illustrate and confirm what is clearly taught elsewhere, and in nonsymbolic language." See also, pp. 22, 24, 293, for similar statements.

140 For such caveat, see ibid., p. 134.

141 See nn. 92, 93 of the present study for proponents of this view.

sidered careless or historical inaccuracies. For example, the author is charged with mistakenly locating the altar of incense in the Most Holy Place (9:3-4).[142]

Finally, it is argued that the only ultimate norm for interpreting the OT sanctuary types is the book of Hebrews, particularly chapter 9. It is maintained that "Only in Hebrews 9 do we find the New Testament's interpretation of the first apartment ministry, the Day of Atonement, and the nature and timing of the cleansing of the sanctuary."[143] Again, "Hebrews 9 is the divine Word on the meaning of the sanctuary ritual, and anything that conflicts with that explanation cannot be urged upon others as a doctrine to be believed and taught."[144] Allowing only Hebrews 9 to function as a basis for interpretation severely circumscribes the discussion of the meaning of the sanctuary ritual.

These assertions challenge Adventist views on the relationship between type and antitype in Hebrews. They cause us to look more closely at the Epistle itself to see if the allegations can be sustained.

Analysis and Explanations

In this concluding section we will give attention to the hermeneutical issues that have been raised regarding the relationship between type and antitype in Hebrews. Chapter limits do not allow for full exegetical treatment of crucial passages, but the broad contours of the present writer's understanding can be summarized and the way pointed for further study.

Typology and Doctrine

The first issue concerns the use of typology to establish doctrine. Is it a valid rule that typology may not be employed to inform any part of the sanctuary doctrine, but only to illustrate what is taught elsewhere in explicit, nonsymbolic, didactic language?

---

142 See Myles M. Bourke, "The Epistle to the Hebrews," *The Jerome Biblical Commentary*, ed. Raymond E. Brown, Joseph A. Fitzmeyer, and Roland E. Murphy (Englewood Cliffs, NJ, 1968), p. 396, regarding Hebrews 9:4: "It seems that the author has made a mistake here, caused probably by the fact that he was not speaking from personal knowledge of the Temple, which replaced the Mosaic Tabernacle, but was merely repeating, and in this case misinterpreting, the description of the Tabernacle found in Ex." So also Alexander C. Purdy, "The Epistle to the Hebrews: Exegesis," *IB*, ed. George A. Buttrick (New York, Nashville, 1955), 11:686-87, regarding the same passage: "Either the author has other sources unknown to us, or else, as is more likely, he was not quite at home here, deriving his knowledge solely from books, and in this case using his books carelessly."

143 Ford, p. 157.

144 Ibid., p. 22.

We immediately observe that the author of Hebrews himself provides us with a clear example of the very methodology which is being charged as illegitimate. In Hebrews 9:23 the doctrine of the cleansing of the heavenly sanctuary is based solely on the typological correspondence with the cleansing of the earthly. Granted the inspiration of the author of Hebrews, it must still be recognized that he does not provide a didactic statement for the cleansing of the heavenly sanctuary, but rather a *typological argument.* He expects his readers to believe him, not because of his inspiration (to which he does not appeal), but because of the typological correspondence which they can recognize as valid.

OT Type to NT Antitype

The above reference to Hebrews 9:23 leads to a related issue. In this passage the author of Hebrews is clearly engaging in what some have considered to be illegitimate: arguing from OT type to NT antitype. In this instance the argument moves from the cleansing of the earthly copy to the *necessity* ("must needs be") for the cleansing of the heavenly reality.

Another example of this same approach is found in chapter 8:1-5. Here the author argues from the sacrifices offered by the OT earthly priests to the necessity for the sacrifice offered by the NT heavenly High Priest.

Actually, the correspondences between type and antitype function as a two-way street. This is particularly true of the relationships between the earthly and heavenly sanctuaries. While the heavenly reality does, indeed, shed great light on the earthly illustration, the earthly illustration likewise provides insights into the function of the heavenly reality.

We have used the phrase "arguing from OT type to NT antitype." To be more precise, in the book of Hebrews the OT earthly sanctuary is designated the "antitype" (*antitupos*) and the heavenly reality the "type" (*tupos*).[145] So to those who insist that one must not argue from type to antitype, but only from antitype to type, it should be pointed out that such is precisely what the author is doing when he argues from the earthly (antitype) to the heavenly (type)!

OT/NT Sanctuary Continuity

Of course, underlying this issue is more than semantics. We must face the crucial question: Upon what basis does the author utilize his detailed argumentation from the OT sanctuary to the NT reality? Is it solely

---

145 See pp. 145-48 of the present study.

because he is inspired and, therefore, can single out those valid points of correspondence between antitype and type? Or is it also because he posits a fundamental continuity between the two? The present writer is convinced that the latter is the correct response.

That the writer of Hebrews conceives of a continuity between the basic contours of the earthly and heavenly sanctuaries seems clearly evident from the citation of Exodus 25:40 (Heb 8:5) and from the use of terminology in Hebrews 8:5 and 9:24 (copy/shadow). As we have already noted above,[146] the use of *tabnît* (*tupos,* LXX) in Exodus 25:40 indicates a vertical correspondence between the earthly sanctuary and (a miniature model of) the heavenly sanctuary. The author of Hebrews remains faithful to this usage in his Epistle.

Furthermore, we have seen how in the NT the use of *tupos* as a hermeneutical term encompasses the linear dynamics of its original meaning of "hollow mold." With a hollow mold, the *antitupos* conforms to the basic contours of the *tupos.* So in biblical typology, the "antitype" corresponds in its essential contours to the "type."

What is clear with regard to horizontal typology (1 Cor 10, Rom 5, 1 Pet 3)—in which the "type" is the OT reality and the "antitype" is the NT fulfillment—is even more evident in vertical typology (Heb 8 and 9)—where the earthly sanctuary is the "antitype" corresponding to the previously existing "type," the heavenly sanctuary (and/or its miniature model). In horizontal typology the OT person/event only *prefigures* an eschatological reality yet to appear in the future. But in vertical (sanctuary) typology the OT earthly sanctuary not only *points forward to* a future heavenly reality functioning in a certain manner, but actually *derives itself from* the already existing heavenly original.

Of course, the author of Hebrews is aware that the earthly sanctuary is not an exact duplicate of the heavenly original. In horizontal typology there is the absolute eschatological intensification of the type in the NT fulfillment. In vertical (sanctuary) typology the earthly is described as a "copy" (*hupodeigma*) and "shadow" (*skia*) of the heavenly sanctuary (Heb 8:5). We may thus expect an intensification between earthly copy/shadow and heavenly original/true. But at the same time these word pairs indicate a continuity of basic contours. A "copy" corresponds to its "original" and a "shadow" reveals the basic contours of its "substance."

Those who argue against a basic continuity sometimes point to the many

---

146 See pp. 151-63 of the present study.

differences between the Mosaic tabernacle and the Solomonic temple (and they might have added Ezekiel's vision of a new temple—Ezekiel 40-48), which were built (or to be built) according to the divinely provided pattern.[147] But such argument can be turned on its head.

The very fact of differences in the Israelite sanctuaries provides an OT indication of what constitutes the essential contours—those which remain constant throughout. Although there may be variance in size, material, and number of articles, the basic design of the sanctuaries remains the same. There are the two apartments (holy place and Most Holy Place), the same dimensional proportions, and the same articles of furniture. It is this basic design that is described in Hebrews 9:1-5.

Resolving Continuity/Disparity Conflict

The next crucial question is this: If the linguistic evidence points to the existence of a fundamental correspondence/continuity between antitype and type, how can we explain the "tremendous disparity" between them that some claim? Are such claims unfounded? It would be appropriate at this juncture to look more closely at the passages cited as evidence of contrasts and deviations in the typology of Hebrews.

Leaving Hebrews 9 for the moment (to be examined later), we note the following passages which are frequently used to substantiate discontinuity: Hebrews 7:11-14; 8:1-3; 10:1-14.[148] The contrasts between type and antitype in these passages have been summarized as follows:

> In the type, the priest was a sinner whose ministry was imperfect and terminated by death. He was forever offering, and knew no successful climax to his work. He belonged to the tribe of Levi and at the best could only enter the presence of God once a year. What a contrast to our Priest in the true sanctuary above. Christ does not belong to the tribe of Levi, His ministry is perfect and is never interrupted by death, and belongs to "a greater and more perfect tabernacle." He needs not to offer sacrifices continually, but after a single "once for all" offering sat down as priest-king at the right hand of God, forever in the presence of His Father.[149]

This summary has rightly pointed out elements of stark contrast, clear deviations from the OT type to the NT antitype. We may outline the major points of difference in these passages (and their contexts), some of which are not mentioned in the preceding quotation:

---

147 See, Ford, pp. 137-38.
148 See ibid., p. 101.
149 Ibid., pp. 108-9.

	OT Type	NT Antitype
A. Priesthoods contrasted (Heb 7)	1. Tribe of Levi	1. Order of Melchizedek
	2. Mortal	2. Eternal
	3. Sinful	3. Sinless
B. Sacrifices contrasted (Heb 8:1-6; 10:1-14)	1. Ineffective sacrifices	1. "Better" sacrifices
	2. Blood of animals	2. Priest offers own blood
	3. Offered repeatedly	3. Offered once for all
C. Covenants contrasted (Heb 8:6-13)	1. First covenant	1. New covenant
	2. Covenant promises	2. "Better" promises
D. Sanctuaries contrasted (Heb 8:1-5)	1. Earthly sanctuary	1. Heavenly sanctuary
	2. Copy/shadow	2. Original/true

How can the author of Hebrews posit such deviations between OT "type" and NT "antitype" and still maintain a fundamental continuity between the two? The answer is at once simple and striking: *In each of the passages cited above the author of Hebrews introduces a departure from the Levitical type, but he substantiates such a change from the OT itself!*

Christ's priesthood does indeed differ in essential features from the Aaronic priesthood, but the author shows how these differences are already indicated in Psalm 110. Christ's sacrifice differs from the animal sacrifices of the OT ritual service, but this alteration of the type is already set forth in Psalm 40. The new covenant does contain better promises than the old, but these are already pointed out in Jeremiah 31. And finally, the heavenly sanctuary is indeed the "greater and more perfect tabernacle," but this is already indicated in Exodus 25:40.

In each of these changes from the Levitical system, the author of Hebrews does not engage in an arbitrary manipulation of the OT type. Rather he provides a "sound piece of exegesis" of OT control passages in order to demonstrate the "self-confessed inadequacy of the old order."[150]

---

150 Caird, p. 47. Caird refers specifically to Psalm 110 and Jeremiah 31 (along with Psalms 8 and 95). See our analysis of Exodus 25:40 on pp. 151-63 of the present study. The present writer has also found Caird's statement applicable to the author of Hebrews' use of Psalm 40. The central section of Psalm 40 (vss. 6-10, the heart of the chiastic structure) does appear to move into the realm of direct Messianic discourse, and the author of Hebrews has (10:5-10) rightly recognized

Thus the author of Hebrews does not collapse the continuity between type and antitype. The fact is, he regards this continuity so highly that wherever the NT antitype moves beyond intensification to an actual modification of the OT type, he feels constrained to demonstrate that such an alteration was already indicated in the OT.

Hebrews 9

Do we find this same high regard for continuity between type and antitype when we move from Hebrews 7, 8, and 10 to the debated passage of Hebrews 9:1-9? Or does Hebrews 9, as claimed by some, contain repeated modification of the OT type—in the form of conscious manipulation of the type to fit the antitype or of historical inaccuracies in description?

Golden altar. Taking up the question of descriptive inaccuracies first, we refer briefly to an alleged example: "Behind the second curtain stood a tent called the Holy of Holies, having the golden altar of incense. . ." (Heb 9:3-4).

At first sight the author does seem to describe the Most Holy Place inaccurately as "having the golden altar of incense (*echousa thumiatērion*)."[151] Some have sought to explain this difficulty by translating *thumiatērion* as "censer" instead of "altar of incense."[152] This is a possible translation. It seems highly unlikely, however, that the author should mention the censer and omit any reference to "one of the most conspicuous and significant of the contents of the tabernacle," namely, the altar of incense.

A satisfactory explanation is seen by the shift in phraseology from verse 2 to verse 4. In verse 2 the author indicates *spatial position* when he refers to the holy place, "in which (*en hē*) were the lampstand and the table and the bread of the Presence." But in verse 4, as B. F. Wescott has rightly noted, "the substitution of *echousa* ['having'] for *en hē* ['in which'] itself points clearly to something different from mere position."[153] By using the term *echousa* ("having"), the writer of Hebrews seems to indicate that the altar of incense is "properly belonging to"[154] the Most Holy Place in

---

the dramatic juxtaposition between the obsolete animal sacrifices and the announcement of the Messiah that He has come to accomplish what the sacrifices never could. See the unpublished study of Jacques Doukhan for further discussion of this important Psalm.

151 See n. 142 above for illustrative citations to this effect. As another example, see Homer A. Kent, Jr., *The Epistle to the Hebrews* (Grand Rapids, 1972), p. 84: "He [the author of Hebrews] thought that the golden altar was inside the veil."

152 See Brooke Foss Wescott, *The Epistle to the Hebrews* (Grand Rapids, 1950), p. 247, for a survey of the usage of this term and listing of proponents of the "censer" interpretation.

153 Ibid.

154 Ibid.

function, although not actually located in the Most Holy Place.

Such a conception of the *functional relationship* between the altar of incense and the Most Holy Place is already at home in the OT. In 1 Kings 6:22 the altar of incense is described as "belonging to the inner sanctuary" (*'ašer-ladbîr*)—the Most Holy Place (vs. 16). Elsewhere in the OT the ark of the covenant and the altar of incense are placed in close connection.[155] Furthermore, it is instructive to note that in the directions for the building of the sanctuary (Exod 25-40), only with regard to the altar of incense is there a mention of the yearly Day of Atonement, a function that focused in the Most Holy Place (Exod 30:10).

It is possible, therefore, to conclude that the author of Hebrews did not describe inaccurately the location of the altar of incense. He simply moved beyond the locative to the functional to capture the OT perspective that the golden altar "belongs to" the Most Holy Place.

The question of descriptive accuracy is not, however, the crucial issue in the dispute over the interpretation of Hebrews 9. Some recent commentators insist that in Hebrews 9 the author deliberately deviates from the earthly type (the bipartite earthly sanctuary) in his description of the heavenly sanctuary.[156] The focus is upon verse 8. Here it is suggested, the author argues that the earthly holy place typifies the entire OT order and the earthly Most Holy Place corresponds to the NT heavenly sanctuary.

While it is not the purpose of this chapter to provide a detailed exegesis of Hebrews 9, significant contextual and exegetical considerations may be pointed out which make such an interpretation untenable.

No change indicated by OT citation. It is illuminating to note, first of all, that Hebrews 9 (unlike chapters 7, 8, and 10) gives no OT citation to substantiate a deviation from type to antitype. We would not press the argument of consistency unduly. However, it should caution us against too easily positing radical deviations between the earthly sanctuary and the heavenly when the passage cites *no* OT evidence to indicate such changes.

The larger context. A number of recent studies,[157] arguing that the

---

155 See Exod 30:6; 40:5; cf. Lev 4:7; 16:12, 18. For further discussion of the Most Holy Place function of the altar of incense, see M. L. Andreasen, *The Book of Hebrews* (Washington, DC, 1948), pp. 321-22.

156 See Ford, Appendices 6 and 8, for a convenient collection of statements by various commentators supporting this view.

157 See especially F. F. Bruce, *Commentary on the Epistle to the Hebrews,* NICOT (Grand Rapids, 1964), pp. 181-98; Aelred Cody, *Heavenly Sanctuary and Liturgy in the Epistle to the Hebrews* (St. Meinrad, IN, 1960), pp. 147-48; Jean Héring, *The Epistle to the Hebrews* (London, 1970), pp. 70-75; Spicq, 2:253-54; and the unpublished paper by Gerhard Hasel, "Some Observations on Hebrews 9 in View of Dr. Ford's Interpretation," pp. 6-8. Cf. William Lindsay, *Lectures on the*

larger context is making a comparison between the old and new covenants (8:1-2, 13; 9:1), underscore the point that each of the covenants had a sanctuary. Thus, Hebrews 9 compares the whole (bipartite) earthly sanctuary of the first covenant—which is a *parabolē* standing for the Mosaic system—and the whole heavenly sanctuary of the new covenant, "the greater and more perfect tabernacle" (9:11). Chapter 9:1-7 constitutes a description of the former, or earthly sanctuary (*prōtē skēnē*), and then verse 8 moves away from the earthly sanctuary and introduces the heavenly sanctuary (*tōn hagiōn*).

The words *prōtē skēnē* in verse 8 should be understood, then, in the *temporal sense* of "former sanctuary," just as *prōtē* ("former") is used in verse 1. It should not be construed as continuing the *spatial meaning* of "first sanctuary" (for example, the holy place), as in verses 2 and 6.[158] Thus the author employs a chiastic literary pattern of A:B: :B′:A′ to bring the reader back to the main point introduced in verse 1. Note the chiasm in the following outline of the passage:

Hebrews 9:1-8 Chiasm

A   "Former" (*prōtē*) "covenant"; [Former] earthly sanctuary vs. 1

B   "First" (*prōtē*), "outer"—first apartment
    [Second] (*deuteros*) "inner"—second apartment   vss. 2-5

B′ "First" (*prōtē*) "outer"—first apartment
    "Second" (*deuteros*) "inner"—second apartment   vss. 6-7

A′ "Former" (*prōtē*), Earthly sanctuary   vs. 8

Epistle to the Hebrews, 2 vols. (Philadelphia, 1868), 2:22-23; Ronald Williamson, *The Epistle to the Hebrews* (London, 1964), p. 84.

158 So Bruce, pp. 194-95: "It is further to be noted that, whereas hitherto our author has used 'the first tabernacle' of the outer compartment of the sanctuary, here [in 9:8] he used it to mean the sanctuary of the 'first covenant' [9:1], comprising the holy place and holy of holies together." Again, Cody, pp. 147-48: "The first tent [of 9:8] becomes the old, earthly tent in its entirety, including both the Holy and Holy of Holies, and . . . the 'better and more perfect tent' of vs 11, becomes the celestial sanctuary"; Williamson, *Hebrews,* p. 84: "This 9:8 is not a reference to the Holy Place of the sanctuary, but stands for the whole Jewish system that has been described." Lindsay, 2:22-23, remarks similarly: "By the first tabernacle, in this verse [9:8], we are not to understand, as in vers. 2 and 6, the outer division of the ancient tabernacle as distinguished from the inner, but the Jewish tabernacle as distinguished from the Christian. . . . It would serve no purpose to define a period by the continuance of the outer apartment particularly, when the inner existed for precisely the same time. . . . It is plainly the Jewish tabernacle as a whole that is meant, to which a contrast is presented in the greater and more perfect tabernacle mentioned in ver. 11." The NEB has captured the proper sense of *prōtē skēnē* by translating as "earlier tent." We may note that Josephus (Contra Apion II.12) uses *prōtē skēnē* in this same temporal sense of "former tabernacle" (i.e., the earthly sanctuary preceding the Solomonic temple).

Ta hagia. At this point the author of Hebrews also provides a transition to the discussion of the heavenly sanctuary by introducing the term *ta hagia.* As A. P. Salom has convincingly demonstrated, *"ta hagia* in Hebrews (apart from 9:2-3) should be regarded as referring to the sanctuary as a whole,"[159] not simply to the Most Holy Place.

Perhaps the most weighty consideration in support of the contextual, structural, and linguistic points just mentioned is the nature of biblical typology.

Difference between type and symbol. Those who argue for a disparity between type and antitype in this passage generally consider the word *parabolē* in Hebrews 9:9 as a synonym for *tupos,* referring to typology.[160] They see a typological relationship between the earthly holy place and the whole OT Mosaic order, and between the earthly Most Holy Place and Christ's ministry in the heavenly sanctuary. But in the light of the typological structures we have studied (summarized in the first two parts of this chapter), we must conclude that *parabolē does not refer to a typological relationship.*

At this point the author of Hebrews has carefully chosen the word *parabolē* rather than *tupos* or *antitupos.* The *prōtē skēnē* (regardless of whether it denotes the first [former] sanctuary or the first apartment of this sanctuary) only *symbolizes* or *stands for,* but does not *point forward to* or *prefigure* the "present age" of which it is a part. Thus there is no prophetic structure operating in this verse. Likewise the eschatological structure is missing. The "present age" is not the eschatological fulfillment foreshadowed by the earthly sanctuary.

Because these crucial typological structures are lacking, one cannot speak of a typological correspondence between the earthly sanctuary (either as a whole or in part) and the old order for which it stands. This first correspondence is not typological but symbolic. It is not sound exegetical procedure to place this *symbolic* correspondence in direct parallel with the clear *typological* correspondence between earthly and heavenly sanc-

---

159 A. P. Salom, *"Ta Hagia* in the Epistle to the Hebrews," *AUSS* 5 (1967): 64-65; see pp. 59-70 for full discussion and evidence. Along with the comparative evidence from the LXX cited by Salom, note also how other Greek writers use the plural *ta hagia* to denote the entire sanctuary: Philo (Fuga 93) and Josephus (Jewish Wars 2.341) apply it to the whole earthly sanctuary, while Sibylline Oracles, 3:308, applies it to the entire heavenly sanctuary. For further discussion on the possible implications of the plural, see Hasel, "Observations on Hebrews 9," pp. 3-5; see also Appendix A in this volume for a reprint of Salom's study.

160 See Kent, p. 168; J. H. Davies, *A Letter to the Hebrews,* Cambridge Bible Commentary, ed. P. R. Ackroyd, A.R.C. Leaney, and J. W. Packer (Cambridge, 1967), p. 86.

tuary that functions in the wider context of this passage.

One cannot say, therefore, that the holy place of the earthly sanctuary is a *symbol* standing for the present age, but that the Most Holy Place of the same sanctuary is a *type* pointing forward to the NT heavenly sanctuary. This is mixing apples and oranges. The only way to be consistent to both the symbology and typology of the passage is to recognize that (1) the whole earthly sanctuary symbolizes or stands for the old order in which it functions, and (2) that this whole earthly sanctuary (and the old covenant order for which it stands) points beyond itself typologically to the NT fulfillment in the heavenly sanctuary (and the new covenant order in which it functions).

It should not be inferred from our discussion that the author of Hebrews is *trying to prove* the existence of a bipartite heavenly sanctuary that corresponds to the earthly counterpart. What we are saying is that in his argument, he remains faithful to the idea of continuity between type and antitype. It would be fair to say that, in harmony with the idea of correspondence (basic contours) between type and antitype as expressed by the terms *tupos* and *antitupos,* the author assumes such a bipartite sanctuary in the original as well as in the copy. This, however, is not explicitly stated and is not the point at issue in his argument.

Transition point. What we may expect the author to indicate, as he compares the sanctuaries of the old and new covenants, is some reference to the point of transition between the old and new covenants, to the commencement of the new covenant ministry and the inauguration of the new covenant sanctuary. Such is precisely what comes explicitly to the fore in Hebrews 10:19, 20, where the verb *egkainizo* ("inaugurate") is employed to describe Christ's entrance into the heavenly sanctuary. Just as the OT sanctuary was inaugurated or consecrated before its services officially began (Exod 40; Lev 8), so the heavenly sanctuary is inaugurated as Jesus begins His priestly ministry in its precincts.

George Rice has shown that Hebrews 10:19, 20 is part of a chiastic structure (encompassing 6:19–10:39) and that Hebrews 10:19 and onward (the second limb of the chiasm) is the explanatory development of the parallel or first limb of the chiasm, Hebrews 6:19.[161] Therefore, in the light of the clear reference to the inauguration of the heavenly sanctuary in 10:19, 20, it appears possible to conclude that the same event is in view in

---

161 George Rice, "The Chiastic Structure of the Central Section of the Epistle to the Hebrews," *AUSS* 19 (1981): 243-46.

the description of Jesus' entrance into the heavenly sanctuary in 6:19, 20. Regardless of which veil(s) the author has in mind in these passages,[162] the continuity between type and antitype is maintained, inasmuch as the entire sanctuary was inaugurated at the commencement of its services.

It may be possible to argue that inauguration imagery—and not primarily Day of Atonement imagery—is alluded to in Hebrews 9:12-21.[163] The "blood of goats and calves" (vs. 12) seems to have reference, not to Day of Atonement services, but to the inauguration/commencement of the Aaronic high priesthood and the beginning of the services of the sanctuary. At that time such offerings were sacrificed (Lev 9:8, 15, 22; cf. Heb 9:19). Thus again the author of Hebrews remains faithful to the basic contours of the OT type. It seems possible to infer that when he makes specific reference to Jesus' entering the heavenly sanctuary after His ascension, the event in view is the antitypical inauguration of the heavenly sanctuary.

The author of Hebrews depicts the continuing work of Christ after the inauguration in terms consonant with the first apartment priestly ministry in the earthly sanctuary. For example, Christ "ever lives to make intercession for us" (7:25), reflecting the ministry of the earthly priest who offered up "perpetual incense before the Lord" (Exod 30:8) in the daily (holy place) ministry. Other passages pertaining to Christ's priestly ministry in heaven and corresponding to the daily (holy place) ministry in the earthly sanctuary, include the following: Hebrews 2:17, 18; 8:2, 6; 9:15, 24; 10:21; 12:24; 13:15.[164] At the same time, in harmony with the OT control passage of Psalm 110, Christ is described in terms of His kingly status as well as His priestly function; He sits at the Father's right hand to wait till His enemies

---

162 For a helpful discussion of the issue of the "veil" in Hebrews 6 and 10, and the related matter of access to the presence of God, see especially Hasel, "Observations on Hebrews 9," pp. 14-19. It becomes apparent from various philological considerations that the references to entering within the veil in 6:19 and 10:20 may encompass something broader than just the veil before the Most Holy Place; at the same time, it is seen that the presence of God is not limited to the Most Holy Place. In light of the fact that the author of Hebrews in 9:3 uses the qualifying "second curtain" when specifically referring to the veil before the Most Holy Place, it is very possible that in 6:19, 20 the reference is to the veil before the holy place, or perhaps in the collective sense to the veil(s) both before the holy and Most Holy Places. But even if the author of Hebrews remains consistent with LXX usage in 6:19, and has the veil before the Most Holy Place exclusively in mind, this would still correlate with the inauguration typology, which in the OT "type" included the entering within the Most Holy as well as the holy place.

163 This is contrary to Ford who argues that "verses 13-22 of Hebrews 9 do not wander away from the Day of Atonement" (p. 146). See Hasel, "Observations on Hebrews 9," pp. 9-12, for further discussion of this issue. For arguments against an inauguration view, see Johnsson, pp. 91-92 in this volume.

164 Note also Hebrews 7:27 and 10:11, where the daily services of the earthly sanctuary (in particular the daily sacrifices) are compared with Christ's work.

are made a footstool for His feet (Ps 110:1; Heb 1:3, 13; 10:12, 13).[165]

Better blood. But neither inauguration nor the heavenly work of Christ as priest/king is the primary concern of the Epistle and the cultic argument of the central section. William Johnsson has persuasively argued that the major concern is with "the relative value of sacrifice."[166] Those Hebrew Christians, tempted to Judaism, the author of Hebrews assures that only in Jesus can they find the "better blood," the one all-sufficient and efficacious sacrifice that can purify the conscience of the believer (9:13-14; cf. 10:4). If they turn away from Him, where will they go?

The author indicates from Psalm 40 (10:5-10) that all the sacrifices of the OT coalesce into the one great sacrifice in the person of Jesus. Because all the sacrificial types of the OT converge upon Jesus, the author in Hebrews draws upon the various sacrificial imagery of the OT ritual. He alludes to both the daily and the yearly (Day of Atonement) and other important blood rituals (7:27; 10:11; 9:13, 18-22, 25). The argument is simple—even at its high point (such as the Day of Atonement) OT sacrificial blood is not able to purify the conscience, as is evidenced by the fact that it must be repeated continually in the rituals (10:3-4). But Christ's blood is far superior. His all-sufficient sacrifice was made once, for all time (7:27; 9:26, 28; 10:10, 14).

Thus in the allusions to the Day of Atonement in the Epistle, the point at issue is the efficacy of sacrifice, not the issue of time. Obviously, all the blood rites (daily and yearly rituals) *met their sacrificial aspect* at the Cross. But all other aspects find their respective fulfillments in the course of Christ's priestly ministry.

Although the timing of the antitypical day of atonement services is not a point at issue, the author does provide hints of it by his reference to the cleansing of the sanctuary (9:23), followed by reference to a future judgment (vs. 27) and the second coming of Christ (vs. 28). Five additional passages refer to a future judgment (2:2-4; 4:1-3; 6:7-12; 10:28-39; 12:26-29). These passages suggest an investigative (4:12; 6:10; 10:28-30) as well as executive judgment involving the professed people of God. These hints regarding timing are consistent with the OT type.

Sources for interpretation. A final issue calls for brief attention as we

---

165 For the kingship motif, see also Hebrews 1:5, 8, 9; 2:7; 8:1; 12:2. The references to "sitting at the right hand" of the Father serve to indicate, not so much Christ's actual physical position, as His rightful position and authority. Cf. Ps 45:9; 109:31; 110:1, 5; Matt 20:21, 23; 26:64; Mark 16:19; Acts 2:34; Col 3:1; 1 Pet 3:22.

166 William Johnsson, "Day of Atonement Allusions," chap. 6 in this volume.

complete this study. Those who find a discontinuity between sanctuary type and antitype in Hebrews claim that only Hebrews (and especially Hebrews 9) provides "the divine Word on the meaning of the sanctuary ritual."[167] But if there is a basic continuity between OT type and NT antitype, as we have argued in this chapter, then the necessity no longer exists for such a constricted final norm in the NT. As a matter of fact, the Epistle of Hebrews nowhere claims to represent the only inspired interpretation of the sanctuary ritual.

In order to put the typology of Hebrews in proper perspective we must stress that the interpretation of the Levitical system given in Hebrews is only part of the rich typological mosaic which includes the total witness of Scripture. Along with Hebrews, other biblical material—in particular the visions of Daniel and Revelation—must be consulted for a complete picture of the nature and timing of the fulfillment of sanctuary typology.

Summary and Implications

We have seen that throughout the Epistle to the Hebrews the author upholds the basic continuity/correspondence between sanctuary type and antitype. This fundamental continuity is seen in the author's—

1. Use of typological terminology (*tupos, antitupos, hupodeigma,* and *skia*).

2. Citation of Exodus 25:40 in Hebrews 8:5.

3. Freedom to argue from type to antitype to establish doctrinal points.

4. Use of OT control passages to legitimize those instances where the NT antitype moves beyond eschatological intensification to actual modification of the OT type.

5. Consistent employment of typological correspondences in passages where no OT control texts are cited.

6. Refusal to set forth his interpretation of the sanctuary ritual as the only complete "divine Word" on the subject.

The implications of this section of the study are especially significant for the recent discussion of the relationship between type and antitype. In the light of what Hebrews itself reveals, it appears possible to maintain the traditional Adventist position that (1) a basic continuity exists between the essential contours of the OT sanctuary type and NT antitype;[168] and therefore, (2) the earthly sanctuary may be regarded as instructive for

---

167 For full citation, see above, p. 168, n. 144.
168 So, *Early Writings,* pp. 252-53: "I was also shown a sanctuary upon the earth containing two apartments. It resembled the one in heaven, and I was told that it was a figure of the heavenly."

clarifying essential features of the heavenly sanctuary, while at the same time recognizing the eschatological intensification that occurs between type and antitype.[169]

Conclusions

We now summarize the major hermeneutical conclusions reached in our discussion of the four areas of concern regarding the nature of typology in Hebrews:

1. Biblical typology is characterized by the presence of certain structures which may be listed as historical, eschatological, Christological-soteriological, ecclesiological, and prophetic in nature. These characteristics, found in representative typological passages, coincide with traditional views on typology. The biblical view differs with the more recent positions taken by scholars in postcritical neotypology.

2. The sanctuary typology of Hebrews possesses unique vertical and cultic dimensions. Nonetheless, it is comprised of the same conceptual structures found in representative typological passages elsewhere in Scripture. Vertical sanctuary typology, therefore, is part of the fundamental biblical perspective on typology. It is not a vestige of alien mythic or dualistic thought forms.

3. The word *tabnît* in Exodus 25:40 implies a vertical correspondence between the earthly and heavenly sanctuaries. Therefore, the author of Hebrews has interpreted Exodus 25:40 correctly when he appeals to it as an OT basis for vertical sanctuary typology.

4. The author of Hebrews recognizes and maintains a basic continuity between the essential contours of sanctuary type and antitype. This high regard for typological continuity allows him to argue from type to antitype in his doctrinal exposition. Furthermore, it leads him to provide OT indicators (control passages) for those instances where the NT fulfillment moves (beyond eschatological intensification) to an actual modification of the OT type.

---

169 So, ibid., p. 253: "And in the wisdom of God the particulars of this work [in the earthly sanctuary apartments] were given us that we might, by looking [back] to them, understand the work of Jesus in the heavenly sanctuary."

Chapter VIII

Antithetical Or Correspondence Typology?

Alberto R. Treiyer

Editorial Synopsis. Even a casual reading of Hebrews indicates that its apostolic author is comparing and contrasting the Levitical system (first covenant; earthly sanctuary; animal sacrifices; human priesthood) with the new system of worship inaugurated by Christ (new covenant; heavenly sanctuary; Christ's own atoning death and priesthood).

Scholars who regard the Epistle as influenced by Greek thought interpret it as a thoroughgoing attack on the Levitical system and see it as a unique example of antithetical typology. The break between the Levitical sanctuary system and Christ's heavenly ministry is considered too profound to permit any significant links of correspondence between the two. Carried to its logical conclusion such a position would reject a two-phased priestly ministry for Christ.

In this chapter the writer demonstrates the falseness of the antithetical typology position and argues for a typology of correspondence. While the contrasts between the two systems underscore the "better" covenant and sanctuary and the "better" sacrifice and priesthood of the Christian era, "better" does not mean "in opposition to" but simply indicates something "superior," something "more definitive."

The apostle Paul portrays the Christian system as "more glorious" in contrast to the Levitical system which he describes as "glorious" (2 Cor 3:6-18). Both are "glorious" because both reveal the light of the gospel. The Levitical system did not erect a barrier to prevent Israel from approaching God. On the contrary God requested His people to build Him a sanctuary so that He might dwell among them (Exod 25:8), and the sinful people had access to Him through the ministrations of a certified priesthood. Even now in the new dispensation—as in the old—no believer can enter *bodily* into the presence of God. In either dispensation we enter by means of a priest whether an Aaronic priest or Christ Himself.

The weakness in the Levitical system was not that it obstructed an approach to God. Rather, the weakness lay in the fact that it was only a shadow-type. As such, it was unable to deal permanently with the sin problem. It could only point the faith of the believer to the coming better sacrifice and priesthood of the Messiah who alone could take away sin.

All shadow-types—whether of the Davidic monarchy, the Melchizedek priesthood, or the Levitical system—had limitations and incomplete aspects. The evidence is sufficient to demonstrate that the author of Hebrews wrote under the assumption of typological correspondences between the two systems in every instance possible. When he did touch on a detail in the Levitical system that did not fit perfectly the ministry of Christ, he observed that such points were already foreseen and resolved in the OT Scriptures.

Since the author of Hebrews does, indeed, relate the new system typologically to the old, we move on a sound biblical basis to see the two phases of Christ's priestly ministry foreshadowed in the daily and yearly ministrations of the earthly sanctuary.

Chapter Outline

I. Introduction
II. Correspondence in Contrasts
III. Limitations in Typology
IV. Sacrifice: Contrast and Correspondence
V. Levitical Sanctuary: Not a Barrier to God
VI. Basic Limitations of the Ancient System
VII. Conclusions

* * * * * * *

Introduction

The writers who believe in an Alexandrian influence on Hebrews see little if any relation between the Levitical typology and the heavenly ministry of Christ. According to this opinion, the purpose of the Epistle was to show the "antithesis" or contrast between the two systems.[1] The

---

1 J.-C. Verrechia, *Le Sanctuarie dans l'Épître aux Hébreux* (doctoral thesis, Strasbourg, 1981), pp. 240-54; V. R. Christensen, *Exegesis of Hebrews 8 and 9* (Lisarow, s/d), pp. 4-6; S. J. Kistemaker,

entire Levitical ritual is viewed as a hindrance to man's approach to God; whereas the new system, established by Christ, is viewed as eliminating these barriers.[2] In short, if one desires to speak about typology in Hebrews, it is argued that he should speak about a typology of opposition and not one of correspondence.

It cannot be denied that the author of Hebrews does indeed contrast the new system with the old. For example:

1. The OT high priests "were many in number, because they were prevented by death from continuing in office." By contrast Christ "holds his priesthood permanently, because he continues for ever" (Heb 7:23-24).

2. The OT high priests had "to offer sacrifices daily"—first for their own sins and then for the sins of the people. By contrast Christ had no need to offer sacrifice for Himself, and He made but one sacrifice when He offered up Himself (Heb 7:27).

3. The OT high priests functioned "in their weakness." By contrast Christ, as God's appointed priest, was "made perfect for ever" (Heb 7:28).

4. The OT high priests could not take away sin; hence, the repetition of sacrifices year after year (Heb 10:1-4). By contrast Christ offered Himself once for all time to take away sin (Heb 10:10-12, 14).

5. The OT high priests served "a copy and shadow of the heavenly sanctuary" (Heb 8:5) and of "the good things to come" (Heb 10:1). By contrast Christ officiates in "the heavenly sanctuary" itself, the true original (Heb 8:2, 5).

But why does the apostle make these comparisons? Answer: These contrasts enable the reader to see that the ministry of Christ is better and fuller than that of the earthly priests. His purpose is not to deny the typological correspondence between the two systems.

There is now "a better covenant," "founded on better promises," which allows a "more excellent" ministry (Heb 7:22; 8:6), and has "better sacrifices" (9:23). The idea of better things does not mean opposition necessarily, but rather something superior, of greater worth, something more extensive and definitive.

Exposition of the Epistle to the Hebrews (Grand Rapids, 1984), pp. 263-65.

2 Verrechia; A. Vanhoye, *Le message de l'épître aux hébreux* (Paris, 1977), pp. 49-50, 54-55; Leon Morris, *Hebrews* (Grand Rapids, 1981), pp. 46, 84, etc.

Correspondence in Contrasts

It is evident that the earthly pattern can never embrace the fullness of the heavenly reality.[3] For instance, the earthly priests were sons of Levi. The Messiah, however, must reign at the same time as the "son of David." How could Jesus meet these two Levitical and Davidic types so as to fulfill the announced role of the Messiah in the OT?[4]

In order to explain this apparent typological incongruence, the apostle appeals to an OT prophecy that justifies it, and at the same time completes the Messianic picture which Jesus must accomplish in the heavenly sanctuary. Actually, David himself solved this tension when he prophesied about the Messiah: "You are a priest for ever after the order of Melchizedek." Melchizedek was both a king and a priest and thus a suitable type for the Messiah's double role as king-priest.[5]

This demonstrates that the author of Hebrews had no intention of breaking with biblical tradition. On the contrary, each time a contrast between both systems appears, he finds his argument in the OT to show that although some details of the Levitical system cannot perfectly fit the ministry of Christ, they were foreseen and solved beforehand in the prophetic messages.[6]

The typological scheme is then resumed. The old is projected to the new. There is correspondence between both. Both Melchizedek and David are taken as types or figures of a dimension in the future ministry of the Messiah that the Aaronic or Levitical priesthood could not adequately typify.

Limitations in Typology

This is not to suggest that the Aaronic ministry does not correspond with that of Christ's ministry, because the inverse is also true. In other

---

3 Cf. Heb 7:11.

4 Cf. Heb 7:14.

5 Ps 110:1, 4; Heb 5:6; cf. Gen 14:18. When Jesus was made king before His Father, according to the Davidic lines (Ps 2:7; Acts 13:33; Heb 1:5, 8-9), He was set at the same time as high priest (Heb 5:5). His double function is described as normal in Acts 13:22-23, 32-39.

6 Cf. Heb 8:3-5; Exod 25:40. R. M. Davidson, "Typology and the Levitical System," in *Ministry,* April 1984, pp. 11-12, who follows G. B. Caird, "The Exegetical Method of the Epistle to the Hebrews," in *CJT* 5 (1959), p. 47, in his analysis of the details of the old system that the apostle obviously cannot apply to the new. Thus Psalm 110 solves beforehand the problem presented in Hebrews 7; Jeremiah 31 is quoted in order to justify the exposition of Hebrews 8; Psalm 40 serves to sound the argument of Hebrews 10; and Exodus 25:40 speaks of the "greater and more perfect tent," the heavenly sanctuary (Heb 9:11; cf. 8:5).

passages of the Epistle the Aaronic priesthood is taken as type or shadow of Jesus in a dimension that neither David nor Melchizedek could prefigure.[7]

For example, did Melchizedek ever offer sacrifices for sins as the Levitical priests offered, and as Jesus Himself did?[8] The answer is, No. There is no biblical record to relate the sin offering to Melchizedek. But Jesus offered Himself as a sin offering in correspondence with the Levitical typology.

On this same point David also is a limited type. Although he offered sin offerings, he never officiated as a priest in such cases. He offered them as all other princes in Israel did when they committed sins.[9] Can his offering be related to the priestly ministry of Jesus? No. Did Jesus offer a sacrifice for His own sins? Never.[10] Thus, it is evident that the Melchizedek and Davidic typologies are also limited in their scope. Modern authors who base their ideas on the different order of genealogy for the priesthood of Melchizedek—thereby denying the typological correspondence of Jesus with the Levitical system—betray their true intentions.

The argument that the inadequateness of the Levitical system proves its typology to be opposed to Christ's real priesthood could be brought against the typology of the Davidic kingdom just as easily. For example, the Davidic institution also produced men who became sinners and apostates,[11] and therefore, could never accomplish the reality prefigured. David himself "died and was buried," and so died all of his descendants.[12] In contrast to the Davidic monarchy Jesus was resurrected, and His kingdom cannot be taken from Him, either by death or by any other power.[13]

If the apostle does not discuss the limitations of the Davidic monarchy in his Epistle, it is because the institution no longer existed in Israel; its Messianic fulfillment was yet in the future. This is why the Gospels assert that Jesus was the "Son of David,"[14] and Paul will later affirm that Jesus is the Son of David "according to the flesh."[15] Even after His resurrection and ascension to heaven, John continues to identify Jesus with David.[16]

---

7 Cf. Heb 3:5; 4:2; 4:14-16; 5:1; 8:3, 5; 9:9-12, 23; 10:1; 12:18-24; 13:11-12.
8 Heb 7:27; 8:3; 10:11-12; etc.
9 Cf. Lev 4:22-26.
10 John 8:46; 2 Cor 5:21; 1 Pet 2:22; cf. Isa 53:9; 1 John 3:5.
11 Cf. Heb 7:27-28.
12 Acts 2:29; cf. Heb 7:3.
13 Acts 2:30-36; cf. Heb 7:24-25, 28.
14 Luke 1:32; 2:11; John 7:42; Matt 21:9.
15 Rom 1:3; Acts 13:22-23; 2 Tim 2:8.
16 Rev 5:5; 22:16; cf. Heb 1:5.

In spite of these correspondences the ministry of Jesus is greatly superior to that of David. In correspondence with David, but on a larger, grander scale, Jesus "will rule" the nations "with an iron scepter" at His second coming.[17] This demonstrates that in spite of the limitations of the Davidic kingdom to represent Christ, the real ministry of Christ in heaven and on the renewed earth corresponds with that of David and is not opposed to it.[18] David reigned in Israel and subjugated all the enemy nations; Jesus reigns today in His church—spiritual Israel[19]—and will subjugate the nations at His coming.[20]

What is the problem then that the apostolic writer faces in Hebrews? Must he break all links with the "figure," "type," "shadow," and "parable" of the Levitical system? Not at all. Instead he shows that in spite of the fact that Jesus did not belong to the tribe of Levi, He can and does fulfill the Levitical types because He is at the same time both a king as well as a priest.

As typology, the Melchizedek priesthood also had limitations which contrasted with the reality of Christ's priesthood. We have noted earlier the absence of sin offerings. We note another example. The Bible writers, especially Matthew and Luke, go to some lengths to record the genealogy of Jesus. But none is recorded for Melchizedek.[21] Must we then consider Melchizedek to be superior to Christ? By no means.

The change of the Levitical law pertaining to the priesthood (that is, its abolition, Heb 7:11-19), which the instituting of the Melchizedek order brought about, had to do with its hereditary aspect. Only a priest of Aaronic descent could legitimately function. In order to establish the legitimacy of this change in priesthood, yet at the same time to preserve the typological correspondence between Christ's priesthood and the Aaronic priesthood, the apostle lays out three fundamental lines of evidence.

1. Although Christ belongs to the tribe of Judah, He can fulfill the types represented by the Levitical priesthood, because—like Aaron—God Himself called Him to be a high priest (Heb 5:4-6).

2. The change in the order of the priesthood was foretold by God through the prophetic message of David (Ps 110:1, 4).

3. Like Melchizedek who supposedly had "neither beginning of days

---

17 Rev 19:15; cf. Ps 2:9.
18 Cf. Heb 10:13.
19 Eph 1:22; 4:15; 5:23; Col 1:18; etc.
20 Cf. Matt 24:30; Rev 6:14-17; 19:11-21.
21 Matt 1; Luke 3; cf. Heb 7:3.

nor end of life" (Heb 7:3), Jesus can officiate as high priest on the basis of "an indestructible life" (Heb 7:16).

This last aspect of the ministry of Jesus (an endless life) could not be made by the Levitical priesthood (Heb 7:23), nor by the Davidic institution of the kingdom (Acts 2:29); neither could it be made by Melchizedek in reality, but only in type. This is why it is said of Melchizedek, that since he appears in the biblical record without genealogy, that he "[resembles] the Son of God" (Heb 7:3). This proves that Jesus is considered by Hebrews to be not only superior to Levi and David but also to Melchizedek.

Sacrifice: Contrast and Correspondence

An outstanding example of typological correspondence in the Epistle to the Hebrews is given in the sacrifice of Jesus. The sacrifice of Christ is compared with the sacrifice of animals. The latter really could not atone for sin (Heb 10:4). According to the author of Hebrews, this difference in sacrifice was foreseen in the prophetic Word. The body or sacrifice of the Messiah is presented in contrast to the weaknesses and inadequacy of animal offerings.[22]

And so the Epistle itself tries to relate the death of Christ typologically to the system of sacrifices. The correspondences are noted. In both instances the blood is carried "into the sanctuary"—holy and Most Holy Places[23]—and the bodies are viewed as being removed from the encampment.[24] This example demonstrates at the same time that the author of Hebrews uses the term "sanctuary" to refer (as in chapter 9) to its two interior compartments and to all its annual services.

Levitical Sanctuary: Not a Barrier to God

Those who regard the Epistle to the Hebrews as a systematic attack on the Levitical sanctuary order do not understand the fundamental message of the biblical Hebrew worship, and they misinterpret the theology of the apostle. The existence of the earthly sanctuary made tangible to the people the great truth that God was, indeed, in the midst of His people. "And let them make me a sanctuary, that I may dwell in their midst" (Exod 25:8).[25]

Furthermore, the presence of the sanctuary was not designed as a

---

22 Heb 10:4-10; Ps 40:6-8.
23 Cf. Heb 8:3; 9:12, 24-26; 10:19; 13:11-12, 20.
24 Heb 13:11-14; Lev 6:30[23]; cf. 4:5-12; 16:14-16, 27.
25 Cf. Heb 12:18.

barrier to prevent the nation from drawing near to the presence of God. On the contrary the sanctuary ritual taught the people how they could come close to Him and how they could serve Him in an acceptable manner. The system still teaches us today how we may draw near to God.

It is true that—physically speaking—not everyone could enter into the Most Holy Place, nor even into the holy place. But neither does the Epistle to the Hebrews say that Christians can enter bodily into the heavenly sanctuary, "behind the curtain." They draw near to the throne of grace (Heb 4:16), to the mountain of Zion (Heb 12:22), in a spiritual manner. But they do not enter bodily into its interior.[26]

In the old system as well as in the new, the believers enter behind the curtain uniquely in the humanity of the priesthood (Heb 10:20; 7:25)— whether that of Aaron or of Christ—in the substitutive blood that he presents for them before God.[27] This entry into the heavenly realities by God's people has two moments: the present which is spiritual and performed by faith, and the future which is physical and will be realized at Christ's return (Rev 3:12, 21).

This is why the Israelite did not need to enter the inner places of the earthly sanctuary in order to draw near to God.[28] The simple act of coming to the court of the sanctuary put him in the presence of God.[29] The expressions "before the Lord" or "in the presence of the Lord" (lipnē Yahweh) appear in relation to the Most Holy Place,[30] the holy place,[31] the court,[32] and in the exceptional instances beyond the court.[33]

In addition, the service of the sanctuary itself functioned in favor of penitent sinners. Although the sanctuary had fixed times for certain rites, its service was not limited by time. For example, the major office of the priest in the holy place involved interceding for the people by virtue of the rite of incense.[34] The daily ritual was described as tāmîd ("continuous").[35] This was because the incense, as well as the fire of the lamps and the bread of the Presence on the table[36] remained continuously before the Lord.

---

26 Heb 13:14. G. E. Ladd, *A Theology of the New Testament* (Grand Rapids, 1974), p. 576.
27 Heb 5:1-3; 4:14-16; 8:3; 10:19.
28 With respect to the spiritual nature of this access, see Rom 5:2; Eph 2:18; 3:12; etc.
29 Lev 1:3; Judg 21:2.
30 Lev 16:13.
31 Lev 4:6-7; Exod 28:29, 35.
32 Lev 4:4, 15; 16:7, 12.
33 Judg 21:2; 2 Sam 21:9.
34 Exod 30:7-8; cf. Luke 1:9-11, 21.
35 Exod 30:8; 28:29-30, 38, etc.
36 Cf. Exod 25:30; Num 4:7; Lev 24:2-4.

The ever-burning incense on the altar allowed the intercessory ministry of the priest to be made continuously (in a symbolic manner), although he himself did not officiate bodily in the interior every moment of the day. Something similar occurred with the *tāmîd* ("continuous") altar of burnt offering. The merits of the sacrifice were always available day and night because the fire was never allowed to go out.[37]

In this manner the ancient system solved the problem of the human limitation of the priesthood. It even provided a way for those who were prevented from coming to the temple to invoke this ministry so as to appear in a spiritual way before the Lord (1 Kgs 8:44-52). This is why Solomon asked in his inaugural prayer for the eyes of the Lord to stay "night and day" upon His house, attending to the supplications of the people, and consenting to give them forgiveness (1 Kgs 8:29-30). And this was what the apostle in Hebrews also perceived when he briefly interpreted the ancient worship, saying that the priests "go continually" into the holy place to accomplish the offices of worship in favor of the people.

Does this mean then that the apostle misunderstood the message of the ancient system when he put it in contrast with the new one inaugurated by Jesus Christ? Did he really say that the Israelites could not have access at any time to God? Could his message have been accepted in a Jewish milieu with such a gross error in respect to the content and purpose of the ancient worship?

This much can be said about the Levitical worship in regard to the taking away of sins: The earthly "parable" did show that through its ministry sins were taken away from the people and finally thrown out of the encampment on the Day of Atonement, never to return again.[38] Since this is so, what does the apostle mean when he says "the blood of bulls and goats" of the old system can never "take away sins" (Heb 10:4, 11)?

Basic Limits of the Ancient System

There is no doubt but that the Epistle outlines here the basic limit of the ancient cult. This worship was only a parable, a shadow, and figure which illustrated the truths to come; but it could never be the reality itself, which is always superior.[39] Until this reality, which it represented, would arrive, the same sacrifices would be interminably repeated and generations

---

37 Exod 29:38-42; Lev 6:9, 12-13.
38 Lev 16:20-22; see Alberto Treiyer, *Le Jour des Expiations, et la Purification du Sanctuaire* (doctoral thesis, Strasbourg, 1982), pp. 157-62, etc.
39 Cf. Heb 10:1.

of priests would come and go; subject to death they could not continue.

This is the reason ultimately for its uselessness (Heb 7:18) and the necessity for a reform (9:10). When could the sacrifice for sins stop being offered?[40] It is evident that if we seek a total and definitive redemption, the figurative system of sacrifices would have to end sometime (Heb 10:2). This would occur when sin would be taken away in reality—and not figuratively—by a superior ministry.[41]

The superior sacrifice and priestly ministry have now arrived with Christ's first advent. The fact that Jesus offered one sacrifice "once for all" (7:27), and that it will never be repeated, proves that "now," in the new dispensation sin has been completely atoned for (Heb 10:1-14). In addition, His priesthood will not have to be replaced by anyone, because He "continues for ever" (Heb 7:24). Jesus does not need to be entering and going out of the sanctuary to officiate for the people. By virtue of His own sacrifice, which is not repeatable, He "always lives to make intercession for them"[42] "until the time for establishing all that God spoke by the mouth of his holy prophets . . ." (Acts 3:21).

This does not mean that in the new order, in contrast to the old, the believer does not take part in any kind of cleansing. Today it is also necessary to draw near to the sanctuary to cleanse the heart "from an evil conscience," to wash the body "with pure water,"[43] and to offer continually to God "a sacrifice of praise" (Heb 13:15-16).

But instead of drawing near to a symbolic earthly sanctuary from which God already has withdrawn His presence,[44] the believer must draw near directly to the heavenly sanctuary.[45] A service is offered there which, by nature, is able to finish forever with the problem of sin.

In short, it can be said that in contrast with the necessity of repeating interminably the same sacrifices in the old system, Jesus started a unique ministry that is able to purge the sin problem forever with only one sacrifice and ministry. Thus it is clear that Jesus consummated the whole aim projected by the old worship. Limited by its temporary nature, the Levitical system could serve only as a prefiguration of the reality to come.

Thus, it seems clear that neither the OT nor the NT, nor yet the Epistle

---

40 Cf. Heb 10:18.
41 Cf. Heb 9:26.
42 Heb 7:25.
43 Heb 10:21-22; cf. 9:10, 14.
44 Cf. Matt 23:38; 27:51.
45 Heb 10:19-22; 12:22-24; 7:25; 4:16.

to the Hebrews, establishes that the old system impeded an Israelite's approach to God or the forgiveness of his sins. The evaluation that the apostle makes of the sin problem and of its solution in the ancient cult is clever. His emphasis is that this Levitical approach and release of sins in the Jerusalem Temple *could never be definitive* in itself as long as its worship continued to be practiced. Hence the necessity for this service to be replaced by another more efficacious (Heb 10:8-9), by the reality which it prefigured. The author demonstrates the need for faith to pass from the earthly ministry to the heavenly ministry, without which the former was impotent and had no reason for being.

The message of the Epistle is that the announced reality has already arrived. It is now no longer necessary to turn to the earthly shadow-types in order to draw near to God. The earthly solution to take away sin and to draw near to God was a provisory solution. Its ministry was, in spite of that, glorious.[46] But what value could this limited system of types now have in view of Jesus' more glorious ministry in Heaven (Heb 3:3)?

Conclusion

It is true that the Levitical worship had certain limits which did not allow it to accomplish a final deliverance from sin and to effect a definitive approach to God. But these same limits to reflect the whole heavenly reality were also shared by all typological institutions of Israel, including that of the Melchizedek priesthood. Notwithstanding, the correspondences between the Levitical system and that of Christ's are never denied. Even in those instances in which certain incongruences appear, foresights from the OT spelled out the adjustments so as to maintain the general correspondences between the two systems.

Therefore, it is incorrect to refer to the typology of Hebrews as antithetic or oppositional typology and to deny the correspondence that it makes between the Levitical institution and the priesthood of Jesus. It is also incorrect to ascribe this pretended antithesis to a platonic influence on the author. The idea of better things does not involve necessarily the idea of opposition between the heavenly and earthly systems.

Although the Davidic institution contained limitations, no one denies its typical correspondence to Christ's kingship. Likewise, the Aaronic system had limitations, but the author of Hebrews clearly recognized its fundamental correspondences with Christ's priesthood. In spite of Israel's

---

46 2 Cor 3:7-11; cf. Heb 12:18-21.

past history of human weaknesses, Christ was crowned king like David and ordained high priest like Aaron—a king-priest like Melchizedek—in order to accomplish all the types of the OT.

Chapter IX

Sanctuary Theology

Alwyn P. Salom

Editorial Synopsis. The book of Hebrews, along with those of Daniel and Revelation, played an important role in the formulation of the Scriptural foundation of the Seventh-day Adventist people. Its primary teaching about the priestly ministry of Jesus Christ in the heavenly sanctuary sparked new hope and action in our pioneers even as it resolved the perplexing question, Why did Jesus not return in 1844 at the close of Daniel's 2,300 year prophecy? (See *The Great Controversy,* pp. 411-13.)

Through the years Adventists have given extended periods of intense study to Hebrews in the Sabbath School. Three quarters in 1889-1890 were allotted to the examination of Hebrews, using materials prepared by J. H. Waggoner. M. L. Andreasen wrote another three sequential quarters for church study in 1948. In 1976 the world church studied the Epistle with lessons for one quarter by Walter Specht. And more recently, in 1986, the world church again reviewed the teachings of this magnificent Epistle with lessons prepared by W. G. Johnsson.

In these several studies of Hebrews the focus has not always been the same. The issue that dominated the three Waggoner quarterlies in 1889-1890 centered on the covenants. More current writings reflect response to the charge that Hebrews denies the Adventist understanding that Christ's high priestly ministry in the heavenly sanctuary consists of two sequential phases (intercession and the second, additional work of judgment in 1844) as typified by the ministrations that took place in connection with the two apartments of the Israelite sanctuary. The present chapter deals with this latter concern.

A correct method for interpreting the Bible is essential if we would understand aright the teaching of Hebrews for our times. In the first place this means that we must discover (as far as possible) how the first century believers understood its message. Secondly, it means that any application valid for the twentieth century Christian must be a genuine outgrowth of and in harmony with the original message. Inspired writings have a deeper import for subsequent generations, but that import is not detached from the original intent of the writing.

The Epistle to the Hebrews appears to be addressed to Jewish Christians who were confronted with the widening breach between Judaism and Christianity, continued persecution, economic needs, and what they perceived as a delay in the Lord's return. The temptation to abandon the Christian faith and to return to Judaism and its Temple religion was strong.

In response the author of Hebrews exercises a pastoral concern to fix the flagging faith of his brethren on the living Christ who now ministers for them as their high priest in the very presence of God in the heavenly sanctuary. Two major themes are emphasized: (1) The centrality of Calvary for salvation. The "better blood" of Christ's once-for-all-time sacrifice alone is able to purge away the sins of the believer. (2) Direct and free access to God through the high priestly ministry of Christ. These great truths are worked out by contrasting them with the repetitious, ineffectual sacrifices and the limited approach to God as found in Israel's ritual system.

Hebrews underscores the reality of the heavenly sanctuary and Christ's ministry in God's presence, valid truths for today's Christians as well as for those in the first century. The author appears to use Day of Atonement imagery to drive home the fact that Christ's death and priesthood have opened "a new and living way" into the presence of God; all barriers between Heaven and the believer have been removed.

However, the Day of Atonement rite does not constitute a major theme in the Epistle. Both the daily as well as the yearly ritual are alluded to along with other elements in the system. There is no attempt to develop an exposition on any one aspect of the services. Instead, the author's evident objective is to demonstrate to his hearers the total inadequacy of the typical system. Even in its highest and most solemn functions (like the Day of Atonement), the typical system is simply unable to resolve the sin problem.

The only time element touched on in the Epistle emphasizes the temporary nature of the Israelite sanctuary. It was designed to function only until the coming of Christ and the events of His sacrificial death and entrance upon His priestly ministry as a king-priest in the heavenly sanctuary. It is upon Christ that the faith of the author's readers must rest as they run the race of life.

Since this is the thrust of the Epistle, it naturally follows that although

Hebrews provides valuable insights into the doctrine of the sanctuary, it does not speak directly to the subject of Christ's two-phased priestly ministry or to the prophetic time for the commencement of final judgment. But neither does it invalidate these truths found elsewhere in Scripture. Hebrews provided another section in the orange of biblical truth, as it were, but it is not the whole orange. Other truths have their sectional positions in order to form a harmonious whole. Hebrews lifts Christian faith heavenward to focus on our living High Priest—a truth that needs to be heard again and again.

Chapter Outline

* * * * * * *

Introduction

It is a truism to say that the book of Hebrews is of great significance for Seventh-day Adventist "sanctuary" theology. This book discusses the heavenly ministry of Jesus Christ, our great high priest, more frequently and more explicitly than any other in the NT. Outside of Hebrews, in fact, the NT gives little direct information about what Christ has been doing since His ascension.

Thus, it is of considerable importance for Hebrews to be examined in detail to discover what it is saying with respect to specific Adventist theological concerns.[1] Does it make *explicit* statements that relate to the Adventist sanctuary doctrine? What can be *implied* legitimately from

---

1 In this respect, see especially the two studies by William G. Johnsson, "The Heavenly Sanctuary — Figurative or Real?" and "Day of Atonement Allusions," pp. 35-51 and pp. 105-120 respectively, in this book. Because of the nature of this study, documentation has been restricted, as far as possible, to Adventist writers.

Hebrews that has relevance for sanctuary teaching? Is the book *silent* at crucial points; or does it, indeed, *deny* any areas of Adventist teaching? And what refining has taken place in orthodox Adventist thinking on these subjects over the years? These are the basic questions which this study addresses.

Interpretation of Hebrews Today

The correct method for arriving at a valid interpretation of Scripture should be understood before considering what Hebrews may be saying to Adventist theology in the twentieth century.

Meaning for First Readers and Later of Applications

A primary principle of interpretation demands that the interpreter work from the basis of the original meaning and intent of the biblical writer. For example, he must ask, What is the historical setting in which this document is written? What is the occasion for writing, and what purpose is the writer endeavoring to fulfill? What is the meaning of the message for the original readers?[2] Only when this basic information has been assembled (as far as the evidence permits) is it possible for him to discern accurately "the fuller import and deeper meaning"[3] of the biblical document.

While the original meaning of the message is of basic importance, it is also true that God may have had deeper meanings in mind for later generations.

> Although God spoke to the generations contemporary to the writers of the biblical books, He saw to it also that the reader of these books in the future would find therein depth of meaning and relevance beyond the local and limited circumstances in which and for which the original was produced.[4]

Any such later application must grow out of, and be in harmony with, the meaning of the text for the first readers. Says Gerhard Hasel:

> It is important to emphasize that the meaning for the faith of men today cannot be something completely different from the meaning intended by the biblical writers for their contemporaries. Any attempt

---

2 See Donald Guthrie, "Questions on Introduction," *New Testament Interpretation: Essays on Principles and Methods,* ed. I. Howard Marshall (Exeter, 1977), p. 114.

3 Gerhard F. Hasel, "Principles of Biblical Interpretation," *A Symposium on Biblical Hermeneutics,* ed. Gordon M. Hyde (Washington, DC, 1974), p. 185.

4 Ibid., p. 168. See also *The Great Controversy,* p. 344; *Testimonies for the Church,* 6:19-20; *Prophets and Kings,* p. 731; *Education,* p. 183. It should be noted that this study does not take up Ellen G. White's statements relative to Hebrews. These statements warrant a separate study of their own.

to understand the biblical authors that fails to recognize a basic homogeneity between the interpreter's meaning "now" and the meaning of the message "then" fails to bring their inspired messages to men of today.[5]

This principle is of great significance. Any understanding for our day derived from the biblical text must not be alien to the original meaning and intent of the passage. Rather, it must be fully sympathetic with the intent of the author. Hasel rightly emphasizes this principle of interpretation.

> The fuller import and deeper meaning of Scripture is a meaning that is intended or implicit in the words of the Bible whether or not the inspired author is aware of it. The fuller import and deeper meaning is *not a reading into the literal sense and meaning of ideas alien or extraneous to it.* The fuller sense or fuller import and deeper meaning of Scripture is not something that is alien to the intent of the biblical words. To the contrary, it is a characteristic of the fuller import and deeper meaning of Scripture to be homogeneous with the literal meaning and sense; that is to say, *it is a development and outgrowth of what the original inspired writer put into words.*[6]

This principle, with the limitations it contains, must be applied to the passages in Hebrews which may address Adventist theological concerns. That is to say, in arriving at an interpretation of these passages, it is necessary to ensure that the application is homogeneous with the author's original intent. The twentieth century understanding of a given passage must be a development and outgrowth of the original message of the biblical writer.

In order to determine the meaning of Hebrews for its original readers (or hearers?), and thus to establish a base from which to approach the text for a valid interpretation for our day, it is necessary to give attention to the external and internal contexts of the writing.

External Context

The external or historical context is concerned with the people addressed, the circumstances which called forth the writing, the author, and to a lesser extent, the place and time of writing. Allowing for differing interpretations of the evidence, and without discussing the arguments, the following may be taken as a very brief summary of the historical context of

---

5 Hasel, p. 183. See also, pp. 163, 170, 182; and Hasel, *Understanding the Living Word of God.* Adventist Library of Christian Thought 1 (Mountain View, CA, 1980): 78-79; I. H. Marshall, "Introduction," in *New Testament Interpretation,* p. 15.
6 Hasel, "Principles," p. 185 (emphasis mine).

Hebrews:[7] Possibly Hebrews was first composed and delivered as a sermon (13:22; cf. 11:32), or series of sermons, to a Jewish-Christian community in the first century—perhaps prior to A.D. 70. Whether one accepts the author as Paul, Paul's scribe, or someone quite different, there are complex problems to face. It may be best, like William G. Johnsson, to resort to the designation "the apostle" for the author.[8] The one verse which speaks directly to the question of origin and destination is ambiguous (13:24).

Internal Context

A consideration of the circumstances which called forth the writing of Hebrews forms a bridge between the external, historical context and the internal, literary context of any given passage in the book. The first recipients of Hebrews were facing problems caused by the widening breach between Judaism and the young church and by the temptation to return to Judaism. The delay in the Second Advent, continued persecution, and economic problems all added to their trauma and led them to ask whether Christianity was worth what it was costing.[9]

The Message of Hebrews

To answer these problems the apostle makes a series of comparisons between Judaism and Christianity, showing in each case the superiority of the latter. He demonstrates that Judaism is fulfilled in Christianity, and that Christianity is the ultimate revelation of God for man. Christ is the "better priest" ministering within the framework of a "better covenant." His ministry in the heavenly sanctuary is contrasted with the ministry of the Levitical priests in the earthly sanctuary.

Two themes (among others) are of special significance for the recipients to understand: the centrality and uniqueness of Calvary, and the believer's "direct access" to God through Christ.[10] Calvary is important for what it is in itself; but it is also important for what it means as a precursor of the heavenly ministry of Christ.[11] Access to God is emphasized by repeated

---

7 For conservative evaluations of the evidence for the historical context of Hebrews, see Donald Guthrie, *New Testament Introduction,* 3rd ed., rev. (London, 1970), pp. 685-718; Everett F. Harrison, *Introduction to the New Testament,* rev. ed. (Grand Rapids, 1971), pp. 370-80. For an Adventist evaluation of the evidence, see William G. Johnsson, *In Absolute Confidence: The Book of Hebrews Speaks to Our Day* (Nashville, 1979), pp. 15-20, 27-30; Francis D. Nichol, ed., *The SDA Bible Commentary,* 7 vols. (Washington, DC, 1953-1957), 7:387-94.

8 Johnsson, *In Absolute Confidence,* p. 29.

9 See Guthrie, *New Testament Introduction,* pp. 704-5.

10 Heb 7:27; 9:12, 26, 28; 10:10.

11 See Johnsson, *In Absolute Confidence,* pp. 114-18.

contrasts between Christ's heavenly ministry and the Levitical system.[12]

These, then, are the questions to be kept in mind as we approach passages in Hebrews which have particular concern for Adventist "sanctuary" theology. What was the writer saying to the first recipients? What does that mean for us today in the light of the "fuller import and deeper meaning?" Is our interpretation of Hebrews homogeneous with the original message of the passage under consideration? What does Hebrews say explicitly or implicitly that has relevance for Adventist theology? Is Hebrews silent on, or does it deny, Adventist theology at any point? We now address ourselves to the issues.

The Heavenly Sanctuary in Hebrews

Reality of the Heavenly Sanctuary

Hebrews is quite explicit about the existence and reality of the heavenly sanctuary. Johnsson highlights this important aspect:

> While he does not enter upon a description of the heavenly sanctuary and liturgy, his language suggests several important conclusions. First, he holds to their *reality*. His concern throughout the sermon is to ground Christian confidence in objective *facts,* as we have seen. *Real* deity, *real* humanity, *real* priesthood — and we may add, a *real* ministry in a *real* sanctuary.[13]

Referring to the earthly sanctuary as a "copy" (*hupodeigma*) and a "shadow" (*skia* [8:5]), the apostle describes the archetype as "the sanctuary" (*ta hagia*) and "true tent" (*hē skēnē hē alēthinē*) "which is set up not by man but by the Lord" (8:2). The adjective *alēthinos* means "genuine," "real." This word marks the reality of the heavenly sanctuary. It is "true in the sense of the reality possessed only by the archetype."[14]

Hebrews, chapter 9, contains several references to the heavenly sanctuary. Verse 8 says "the way into the [heavenly] sanctuary" has not been made open as long as "the outer tent is still standing." Verse 11 speaks of the heavenly sanctuary as "the greater and more perfect tent (not made with hands, that is, not of this creation)." And verse 24 affirms that Christ has entered "not into a sanctuary made with hands, a copy of the true one, but into heaven itself." Later the author writes, "we have confidence to

---

12 Heb 4:14, 16; 6:19-20; 9:11-12, 24; 10:19-20; cf. 7:23-25; 9:7-8; 10:11-12.
13 Johnsson, *In Absolute Confidence,* p. 91.
14 William F. Arndt and F. Wilbur Gingrich, *A Greek-English Lexicon of the New Testament and Other Early Christian Literature,* 2nd rev. and aug. (Chicago, 1979), p. 37.

enter the [heavenly] sanctuary by the blood of Jesus" (10:19).

For the recipients of Hebrews, these statements concerning the heavenly sanctuary were intended to give assurance.[15] Because of national and family opposition, the Jewish-Christian readers of Hebrews had suffered separation from the religious life of Judaism. And if, as seems likely, the destruction of Jerusalem and its temple was near, all the more would they need such assurances. These verses told them that they had access to a superior "temple"—an heavenly sanctuary where Jesus Christ ministered.

The application of these verses today must grow out of, and develop from, the original intent of the author. As were the first century readers, we need to be assured of our place of worship and of our access to the throne of God in the heavenly sanctuary. In an age which threatens all religious values, we need to know that "we have a great high priest who has passed through the heavens" and that we can "draw near to the throne of grace" to receive mercy and find grace (4:14, 16).

The Nature of the Heavenly Reality: A Caution

While the passages quoted above from Hebrews 8 and 9 affirm the reality of the heavenly sanctuary, they also contain inherent warnings with respect to our interpretation of its *nature*. Hebrews 8:1-5 offers several such warnings. For example, the expression, "set up not by man but by the Lord" (vs. 2), suggests immediately that there is a crucial difference between the earthly and heavenly sanctuaries. That difference lies in the nature of the builder. The limitations of the human builder of the earthly sanctuary do not apply to the Lord. And thus, the heavenly sanctuary is not to be viewed with the restrictions and limitations which an earthly facility might be expected to possess.

The words "copy" (*hupodeigma*), "shadow" (*skia*), and "pattern" *(tupos)* in verse 5 likewise indicate that the earthly sanctuary should not form the basis for attempting a detailed reconstruction of the heavenly sanctuary. The earthly sanctuary is but a shadowy representation of the heavenly reality. While some general conclusions about the heavenly sanctuary may be reached by studying the earthly, care should be taken not to press these points too far. "It is necessary to remember that an earthly 'copy' can never, in all details, fully represent a heavenly original."[16]

Chapter 9 also contains some warnings against pressing to extremes the

---

15 See, for example, Hebrews 10:19 ("since we have confidence to enter the sanctuary").
16 *The SDA Bible Commentary,* 7:445.

parallels between the earthly and heavenly sanctuaries. Hebrews 9:9 identifies the "outer tent" as a "symbol" (*parabolē*). Whether "outer tent" here refers to the first apartment of the sanctuary or the whole Mosaic sanctuary is beside the point for this purpose.[17] What is significant is that the earthly sanctuary *is described as having symbolic value.* This warns us from arguing literalistically from the basis of the earthly sanctuary to establish the *nature* of the heavenly sanctuary.[18]

In Hebrews 9:11 our author speaks of the heavenly sanctuary as "the greater and more perfect tent (not made with hands, that is, not of this creation)." Again we are alerted to the fact that there are essential differences between the earthly and heavenly sanctuaries. The heavenly sanctuary is "greater," "more perfect," "not made with hands," and "not of this creation." It belongs to the celestial order of reality, whereas the Israelite sanctuary belonged to this world (9:1).

In Hebrews 9:24 the earthly sanctuary is described as a "copy [*antitupos*] of the true [*alēthinos*]." The inadequacies of the earthly sanctuary as a representation of the heavenly are once more implied. In this verse a contrast is also drawn between the earthly sanctuary and the heavenly sanctuary ("not . . . made with hands").[19]

Johnsson points out that the writer of Hebrews "is not careful in his description of the Old Testament sanctuary and sacrifices. For instance, he locates the golden altar in the Most Holy and merges the various sacrifices."[20] Such an attitude would hardly be reasonable if the author sought to present the earthly sanctuary as a precise miniature of the heavenly in every respect. This lack of care suggests that these details of the description of the earthly sanctuary are not significant for an understanding of the heavenly sanctuary. Indeed, concerning such things, he says, "we cannot now speak in detail" (Heb 9:5b).

Although his choice of terms leaves something to be desired, Johnsson is correct in drawing a distinction between a "literalistic" and a "literalizing" view of the heavenly sanctuary.[21] He describes the literalistic interpretation as that in which "each term has hard value—for the heavenly sanctuary, the earthly would be a miniature in all respects."[22] The

---

17 See Ibid, p. 451.
18 See *Seventh-day Adventists Answer Questions on Doctrine* (Washington, DC, 1957), pp. 365-68.
19 Cf. Heb 9:11.
20 Johnsson, *In Absolute Confidence,* pp. 16-17; see also, p. 32, n. 10.
21 Id., "The Heavenly Sanctuary," p. 51, in this book.
22 Ibid.

literalizing interpretation is that in which "the reality of the heavenly sanctuary and ministry would be maintained as safeguarding the *objectivity* of the work of Christ, but precise details of that sanctuary would not be clear to us."[23]

With respect to Johnsson's two categories, the weight of evidence supports the latter. "It is therefore apparent that, while we may affirm the *reality* of the heavenly sanctuary in the book of Hebrews, we have comparatively little hard data about its appearance."[24] This is supported by the following: ". . . we should not permit any finite perplexity in visualizing a heavenly sanctuary on the order of the earthly, to blur in our minds the great truths taught by that earthly 'shadow'. . . ."[25]

Function More Important Than Form

The first readers of Hebrews needed to learn that they should place no trust in the magnificent Temple structure in Jerusalem. Its presence and ritual undoubtedly tempted them to abandon their Christian faith. They needed to remember that even the wilderness tabernacle, the spiritual precursor of the Temple, was but a "copy" and "shadow" of the reality of the heavenly sanctuary. Since they were tempted to place importance on external form, the apostle reminds his readers that more important than the *structure* of either the earthly sanctuary or its heavenly counterpart was its *function.* His admonition is still relevant today.

Because the heavenly sanctuary is the "genuine," the "original," "we should see the earthly in light of the heavenly, rather than *vice versa.*"[26] The heavenly sanctuary—the archetype—is to be the basis for our reasoning, not the goal of it. As Johnsson elaborates, "it is the heavenly and not the earthly that is the genuine. The earthly was but a pale shadow, a temporary device pointing to the real. (This point, by the way, is important in interpretation: The real will explain the shadow, and not vice versa.)"[27] Thus, as we look at the earthly sanctuary, we should be constrained to look at the great principles that it encompassed, not at the details of its structure.

---

23 Ibid. Also, "we must not think of a literal tent in heaven, literally pitched by God." — *The SDA Bible Commentary,* 7:444.

24 Johnsson, "The Heavenly Sanctuary," p. 51, in this book.

25 *The SDA Bible Commentary,* 7:468.

26 Johnsson, "The Heavenly Sanctuary," p. 51, in this book.

27 Id., *In Absolute Confidence,* p. 91. This is not to deny that the shadow illustration provides some important insights into Christ's priestly ministry, such as His two phases of ministry which correspond to the ministration in the two apartments. — Ed.

There can be no doubt about the reality of the heavenly sanctuary. Hebrews assures us of that. At the same time, Hebrews provides only limited information about the *nature* of that reality.

The Heavenly Ministry of Christ in Hebrews

Adventists are not unique in recognizing the value of Hebrews for what it teaches about the present ministry of Christ in the heavenly sanctuary. A popular, conservative college text of two decades ago declared:

> The greatest single value of the book of Hebrews is its teaching on the present ministry and priesthood of Christ. There are many references in the New Testament to His ascension and to His place at the right hand of the Father, but with the exception of Romans 8:34 none of these explains what He is now doing.[28]

Anglican Bishop Brooke Foss Westcott, in his classic commentary on Hebrews, wrote of Christ as high priest ministering "in His human nature" and of the heavenly sanctuary as the "archetype" of the earthly sanctuary.[29] In a note on "The Present Work of Christ as High-priest," he described the cleansing work of the Levitical high priest. "Thus we read in a figure," Westcott declares, "the High priestly work of Christ."[30] More recently, George W. Buchanan allowed that "since the heavenly archetype functions just as its earthly imitation," there is provision "to cleanse 'the heavenly things' (Heb 9:23)."[31] In this context, Buchanan speaks of the "cleansing" of the heavenly sanctuary from "sin and defilement."[32]

Adventists have rightly looked to Hebrews for information concerning the heavenly ministry of Christ, for this book provides very important statements about the present work of our Great High Priest. In chapters 8-10, particularly, and in scattered places in chapters 4, 6, 7, and 13, the author describes the heavenly work of Christ.

The "Right Hand of God" Theme

In five places in Hebrews (1:3, 13; 8:1; 10:12; 12:2), our author describes Christ as seated "at the right hand of God" following His ascension. This assertion is part of a larger NT theme which includes a total of 19

---

28 Merrill C. Tenney, *New Testament Survey,* rev. ed. (London, 1961), p. 362.
29 Brooke Foss Westcott, *The Epistle to the Hebrews: The Greek Text With Notes and Essays,* 2nd ed. (London, 1892), p. 257.
30 Ibid., p. 229.
31 George Wesley Buchanan, *To the Hebrews,* AB (Garden City, NY, 1972), p. 162.
32 Ibid.

passages.[33] The context of three texts, Mark 16:19; Ephesians 1:20; and 1 Peter 3:22 clearly indicates that Christ took up this position at His ascension. It is also significant to note that the contexts of a number of the "right hand of God" passages are cultic in nature.[34] This suggests that the expression refers to more than Christ's inauguration, dedication, and exaltation in the heavenly sanctuary. It must at times include as well a reference to His continuing high priestly work.[35]

The repetition of this theme in Hebrews undoubtedly was intended to assure the readers of the significance of Christ's heavenly ministry. Some were wavering in their determination to stand firm in the new faith. The writer assures them that the One whom they have accepted as Saviour is the same One who ministers for them in the very presence of God.

As so often in Hebrews, there is also the implication that if their High Priest is in the presence of God, there is full and free access for His followers also into God's presence.[36] This assurance is still provided by these verses. Primarily, they are still saying that our Lord and Saviour is not separated in any way from the Father—He is in His very presence.

The "right hand of God" theme declares that Christ has been ministering in God's presence since His ascension. This does not deny the possibility of a two-phased heavenly ministry for Christ. However, it would deny any literalistic view of the heavenly sanctuary which would confine Him to an apartment apart from God. This theme brings into focus both the place and nature of Christ's ministry.

The Free Access Theme

Earthly Sanctuary: Limited Access to God

The Levitical cult, to which the recipients of Hebrews were in danger of retreating, was characterized by "limited access" of the worshiper to God. The individual Israelite was separated from the object of his worship by the way the sanctuary system operated. This is spelled out nowhere more clearly than in Hebrews 9:6-8. The Israelite could come only as far

---

33 See also Mark 16:19; Eph 1:20; Col 3:1. Revelation 3:21 says the same thing, with a slight variation. The following passages describe Christ as being at the right hand of God without using the verb "to sit": Matt 22:44 (and parallels—Mark 12:36; Luke 20:42); Acts 2:33-34; 5:31; Rom 8:34; 1 Pet 3:22. Acts 7:55, 56.

34 See A. P. Salom, "Exegesis of Selected Passages in Hebrews 8 and 9" (unpublished paper, Glacier View, 1980), pp. 22-23.

35 For a somewhat differing view, see Daniel and Revelation Committee report in this book, p. 4.

36 See Heb 4:14, 16; 7:19, 25; 10:22.

as the court of the sanctuary to offer his sacrifice. He had no access to the sanctuary proper. The priest had access to the first apartment of the sanctuary, but no access beyond that. The high priest had access to the Second Apartment—but only once a year, and then only when he brought with him the blood of the appropriate sacrifice. Barriers to access confronted the worshiper at every point.

Heavenly Sanctuary: Free Access to God

The Jewish-Christians, to whom Hebrews was addressed, were tending to espouse again their ancient system of worship with its inherent limitations. To enable them to see the futility of such a course, the author of Hebrews emphasizes the freedom of access to God which is now available in the heavenly ministry of Christ and challenges his readers to avail themselves of it. With the entrance of Christ into the presence of God a new and direct method of access has been created. This is the thrust of those passages which speak of Christ's entry into God's presence.

Hebrews 6:19-20 is an example of the "free access" theme at work in an important context.[37] The author assures his readers of their access to God because of Christ's entry into God's presence. On the strength of two unchangeable things—God's promise (vs. 15) and His oath (vs. 17)—they are assured of a free approach to God through Christ. He desires them to believe that in Christ they have "a sure and steadfast anchor of the soul" (vs. 19a). This anchor is the hope "that enters into the inner shrine behind the curtain" (vs. 19b). Then he gives his strongest assurance. Christ, like the Christian's hope, has gone into the very presence of God as a forerunner on our behalf, "having become a high priest for ever after the order of Melchizedek" (vs. 20). By virtue of Christ's access into the presence of God, the readers may also have free access to God.

The immediate context (vss. 13-20) and the "free access" theme reveal clearly the author's intent in 6:19, 20. The phrase, "the inner shrine behind the curtain" (vs. 19), may be understood to be a reference to the Second Apartment[38] without introducing any thought of the second phase of Christ's ministry commencing at the Ascension.[39]

---

37 See also Heb 10:19-20.

38 See Salom, pp. 17-19; and Norman H. Young, "The Checkered History of the Phrase 'Within the Veil'" (unpublished paper, Avondale College, 1974), pp. 1-13. See also, Erwin R. Gane, "Within the Veil: Where Did Christ Go?" *Ministry,* December 1983, pp. 4-7.

39 " 'Within the veil' refers to this symbolic picture of the presence of God in a first-century application of the Day of Atonement imagery rather than the antitypical fulfillment of the Old Testament type. This way of speaking in no way precludes our understanding of Christ's two-

The author's original intent was to assure his readers of the fact that the heavenly ministry of Christ provided the basis for a "better" form of worship than they had experienced in the Levitical cultus and that it provided them with full and free access to God.

> We do not believe that the phrase was intended to mean that from the time of His ascension Christ has been engaged in a ministry equivalent to that which the Old Testament high priest performed once a year in the Second Apartment of the tabernacle on the Day of Atonement, to the exclusion of the daily phase of the priestly ministry. "Within the veil," we believe, was intended to convey the conviction that, *since Christ's ascension, we have full, free, and direct access to the very presence of God.*[40]

The document issued following the Glacier View conference declared:

> There is no intermediate step in our approach to God. Hebrews stresses the fact that our Great High Priest is at the very right hand of God (chap. 1:3), in "heaven itself . . . in the presence of God" (chap. 9:24). *The symbolic language of the Most Holy Place, "within the veil," is used to assure us of our full, direct, and free access to God* (chaps. 6:19-20; 9:24-28; 10:1-4).[41]

Day of Atonement Allusions

The significance of Day of Atonement allusions in Hebrews has been canvassed in several places.[42] Cautiously, Johnsson identifies three "unambiguous" references (9:6-7, 24-25; 10:1-4).[43] Only one of these (9:24, 25) refers to the heavenly ministry of Christ. In addition, he sees eight more "possible" allusions (4:16; 5:3, 7:26-27; 9:5, 8, 13, 27-28; 13:10-11). Of this latter group, all but 5:3 and 9:5 refer to Christ's ministry.[44] A strong case has been made by Norman Young for the existence of parallels between 9:7, verses 11, 12, and verse 25.[45] Thus 9:7, which is patently

---

phased mediatorial ministry in the heavenly sanctuary. . . ." "Statement on Desmond Ford Document" (Glacier View, CO), *Adventist Review,* September 4, 1980, p. 9.

40 Ibid., p. 8 (emphasis mine).

41 Sanctuary Review Committee, "Christ in the Heavenly Sanctuary," *Adventist Review,* September 4, 1980, p. 14 (emphasis mine).

42 See Norman H. Young, "The Impact of the Jewish Day of Atonement Upon the Thought of the New Testament" (Ph.D. dissertation, Manchester University, 1973); "The Gospel According to Hebrews 9," *NTS* 27 (1981): 198-210; Johnsson, "Day of Atonement Allusions," pp. 100-115.

43 Johnsson, "Day of Atonement Allusions," pp. 113-14. Presumably verse 23 belongs with the reference to verses 24, 25.

44 Hebrews 9:7 should be connected with verse 8, and 9:11, 12 with verse 13.

45 Young, "The Gospel," p. 199.

a reference to the Day of Atonement, sets the pattern for the other two passages.

The attention given to the Day of Atonement service in Hebrews (and particularly in chapter 9) was undoubtedly of some significance to the recipients. As Jews, prior to their conversion, they had looked to this day as one of great importance in their religious life, the high point of their cultic experience. Now they considered the possibility of defecting from Christianity back to Judaism.

Because the Day of Atonement was so important to the Jew, the author picks it out for special attention. He is endeavoring to show the inadequacies of the Levitical cult, even at this religious high point in Judaism. While this service promised the supreme example of access to God in the OT ritual, such access was strictly limited (9:7). Furthermore, it was necessary for this service to be repeated annually (9:7, 25; 10:2-3). But more important, it was not effective, in the highest sense, for the purgation of sins (9:9-10; 10:1-4). However, the Day of Atonement pointed to the perfectly adequate heavenly ministry of Christ (if the following are accepted as containing Day of Atonement imagery (9:11, 12, 14, 24-26). "All barriers between God and man have been abolished, so that we may come boldly into the presence of God. At last a sacrifice has been made that is able to provide thoroughgoing purification of sins."[46]

Perhaps the most crucial passage in Hebrews for Adventist sanctuary theology is 9:23-25. Johnsson has pointed out that "the context points clearly to a Day of Atonement allusion."[47] The free access provided by Christ's heavenly ministry (vs. 24), the superiority of His sacrifice (vs. 25), and its unrepeatable nature (vs. 26) are the major thrusts of this passage for the first readers. It is part of the theme of "better" things by which the readers were being encouraged to remain in the Christian faith. This background must be kept in mind as the interpretation for today is sought.

Commentators have backed away from seeing the necessity for a "cleansing" of the heavenly sanctuary to correspond with the Day of Atonement service in the earthly sanctuary. They have tried to evade the issue by suggesting various solutions to the ellipsis in verse 23. The verb "inaugurated" has sometimes been supplied to fill the gap in the second clause. Bishop Westcott, however, has clearly identified the relationship of sin to the heavenly sanctuary, and the need of its "cleansing."

---

46 Johnsson, "Day of Atonement Allusions," p. 119; cf. *The SDA Bible Commentary,* 7:455.
47 Ibid., p. 113.

> The whole structure of the sentence requires that "cleansed" should be supplied in the second clause from the first, and not any more general term as "inaugurated." In what sense then can it be said that "the heavenly things" needed cleansing?

> The necessity for the purification of the earthly sanctuary and its vessels came from the fact that they were to be used by man and shared in his impurity (comp. Lev. xvi. 16).

> Agreeably with this view it may be said that even "heavenly things," so far as they embody the conditions of man's future life, contracted by the Fall something which required cleansing.[48]

Just as the earthly sanctuary was defiled by sin and was in need of purification, so also was the heavenly sanctuary. Thus while the argument of Hebrews does not directly address the issue of the Adventist sanctuary doctrine, "we may say, particularly on the strength of 9:23, that it allows for it."[49]

It should be noted that the Day of Atonement service is not the only service of the sanctuary system which receives attention in Hebrews 9. There are also more casual references to the "red heifer" sacrifice (vs. 13), the ratification of the covenant with blood (vss. 18-20), the dedication of the sanctuary (vs. 21), and sacrifices in general (vs. 22). *Indeed, the allusions to the Day of Atonement actually do not constitute the central theme in the argumentation of Hebrews concerning sacrifice.* They are merely part of a larger complex of references to the Levitical cultus.[50] A recognition of this fact enables us to see these allusions in their proper perspective.

As Johnsson has pointed out so clearly, the real issue of this section of Hebrews is not the Day of Atonement as such, but the superiority of the blood of Christ.[51] "If the sacrificial system falls short at its high point, the complete structure must be branded inadequate. But, says Hebrews, the good news is that of *better blood*!"[52] The repeated Days of Atonement could not do what was done once and for all at Calvary by the sacrifice of Christ—the shedding of the "better blood." And in Hebrews "it is the motif of *haima* ('blood') that links together the various references to daily

---

48 Westcott, p. 270. Buchanan adds, "It also seems a little surprising to think of heaven as a place where there would be sin and defilement that needed cleansing. The author of Hebrews found no difficulty with this, however" (p. 162).

49 Johnsson, *In Absolute Confidence*, p. 116.

50 See Heb 5:1-3; 7:27; 9:9-10, 12-13, 18-21; 10:8, 11, 29; 11:4, 28; 12:24.

51 William G. Johnsson, "Defilement and Purgation in the Book of Hebrews" (Ph.D. dissertation, Vanderbilt University, 1973), pp. 102-361.

52 Johnsson, "Day of Atonement Allusions," p. 118-19.

sacrifices, heifer, inauguration of covenant and Yom Kippur."[53]

What then is Hebrews 9 saying relative to Adventist sanctuary theology when it speaks of Christ's ministry in the context of the Day of Atonement? First it must be pointed out that there is a clear relationship between the Day of Atonement allusions in Hebrews and Christ's heavenly ministry. "There is basic agreement that Christ at His ascension entered into the very presence of God, *as symbolized* by the earthly high priest's entrance on the Day of Atonement."[54]

However, this is not taken to mean that Christ began the second phase of His heavenly ministry at His ascension.[55] The implication of the Day of Atonement allusions in Hebrews is that Christ is located at His ascension, like the high priest on the Day of Atonement, in the presence of God. But Hebrews does not address itself to the question of the two phases of Christ's heavenly ministry, nor to the location of events in time. Says Johnsson:

> The Day of Atonement references of Hebrews, therefore, are *not* designed to show that the antitypical day of atonement began at the Ascension. . . . Rather, the argument swings on the *relative value of sacrifice,* contrasting the apex of the OT cultus with the surpassing achievement of Jesus Christ on Calvary.[56]

Two-Phased Ministry and Events in Time

Without identifying it as such, Hebrews clearly speaks of the first phase of Christ's heavenly ministry. Hebrews 7:25 discusses Christ's intercessory ministry quite explicitly. In addition, 4:14-16 strongly implies His intercession for those who approach the throne of grace seeking "mercy" and "grace."

Sanctuaries — Not Eras Contrasted

The questions of phases of ministry and events in time have been raised in connection with Hebrews 9:6-10, specifically with verse 8. In this verse *tōn hagiōn* is best translated "sanctuary" (RSV).[57] The context indicates that the reference is to the heavenly sanctuary. Verses 1-7 describe the earthly sanctuary and its services, and the author moves next to discuss

---

53 Ibid., p. 118.
54 "Statement," p. 8 (emphasis mine).
55 Ibid.
56 Johnsson, "Day of Atonement Allusions," p. 119.
57 See A. P. Salom, "*Ta Hagia* in the Epistle to the Hebrews," *AUSS* 5 (1967): 59-65, 68. See Appendix A.

Christ's work in the heavenly sanctuary (vss. 11-12). Thus it is quite natural for verses 8-10 to form a bridge passage in which he describes the symbolic value of the earthly sanctuary in light of the heavenly.

The phrase "the outer tent" (*tēs protēs skēnēs*) has elicited much discussion. It has just been used twice (vss. 2, 6) to describe the first apartment of the earthly sanctuary. It is only reasonable that it should be used the same way in verse 8.[58]

This has led some to the incorrect conclusion that the first or outer apartment is symbolic of the age of the OT, and the Second and inner Apartment points to the era of the NT. This would equate the entire period since Calvary with the Day of Atonement.[59] But the contrast in the author's argument is being made between sanctuaries, not eras. Thus the first or outer apartment of the earthly sanctuary is representative of the whole earthly sanctuary as the system of limited access.

Westcott has expressed it as follows:

> The first, the outer, tabernacle, the sanctuary of habitual worship, did in a most impressive way shew the limits which were placed upon the worshipper. While this held a recognised place among divine institutions the people were separated from the object of their devotion. All had not as yet the privilege of priests: all priests had not the right of approach to the Divine throne. Thus the outer sanctuary was the representative symbol of the whole Tabernacle as the place of service.[60]

With this Johnsson agrees: ". . . the 'first tent' here probably points to the entire Sanctuary of the old cultus, in contrast to the genuine or 'true tent' of the heavenly sanctuary (Heb 8:1, 2). That is, the contrast is between the two sanctuaries rather than the two eras."[61]

Verse 9a is closely connected to the comment about "the outer tent" (vs. 8). The earthly sanctuary, represented by its first apartment, was marked by limited access to God (cf. vss. 6, 7). As long as the Temple services continued, this was the situation for those who, like some of the first readers of Hebrews, were in danger of choosing to worship according

---

58 This is one option in *The SDA Bible Commentary,* 7:451. For other comments see, Johnsson, pp. 44-45, 109; Kiesler, pp. 60-62; Davidson, pp. 175-76, in this volume.

59 See Desmond Ford, "Daniel 8:14, the Day of Atonement, and the Investigative Judgment" (unpublished paper, Glacier View, 1980), pp. 183-864.

60 Westcott, p. 252.

61 Johnsson, "Day of Atonement Allusions," p. 114; also, "Thus the *entire* earthly sanctuary, not merely its first apartment, was a parable of the old era, at the time then present . . ." (Id., "The Heavenly Sanctuary," p. 47; *The SDA Bible Commentary,* 7:451).

to the OT sanctuary system. Thus the author describes the first apartment (representative of the entire earthly sanctuary) as a "parable for the present age."[62]

The apostle is saying that the way into the heavenly sanctuary is not yet opened as long as the earthly sanctuary continues to have standing or "retains status" (*echouses stasin*). In light of the problem of the wavering Jewish-Christians, it may thus be that he is speaking here experientially rather than historically—that his emphasis is upon the spiritual experience of his readers rather than on events in time.

Issues Not Addressed

Hebrews does not directly address the question of the two-phased heavenly ministry of Christ. This is not its concern. Johnsson puts the matter well: "We may say that Hebrews *allows* for the two-phased work of Christ but does not develop it. The author alludes to future judgment [9:27; 10:30, 31; 12:25-27] but goes no further—his concern is with what Christ already has done and with His present heavenly ministry."[63]

This view is endorsed by the *SDA Bible Commentary* when, discussing the two phases of Christ's heavenly ministry, it says, "the book of Hebrews is hardly the place to find a definitive presentation on the matter."[64] Another recent Adventist statement took a similar position: "There is also general acceptance that neither Daniel nor a two-phased ministry are referred to in the Epistle to the Hebrews."[65]

Again, Hebrews does not address the question of future time. Apart from references to the Second Advent and general allusions to future judgment, it does not look forward. It is more concerned to look back to what was achieved at Calvary and to make its appeal to its first readers on the basis of that. "He is certain of the reality of Christ's high priestly ministry in the heavenly sanctuary, but his argument basically looks back from his time to what already has happened at Calvary."[66] Hebrews gives no clues on the question of eschatological events in time. "Hebrews is not

---

62 Although the final results are the same, the Daniel and Revelation Committee adopted a different exposition of Hebrews 9:8. See report, p. 4-5.

63 William G. Johnsson, "Hebrews, Adventist Storm Centre," *Collegiate Sabbath School Quarterly,* September 30, 1981, p. 16.

64 *The SDA Bible Commentary,* 7:468.

65 "Statement," p. 8; also, "This way of speaking in no way precludes our understanding of Christ's two-phased mediatorial ministry in the heavenly sanctuary, which the letter to the Hebrews neither teaches nor denies," p. 9.

66 Johnsson, "Storm Center," p. 16. "The apostle here definitely does *not* deal with the work of Christ in the heavenly tabernacle from a time perspective" (Johnsson, *In Absolute Confidence,* p. 116).

in fact concerned with the question of time; it concentrates rather on the all-sufficiency of Calvary."[67]

Conclusions

Hebrews is silent on some matters which intensely interest Adventists. These matters are part of our concerns as we look at the eschatological scene. But they were not concerns of the writer of Hebrews. They are our questions, not the apostle's. We must be careful in the interpretation of this book—as of all Scripture—that we do not seek answers for questions which are irrelevant to the writer's concerns.

Hebrews is quite explicit in its discussion, both of the reality of the heavenly sanctuary, and of Christ's ministry there. It is clear that Christ has opened access which is full, free, and direct into the presence of God, and that He ministers there on our behalf. It is certain that His sacrifice has provided "better blood" than the sacrifice of animals. But Hebrews does not discuss either the two-phased heavenly ministry of Christ or any questions involving time relative to this ministry. "The argument of Hebrews, then, does not deny the SDA sanctuary doctrine, because basically it does not address the issue."[68]

---

67 "Christ in the Heavenly Sanctuary," p. 13.
68 Johnsson, *In Absolute Confidence,* p. 116.

Appendix A

Ta Hagia in the Epistle
to the Hebrews

Alwyn P. Salom

Tα αγια (and its variants) occurs a total of ten times in the NT, all of them in the Epistle to the Hebrews.[1] A casual examination of translations and commentaries makes it evident that there is considerable confusion of expression (if not of thought) among translators and commentators in their handling of this word. Table I illustrates the variety offered by translations ranging from the KJV to Phillips. An attempt was made to choose a representative group, including the committee translation, the modern speech translation, and the paraphrase. Of the ten translations chosen there is complete agreement only at one point (9:1). In six of the verses under consideration (9:2, 8, 12, 25; 10:19; 13:11) there is disagreement whether τα αγια refers to the sanctuary in general or to a specific part of it. Of the 100 translations represented in Table I, 65-69 are in terms of the sanctuary in general, 11-13 are in terms of the outer compartment of the sanctuary, and 20-22 are in terms of the inner compartment.[2] The same division of opinion has been

---

Reprinted by permission from *Andrews University Studies,* January 1967, vol. 5, No. 1, pp. 59-70. Due to printing technicalities accent and breathing marks are omitted from the Greek words used in the body of the text and footnotes. – Ed.

1 Heb 8:2; 9:1, 2, 3, 8, 12, 24, 25; 10:19, 13:11.
2 The variation occurs because, at some places, the intention of the translator is not clear. In order to avoid the confusion introduced by such terms as "Holy Place," "Holy place," "holy Place," "holy place," "holy places," etc., the following terminology is hereinafter used as far as possible: "sanctuary" is used to refer to the Tabernacle or Temple in general; "outer compartment" and "inner compartment" are used of the Holy Place and Holy of Holies respectively. The summary given above in the text can be broken down as follows: 8:2 sanctuary 10 x; 9:1 sanctuary 10 x; 9:2 sanctuary 3 x (?), outer compartment 7 x; 9:3 inner compartment 10 x; 9:8 sanctuary 6 x, inner compartment 4 x; 9:12 sanctuary 5 x, outer compartment 3 x, inner compartment 2 x; 9:24 sanctuary 10 x; 9:25 sanctuary 7 x, outer compartment 2 x; inner

Table I: Translation of τα αγια in the Epistle to the Hebrews[a]

Reference	Greek	Goodspeed	Knox	NEB	ERV	ASV	RSV	KJV	Moffatt	Wuest	Phillips
8:2	των αγιων	1b	1	1	1	1	1	1	1	10	1
9:1	Το τε αγιον	1	1	1	1	1	1	1	1	1	1
9:2	Αγια	1	1	2	2	2	2	1	2	2	2A
9:3	Αγια Αγιων	1A	1A	3	4	4	4	5	4	4	4
9:8	των αγιων	1	1	1	9	9	1	5	6	7	4
9:12	τα αγια	1	1	1	9	9	2	9	2	4	4
9:24	αγια	1	1	1	9	9	1	10	9	10	10
9:25	τα αγια	1	1	1	9	9	2	9	9	10	4
10:19	των αγιων	1	1	1	9	9	1	7	8	4	4
13:11	τα αγια	1	1	1	9	9	1	1	2	4	1

[a]The translations are arranged (reading from the left) in order of consistency of translation. Although it is recognized that this is not a *sine qua non* of translation, it is, nonetheless, one factor of evaluation and for the present purpose a convenient standard of comparison. A study of this Table reveals some expected results, *e.g.*, the close connection between the ERV and the ASV; and the degree of inconsistency of translation in the "expanded" translation of Wuest and the paraphrase of Phillips. It also reveals some surprises, *e.g.*, the consistency of translation of the NEB; and the similarity of Knox to Goodspeed.

[b]
1= "sanctuary"; 1A = "inner sanctuary"
2= "Holy Place," "Holy place," "holy Place"
   2A ="outer compartment"
3= "Most Holy Place"
4= "Holy of Holies," "Holy of holies," "holy of holies"
5= "Holiest of all," "holiest of all"
6= "Holiest Presence"
7= "Holiest," "holiest"
8= "holy Presence"
9= "holy place"
10 = "holy places"

discovered among the commentators[3] where it has been found necessary to explain that "Holy place" in some instances does not refer to the Holy Place, but to the Holy of Holies!

In view of the fact that the *auctor ad Hebraeos* leaned so heavily upon the LXX,[4]

---

compartment 1 x; 10:19 sanctuary 6 x, inner compartment 4 x; 13:11 sanctuary 8 x, outer compartment 1 x, inner compartment 1 x.

3 See *infra,* pp. 66ff.

4 For a recent discussion of the use of the LXX by Hebrews, see Kenneth J.

it would seem that this is the logical place to look for evidence of his meaning in the use of τα αγια. A study of the LXX revealed the results summarized in Table 2. Of the 170 uses of this word which had reference to the Tabernacle or Temple,[5] the overwhelming majority (142) referred to the sanctuary in general. When used in this way τα αγια seemed to appear indiscriminately in the singular or plural, although more than twice as frequently in the plural.[6] At the same time it should be pointed out that when it was used of either the outer or inner compartments it was more usually singular. With only four exceptions this use was found to be articular. This same general pattern seems to be followed (on a much smaller scale) in Hebrews.[7] It is significant that of the 98 places where this LXX expression is a

Table II: The Use of τα αγια in the LXX[a]

	sanctuary	outer compartment	inner compartment
Total number of uses	142	19	9
Singular	45	13	8
Plural	97	6	1
Articular	138	19	9
Anarthrous	4	—	—

[a]The accuracy of these figures is, of course, subject to such factors as variant readings, doubtful uses, and the human factor.

Thomas, "The Old Testament Citations in Hebrews," *NTS* 11 (1965), 303-25. See also B. F. Westcott, *The Epistle to the Hebrews* (London, 1903), pp. 469-80; J. van der Ploeg, "L'exégèse de L'Ancien Testament dans l'Épître aux Hébreux," *RB* 54 (1947), 187ff.; R. A. Stewart, *The Old Testament Usage in Philo, Rabbinic Writings, and Hebrews* (unpublished M. Litt. Thesis, University of Cambridge, 1947); C. Spicq, *L'Épître aux Hébreux* (Paris, 1952), I, 330ff.; F. C. Synge, *Hebrews and the Scriptures* (London, 1959); M. Barth, "The Old Testament in Hebrews," *Current Issues in NT Interpretation*, ed. W. Klassen and G. F. Snyder (New York, 1962), pp. 53ff.

5 In addition there were 16 uses in which it was constructed with τοπος, and 13 in which το αγιον των αγιων (and variants) occurred. These were treated separately.

6 The possible reasons why the plural was used so commonly were not pursued in this study. See F. Blass and A. Debrunner, *A Greek Grammar of the New Testament and Other Early Christian Literature* (tr. and rev. by Robert W. Funk, Cambridge, 1961), p. 78; Nigel Turner in James Hope Moulton, *A Grammar of New Testament Greek* (Edinburgh, 1963), III, 25-28; J. Wackernagel, *Vorlesungen über Syntax mit besonderer Berücksichtigung von Griechisch, Lateinisch und Deutsch* (Basel, 1926), I, 97ff.

7 Of the nine uses in Hebrews which correspond to τα αγια (the construction at 9:3 is Αγια αγιων), eight were in the plural and seven were articular.

translation of the Hebrew, 36 translate מִקְדָּשׁ which designates a sanctuary in general.[8] All of this would suggest that this word had the idea of the sanctuary as a whole for its basic meaning in Hebrews as in the LXX.

It could be argued that, inasmuch as all the uses of τα αγια from Hebrews 9:8 on are found in a Day of Atonement setting, a connection must be made between these six uses (at least) and the seven uses of this same word in Leviticus 16.[9] It is true that these latter references are to the inner compartment of the sanctuary.[10] However, it should be pointed out that each of the uses in Leviticus is singular, while in Hebrews (with one exception) they are plural. If the author of Hebrews was making a conscious borrowing from Leviticus 16 undoubtedly he would have used the singular. Furthermore, it seems far more likely that he was influenced by the general tendency of the LXX (which indicates that τα αγια refers primarily to the sanctuary as a whole), than by a specific part of it.

In addition to the uses of τα αγια already considered, there are two other constructions in which it appears in the LXX. το αγιον των αγιων (and variants) occurs 11 times referring to the inner compartment of the sanctuary.[11] Seven of these are of the order cited above (i.e. singular/plural) and four are plural/plural. All of them are translations of קֹדֶשׁ הַקֳּדָשִׁים. Αγια Αγιων in Hebrews 9:3 is an example of this use and refers to the inner compartment. Although it appears in the LXX more frequently in the articular form (eight such uses), this is not sufficient reason to eliminate the anarthrous example in Hebrews from this category. It appears that the author of Hebrews had a specific reason for omitting the article.[12]

The construction with τοπος is found 16 times in the LXX, all of which are singular.[13] It does not appear in Hebrews but is found in the NT at Matthew 24:15; Acts 16:13; 21:28. In all of its LXX appearances it refers to the sanctuary in general. All three of the NT uses could also be understood in this same way. Acts 21:28 is particularly significant in that τον αγιον τοπον τουτον is parallel to ιερον. The use of this construction in both the LXX and the NT supports the thesis that τα αγια primarily refers to the sanctuary in general.

The use of αγιος in nonbiblical sources reveals that the meaning "sanctuary"

---

8 The remaining 62 were translations of קֹדֶשׁ which parallels αγιος.

9 Lev 16:2, 3, 16, 17, 20, 23, 27.

10 See especially Leviticus 16:2 where "within the veil, before the mercy seat" specifies which part of the sanctuary is referred to.

11 Exod 26:34; 1 Kgs 6:16; 7:36; 8:6; 1 Chr 6:49; 2 Chr 3:8, 10; 4:22; 5:7; Ezek 41:4; Dan 9:24. In addition there are two uses, the meanings of which are debatable: Lev 16:33; Num 18:10.

12 See *infra*, p. 64.

13 Exod 29:31; Lev 6:9 (MT 6:16), 19 (MT 26); 8:31; 10:13, 17, 18; 14:13; 16:24; 24:9; Ps 23:3 (MT 24:3); 67:6 (MT 68:5); Eccl 8:10; Isa 60:13; 2 Macc 2:18; 8:17.

or "temple" was quite widespread. In the Ptolemaic period το αγιον was used for "temple" in the Canopus inscription of Ptolemy III (239 B.C.).[14] Both Philo[15] and Josephus[16] also used it in this sense. Schlatter points out that Josephus used it sparingly in this sense probably because it would have sounded strange in the ears of Greeks who were used to hearing ιερον.[17] Procksch[18] agrees with Flasher[19] that το αγιον and τα αγια were introduced into the LXX to avoid using ιερον which had heathen connotations.

Only three of the uses of τα αγια in Hebrews are anarthros. Of these, Hebrews 9:24 is qualified by the accompanying χειροποιητα so that it has the value of being definite, even though not articular. The remaining 9:2 (Αγια) and 9:3 (Αγια Αγιων) both refer to specific parts of the sanctuary (the outer and inner compartments respectively), as is clearly indicated by the context. Was the author trying to make a distinction between these two (by leaving them anarthrous) and the other uses in Hebrews thus indicating that these two alone referred to specific parts of the sanctuary? Was this a device employed deliberately, to show a difference between the two groups?[20] If this is the case, it constitutes further evidence that τα αγια in

---

14 W. Dittenberger, ed., *Orientes Graeci Inscriptiones Selectae* (Leipzig, 1903-1905), No. 56, line 59. See also U. Wilcken, *Urkunden der Ptolemäerzeit,* 1 (Berlin, 1922), No. 119, line 12 (156 B.C.).

15 *Legum Allegoriae,* iii. 125.

16 Josephus used it both of the Jerusalem temple (*Ant.,* iii. 6.4), of the inner compartment (*Bell.,* i. 7.6), and of the sanctuary with the forecourt and walls of the temple (*Bell.,* iv. 3.10; vi. 2.1; *Ant.,* xii. 10.6).

17 A. Schlatter, *Der Evangelist Matthäus* (Stuttgart, 1929), p. 12.

18 Otto Procksch, *TDNT* (Grand Rapids, 1964), I, 95.

19 M. Flasher in *ZAW,* 32 (1929): 245, n. 2.

20 Westcott, *op. cit.,* p. 245, noted that "the anarthrous form [Αγια in 9:2] in this sense appears to be unique." He also connected it with Αγια Αγιων in 9:3. However, he felt that it fixed attention on the character of the sanctuary. Helmut Koester's puzzlement concerning the use of Αγια here (" 'Outside the Camp': Hebrews 13:9-14," *HThR* 55 [1962]: 309, n. 34) is solved by the above suggestion. His statement that "in all other places the simple Αγια is the technical term for the 'inner tent' " does not take into consideration the peculiarly anarthrous nature of the expression at 9:2, nor does it account for the use of this word at 9:1, 24. His explanation of 9:2, in terms of dependence upon a *"Vorlage"* in the description of the tabernacle, is quite unsatisfactory. Koester himself seems to prefer the suggestion of J. Moffatt, *A Critical and Exegetical Commentary on the Epistle to the Hebrews* (New York, 1924), p. 133, that the words ητις λεγεται Αγια of 9:2 would have been in a better position immediately after η πρωτη. From this, Koester takes the next step to suggest that the words are a marginal gloss "which later came into the text, that is at a wrong place." It is true that there is some textual confusion at this point, but

Hebrews (apart from 9:2, 3) should be regarded as referring to the sanctuary as a whole.

The general conclusion reached from the study of the LXX use of τα αγια and the comparison with the use in Hebrews is that this expression refers basically to the sanctuary in general. The question remaining to be answered is the question of translation. How should it be translated in Hebrews? Should it be left in translation with the emphasis on the basic meaning and thus be translated "sanctuary" each time (as by Goodspeed and Knox)? Or should it be interpreted in the light of its context and the theology of the passage, and translated according to that specific part of the sanctuary which seems to be in the mind of the writer? It is the contention of the present writer that the basic meaning of the word should be uppermost in the mind of the translator and, provided it makes sense in the context, should be used for the translation.[21] Thus "sanctuary" would be the translation throughout Hebrews except at 9:2, 3. It is then the work of the commentator, on the basis of his study of the context and the theology of the passage, to decide what specific part (if any) of the sanctuary was in the mind of the writer.

8:2 των αγιων here refers to the heavenly sanctuary as a whole. This is supported by the epexegetical statement that follows, και της σκηνης της αληθινης.[22] σκηνη is used quite regularly in the LXX for both אהל and משכן representing the tabernacle as a whole. While it is argued by Koester[23] and Hewitt[24] that the author is speaking here of two separate things, their position is not strongly supported. In view of the evidence already presented from the LXX of the use of τα αγια, it would appear that the primary meaning here is the sanctuary as a whole, not the

---

none of the readings suggests a different position for this clause. It should also be pointed out that, while there are readings for articles before both Αγια of 9:2 and Αγια Αγιων of 9:3, the evidence is not strong for either.

21 The general principle as applied to the question of ambiguity in translation is discussed by the following: Robert G. Bratcher and Eugene A. Nida, *A Translator's Handbook on the Gospel of Mark* (Leiden, 1961), pp. 63, 69; Theophile J. Meek, "Old Testament Translation Principles," *JBL* 81 (1962): 143-45; F. F. Bruce, *The English Bible: A History of Translations* (London, 1961), p. 222.

22 Spicq, *op. cit.*, II, 234, "Mais il désigne nettement le temple dans ix, 8, 12; x, 19; xiii, 11, et il est fréquemment l'équivalent de ιερον dans les LXX (cf. Lev v, 15; 1 Macc iv, 36; xiv, 15). De fait, il est parallèle ici à της σκηνης." It is worth noting that Philo uses the exact phrase *(Leg. Alleg.* iii. 46), λειτουργος των αγιων, of Aaron. He uses it, however, in the sense of "holy things."

23 Koester, *loc. cit.*, "This is not a hendiadys, but expresses that Christ's office includes both the service in the sanctuary of heaven itself (τα αγια) *and* the entering by passing through the heavenly regions (η σκηνη) = the ascension!"

24 Thomas Hewitt, *The Epistle to the Hebrews* (Grand Rapids, 1960), p. 135.

inner compartment (the basis of the arguments of Koester and Hewitt). Moffatt strongly supports this conclusion.[25]

In the larger context of the author's argument the emphasis is here being placed on the *existence* of the heavenly sanctuary. Just as Israel had its place of worship and high priest, so (says the *auctor*) Christianity, on a grander scale, has the same. In the words of Moule, "sanctuary and sacrifice are ours."[26] Now it is true, both that the reference in the context is to the high priestly function (8:1, 3), and that the unique function of the high priest was concerned with the inner compartment of the sanctuary. Thus, while "sanctuary" must rightly be regarded as the translation of των αγιων, on a secondary level, at least, the author may be considered to have had a specific part of the sanctuary in view.

9:1 Coming as it does, at the beginning of a detailed description of the parts and functions of the earthly sanctuary, το αγιον κοσμικον obviously is a reference to the sanctuary in general and should be translated accordingly. As Bruce points out, the author bases his description on "the wilderness tent described in the book of Exodus . . . the sanctuary of the old covenant."[27] Westcott emphasizes that it gives naturally "the general notion of the sanctuary without regard to its different parts."[28] The singular το αγιον is not found elsewhere in Hebrews; however, it is found quite frequently in the LXX.[29]

9:2 Provided the reading Αγια is correct (τα Αγια B sa), this use is unique. The significance of this has already been discussed.[30] Montefiore notes that the anarthrous form is unparalleled in Hebrews but fails to see any significance in it.[31] Unaccountably (unless there is a printing error, or he is following the *Textus Receptus*), he identifies the word as αγια and then discusses whether it is neuter plural or feminine singular. He decides in favor of feminine and considers that it is an adjectival use qualifying σκηνη. However, it would appear rather to be a neuter form and a substantival use referring to the outer compartment (η πρωτη σκηνη)

---

25 Moffatt, *op. cit.*, p. 104: "But the writer uses τα αγια elsewhere (9[8f] 10[19] 13[11]) of 'the sanctuary,' a rendering favoured by the context. By τα αγια he means, as often in the LXX, the sanctuary in general, without any reference to the distinction (cp. 9[2f]) between the outer and the inner shrine."

26 C.F.D. Moule, "Sanctuary and Sacrifice in the Church of the New Testament," *JThS*, N.S., 1 (1950): 37.

27 F. F. Bruce, *The Epistle to the Hebrews* (Grand Rapids, 1964), p. 182.

28 Westcott, *op. cit.*, p. 244. See also Moffatt, *op. cit.*, p. 112; Spicq, *op. cit.*, p. 248 ("il désigne ice l'esemble de ce lieu saint sans distinction de l'une ou l'autre de ses parties").

29 E.g., Exod 36:3; Lev 4:6; 10:18; Num 3:47; Ps 62:3 (MT 63:2); Ezek 45:18; Dan 8:11, etc.

30 *Supra*, p. 64.

31 Hugh Montefiore, *A Commentary on the Epistle to the Hebrews* (New York, 1964), p. 146.

of the sanctuary. The contents of the room as described in the verse support this.

9:3 This is the most straightforward of the uses of τα αγια in Hebrews. The form Αγια Αγιων (both neuter plural) is equivalent to the Hebrew superlative קֹדֶשׁ קָדָשִׁים ("Holiest") and thus refers to the inner compartment of the sanctuary.[32] Like 9:2, the expression in this verse is anarthrous,[33] and like 9:2, it refers to a specific part of the sanctuary. This, of course, is confirmed by the context (9:4) which describes the contents of this compartment.

9:8 Again, the basic meaning of τα αγια must be considered foremost in translating, so that "sanctuary," as given by Goodspeed, Knox, RSV, and NEB, is correct. The comprehensive meaning which includes both the outer and inner compartments of the sanctuary explains the use of η πρωτη σκηνη.[34] The sanctuary here described is the heavenly sanctuary of which the inner compartment of the earthly sanctuary is symbolic.[35]

The means of access to the heavenly sanctuary was historically not available as long as the outer compartment had standing or retained its status.[36] This outer compartment represents the customary limit of access to God in the experience of Israel. Westcott's comment is pertinent: "the outer sanctuary [i.e., compartment] was the representative symbol of the whole Tabernacle as the place of service."[37] When the earthly sanctuary fulfilled its purpose at the death of Christ, the means of access was historically provided into the heavenly sanctuary.

9:12 The translations of the KJV, ERV, and ASV ("the holy place") and of Moffatt ("the Holy place") and the RSV ("the Holy Place") are definitely misleading. The characteristic service of the Day of Atonement here referred to (cf. vs. 7), was located in the inner compartment of the earthly sanctuary. However, inasmuch as the high priest had to pass through the outer compartment, it could be said that he "employed" (cf. vs. 11, δια της μειζονος και τελειοτερας σκηνης) the whole sanctuary in this service. "Whereas Aaron and his successors went into the earthly holy of holies on the Day of Atonement . . . Christ has entered the heavenly sanctuary."[38] It is suggested, then, that τα αγια once more be rendered

---

32 P[46] has αγια here and αγια αγιων in 9:2. This appears to be the result of some primitive disturbance of the text.

33 א[C] B D[C] K L read τα αγια των αγιων. This could be an assimilation to the LXX use of this phrase which is always articular.

34 η πρωτη σκηνη (as in 9:2, 6) refers to the outer compartment. See Moffatt, op. cit. p. 118; Westcott, p. 252.

35 Spicq, op cit., p. 253.

36 Bruce, The Epistle to the Hebrews, p. 192, n. 48: "It is not necessarily implied that the earthly sanctuary, as a material structure, no longer existed; what is implied is that, with Christ's passing 'through the heavens' (ch. 4:14) into the presence of God, the earthly structure has lost its sanctuary status."

37 Westcott, op. cit., p. 252.

38 Bruce, The Epistle to the Hebrews, p. 200. See also Montefiore, op. cit., p. 153.

"sanctuary," referring to the heavenly sanctuary.

9:24 If in 9:12 τα αγια is to be translated "sanctuary," clearly it should be the same in 9:24, for the same locale is described. It is not a specific part of the heavenly sanctuary that is in the mind of the author, as is evident from his adversative phrase αλλ εις αυτον τον ουρανον. Commentators are almost unanimous in considering this use of αγια a reference to the heavenly sanctuary in general.[39]

9:25 As in 9:12, the translation "Holy Place" (and variants) is misleading. The reference in the context of the Day of Atonement service of the earthly high priest is not to the outer compartment of the sanctuary. His characteristic service on that day was carried on in the inner compartment. However, once more, because the whole sanctuary is involved in these services, "sanctuary" is to be preferred as the translation, thus emphasizing the basic meaning of the expression. This leaves with the commentator the task of pointing out that the inner compartment was the place where the significance of that day resided.[40]

10:19 Unquestionably, the context (vs. 20) indicates that the author here is referring to the Christian's privilege of free access into the very presence of God, access which was denied both the worshipper and the ordinary priest in the earthly sanctuary. But again it is recommended that the translation of των αγιων be left as "sanctuary," allowing the reader or commentator, on the basis of the literary and theological context, to draw his conclusions as to what part of the sanctuary is particularly in the mind of the author.

13:11 Although Westcott allows that this verse may apply to other than the Day of Atonement ritual,[41] it is likely in view of chapter 9 particularly, that the author has this day in mind. From Leviticus 16:27 (cf. vs. 2) it is possible to discover that on the Day of Atonement the blood of the sacrificial animal was carried into the inner compartment of the sanctuary. Thus this part of the sanctuary was in the mind of the author. But the LXX use of τα αγια and the manner in which it has been used in Hebrews would lead us to render it once more in the neutral sense, "sanctuary."

---

39 See Montefiore, *op. cit.* p. 160; Bruce, *The Epistle to the Hebrews,* p. 220; Spicq, *op. cit.,* p. 267; Westcott, *op. cit.,* p. 271; F. W. Farrar, *The Epistle to the Hebrews,* Cambridge Greek Testament (Cambridge, 1888), p. 123.

40 F. D. Nichol, ed., *The SDA Bible Commentary* (Washington, DC, 1957), 7:456: "*Ta hagia* may, in this context, be regarded as referring particularly to the most holy place, or in a general sense to the sanctuary as a whole, as in ch. 8:2."

41 Westcott, *op. cit.,* p. 440.

Appendix B

Hebrews 6:19
Analysis of Some Assumptions
Concerning *Katapetasma*

George E. Rice

Commentators on the book of Hebrews are practically unanimous regarding four assumptions upon which they base their interpretation of the term *katapetasma,* "veil," at 6:19 (and also elsewhere in the book). These are (1) that *tou katapetasmatos* in the phrase *eis to esōteron tou katapetasmatos* at 6:19 is the second veil of the tabernacle structure, namely the veil that separates the holy place from the Most Holy Place; (2) that to *esōteron,* "the [place] within," in the same phrase refers to the inner shrine or Most Holy Place; (3) that God the Father's presence within the OT sanctuary was to be found only in the Most Holy Place; and (4) that *ta hagia* (lit., "the holies") in chapter 9 refers to the Most Holy Place.

In other words, it is assumed that the sanctuary language and imagery of the book of Hebrews reflects the second-apartment and Day-of-Atonement ritual. Space will not permit an examination here of all four of these assumptions, but only the first two — those regarding the meaning of the terms *katapetasma* and *esōteron* in Hebrews 6:19. If there is doubt as to the validity of these first two assumptions, then the third and fourth ones are also open to question and will demand new investigation.

1. *Katapetasma*

Otto Michel reflects the thinking of commentators in general on *katapetasma* in the book of Hebrews when he states that "when Hebrews speaks of 'veil,'... then the veil before the Most Holy Place is meant, in harmony with a broader usage of the language."[1] The commentators support this sort of position by appealing to

---

Reprinted by permission from *Andrews University Studies,* Spring 1897, vol. 5, No. 1, pp. 65-71, with corrections by the author.

1 Otto Michel, "Der Brief an die Hebraer," in *Kritisch-Exegetischer Kommentar uber das Neue Testament* (Göttingen, 1975), p. 254.

Philo and/or to the LXX wording in Leviticus 16:2.[2]

Philo *(De Vit. Mes.* 3.5), Marcus Dods tells us, makes a distinction between the two veils of the sanctuary by identifying the first veil with the term *kalumma* and reserving *katapetasma* for the inner veil. Dods then suggests that this is the way *katapetasma* is to be understood in the NT.[3]

However, B. F. Westcott points out that Philo uses these terms "for a spiritual interpretation."[4] Philo may be free to make this clear distinction by the exclusive use of *kalumma* and *katapetasma* in his allegory, but does his allegory reflect what existed in reality? One wonders, on the basis of Hebrews 9:3, where the inner veil of the earthly sanctuary is called the *deuteron katapetasma,* "second veil." If the numerical adjective *deuteron* is required to identify this veil, is it possible that the word *katapetasma* was *not* reserved for the inner veil as Philo and Dods suggest?

With regard to the LXX of Leviticus 16:2, its wording, *eis to hagion esōteron tou katapetasmatos,* and that of Hebrews 6:19, *eis to esōteron tou katapetasmatos,* are indeed close. This fact has led James Moffatt to conclude that Hebrews "uses language from the ritual of Lv 16^{2f}," thus indicating that the veil of Hebrews 6:19 is the inner veil.[5]

However, the contexts of the two passages are entirely different. Leviticus 16 presents the Day of Atonement – a day of reckoning and judgment. Hebrews 6:13-20 deals with the Abrahamic covenant and the dispensing of its promises to Abraham's heirs. Are we to impose the context of the Day of Atonement of Leviticus 16 upon Hebrews 6 in an attempt to identify the veil of Hebrews 6:19? Is the fact that the earthly high priest passed within the inner veil during the ritual of the Day of Atonement sufficient reason to understand *katapetasma* at Hebrews 6:19 as being the inner veil? Or should we allow *eis to esōteron tou katapetasmatos* to stand within its own context, free from the baggage of Leviticus 16?

Appealing to Philo for the distinction between the inner veil (*katapetasma*) and the outer veil *(kalumma)* of the sanctuary, Westcott admits that this "distinction of the two is not strictly preserved in the LXX."[6] The problem with Westcott's observation is that he fails to inform his readers as to the degree to which that distinction is not preserved in the LXX.

Other commentators recognize a disparity between the use of *katapetasma* in the LXX and the generally accepted thesis that when this word is read we must understand the inner veil. Herbert Braun, for example, uses the term "meist" in

---

2 Cf. George Wesley Buchanan, *To the Hebrews,* AB 36 (Garden City, NY, 1985), p. 116; Michel, pp. 253-54; James Moffatt, *A Critical and Exegetical Commentary on the Epistle to the Hebrews,* ICC (Edinburgh, 1979), p. 89; Brooke Foss Westcott, *The Epistle to the Hebrews* (Grand Rapids, MI, 1970), p. 163.
3 Marcus Dods, "The Epistle to the Hebrews," in *The Expositor's Greek Testament,* ed. W. Robertson Nicoll (Grand Rapids, 1970), p. 305.
4 Westcott, p. 163.
5 Moffatt, p. 89.
6 Westcott, p. 163.

this sense when commenting on *tou katapetasmatos* at Hebrews 6:19: In the LXX, he informs us, this term is used "mostly [meist] for the veil between the Holy and Most Holy."[7] If by "meist" Braun means that *katapetasma* is the word that is *almost always* chosen for the inner veil in opposition to any other word, there is no quarrel with his statement. But if he means that *katapetasma* is used for the inner veil and *almost never* used for the courtyard veil nor for the first veil of the sanctuary, then his statement comes into serious question. Unfortunately, Braun does not clarify his use of "meist."

R.C.H. Lenski, on the other hand, leaves no alternative when he declares: "The καταπετασμα τον ναον is the inner curtain or veil that hangs between the Holy and the Holy of Holies, as the readers, being Hebrews, well knew. . . . But the regular term for the outer curtain was καλυμμα and only occasionally was the other term used."[8]

Because the wilderness tabernacle forms the basis for the sanctuary discussion in the book of Hebrews, an examination of *katapetasma* and *kalumma* in the LXX will prove interesting. Looking at the references to these two words in Hatch and Redpath, one receives quite a surprise. Out of six references to the courtyard veil, *katapetasma* is used five times[9] and *kalumma* once.[10] In 11 references to the first veil of the sanctuary, *katapetasma* is used six times,[11] *kalumma katapetasma* once,[12] *katakalumma* twice,[13] *kalumma* once,[14] and *epispastron* once.[15] Of the 25 references to the inner veil, *katapetasma* is used 23 times,[16] *to katakalumma tou katapetasmatos* once,[17] and *katakalumma* once.[18]

Certainly, *katapetasma* is used *almost* exclusively for the inner veil (23 out of 25 times). But the same can be said for the courtyard veil (five out of six times)! *Katapetasma* is also the majority choice for the first veil of the sanctuary as well (six out of eleven times).

In other words, out of the 42 references in the LXX to the three veils of the wilderness sanctuary, *katapetasma* is used 34 times. Or put another way: In only

---

7 Herbert Braun, "An die Hebraer," in *Handbuch zum Neuen Testament*, 14 (Tübingen, 1984): 191. The original German reads, "In LXX unübertragen, meist für den Vorhang zwischen dem Heiligen und dem Allerheiligsten."

8 R.C.H. Lenski, *The Interpretation of the Epistle to the Hebrews and of the Epistle of James* (Columbus, OH, 1938), pp. 205-6. Lenski is here using the wording of the Synoptic Gospels (Matt 27:51; Mark 15:38; Luke 23:45) in commenting on Hebrews 6:19.

9 Exod 37:26; 39:19; Num 3:26; 4:32; 3 Kgs 6:36 (1 Kgs 6:36).

10 Exod 27:16.

11 Exod 26:37; 37:5 (36:37); 39:19 (40); Lev 21:23; Num 3:10; 18:7.

12 Exod 40:5.

13 Num 3:25; 4:31.

14 Num 4:25.

15 Exod 26:36.

16 Eoxd 26:31, 33 (three times), 34, 35; 27:21; 30:6; 35:12; 37:3 (36:35); 38:18 (36:36); 39:4 (38:27); 40:3, 22, 26; Lev 4:6, 17; 16:2, 12, 15; 24:3; Num 4:5; 2 Chron 3:14.

17 Exod 40:21.

18 Num 3:31.

eight instances among these 42 references to the sanctuary veils is *katapetasma* not used by itself. Furthermore, in two additional instances *katapetasma* is combined with *kalumma,* thus leaving only six instances out of 42 where the word does not appear.

Thus, without a doubt, *katapetasma* is the hands-down favorite, not only for the inner veil, but for the first veil and the courtyard veil as well. And in view of this use of *katapetasma* in the LXX, we are forced to conclude that assumptions such as Lenski's must be reexamined. Certainly, Hebrew readers of the LXX were aware that *katapetasma* was thus used overwhelmingly for all three veils, and it is undoubtedly for this very reason that Hebrews 9:3 identifies which *katapetasma* is being addressed by using the numerical adjective *deuteron*.

2. To Esōteron

As we next analyze the assumption that an analogy with Leviticus 16:2 *to esōteron* at Hebrews 6:19 must refer to the inner shrine, it is important to note that omission of *to hagion* from the phrase contained in Hebrews creates a different syntax from what is found in Leviticus 16:2. In *eis to hagion esōteron tou katapetasmatos* in Leviticus 16:2, *to hagion* is a substantive adjective and object of the preposition *eis*. The word *esōteron* appears to be an improper preposition followed by the genitive of place, as is also true in Leviticus 16:12, 15. In *eis to esōteron tou katapetasmatos* at Hebrews 6:19, however, *to esoteron* becomes a substantive[19] and thus the object of the preposition *eis*; and the phrase *tou katapetasmatos* is, again, a genitive of place.

Paul Ellingworth and Eugene A. Nida say that "shrine" (RSV) or "sanctuary" must be understood with the substantive *esōteron,* thus giving "inner shrine" or "Most Holy Place."[20] But this is true only if one thinks *katapetasma* identifies the second veil. However, we have seen that *katapetasma* is used overwhelmingly for all three veils. Therefore, the *esōteron* behind the veil could just as well be the first apartment of the sanctuary as the "inner shrine," since there is nothing in the context of Hebrews 6 that directly identifies which veil is being addressed.

Neither should the comparative form of *esōteron* in Hebrews 6:19 be understood as identifying the "inner shrine." The comparative forms in Greek at this point in time were not strictly adhered to. This can be seen in Leviticus 16:2, where the context for the phrase *eis to hagion esōteron tou katapetasmatos* identifies *to hagion* as the room where the ark of the covenant stood, with *tou katapetasmatos* therefore being the second veil standing before the ark. *Esōteron* here is understood as the simple *eso* and is translated "within." The context prohibits any other understanding of the word *esoteron*. Likewise at Hebrews 6:19, *esōteron* may be

---

19 Cf. Braun, p. 191.
20 Paul Ellingworth and Eugene A. Nida, *A Translator's Handbook on the Letter to the Hebrews* (New York, 1983), p. 131.

understood as simply "within." The comparative form should not be pushed in an attempt to identify which apartment stood behind the veil.[21]

3. The Context of Hebrews 6:19

G. W. Buchanan makes the following statement that is somewhat difficult to understand:

> The LXX has *to hagion esōteron*, "the Holy innermost place." The author [of Hebrews] either used a different text or chose to omit this word, but the context requires that the place be understood as the holy of holies. The LXX passage refers to the conduct of Aaron on the Day of Atonement. The author's reason for quoting this passage was in continuation of his previous discussion. The hope for which other generations had expected fulfillment since the promise was first made to Abraham might be fulfilled for the author's generation.[22]

Buchanan does not inform us how the Day of Atonement of Leviticus 16 relates to the context of Hebrews 6 and the fulfillment of the Abrahamic covenant. Nor does he point out how or why the context of Hebrews 6 requires us to understand the Holy of Holies, the place that is clearly indicated within the context of Leviticus 16. It appears that Buchanan is claiming the context of Leviticus 16 as the basis for our understanding of Hebrews 6:19. But Hebrews 6:19 has its own context, and we must allow the term "veil" to stand on its own merits within that specific context.

In Leviticus 16:2, the context identifies *katapetasma* as the second veil and *to hagion* as the "inner shrine." Also, in Hebrews 9:3 the general context and the use of the numerical adjective *deuteron* identify *katapetasma* as the second veil. But the contexts of Leviticus 16 and Hebrews 9 do not exist in Hebrews 6. The fact that the term *katapetasma* appears in Hebrews 6:19 does not allow us to assume that the second veil is meant, for we have seen that this word is freely used for all three sanctuary veils.

Does, then, the context of 6:19 give us any help in identifying the word *katapetasma*? Hebrews 6:13-20 deals with dispensing the blessings of the Abrahamic covenant to Abraham and his children: (1) God swore by Himself to fulfill His promises (vss. 13-16). (2) In order to convince the heirs of the covenant that He would fulfill His word, God interposed with an oath (vs. 17). (3) So by two

---

21 A. T. Robertson observes that the original meaning of comparative adjectives which are built on adverbs "was not the comparison of greater or less, not a matter of degree, but a question of contrast or duality." "So προτερος (from the adverb προ) is not 'more forward,' but 'forward' in opposition to υστερος, 'backward.'... So εξωτερος is 'outside,' not 'more outside.' " (*A Grammar of the Greek New Testament*, p. 662.) The notion of degrees came later (p. 663).

The context for *esōteron* at Leviticus 16:2 and Hebrews 6:19 seems to favor the original emphasis of contrast. Therefore, the substantive *esōteron* (which is built on the adverb *esō*) at Hebrews 6:19 should be understood simply as speaking of that which is "within" (not as a matter of degree — "inner shrine") in opposition to *exōteros*, that which is "without."

22 Buchanan, p. 116.

unchangeable things we have strong encouragement to seize the hope (fulfillment of God's promises) set before us (vs. 18). (4) The hope enters "within the veil," where Jesus has gone on our behalf as priest after the order of Melchizedek (vss. 19-20).

This context does not deal with the sanctuary per se—i.e., its apartments, furniture, services, etc.—nor does it contain any reference to the Day of Atonement, as do the contexts of Leviticus 16:2 and Hebrews 9:3. At 6:19, *katapetasma* is simply dropped into a discussion of the Abrahamic covenant and the dispensing of the blessings of that covenant. There is nothing here that would identify the veil with which we are dealing, but *katapetasma* is introduced simply to locate where Jesus is ministering—the place where the hope of the covenant people is centered and from whence the covenant blessings are dispensed. Within the broader context of the discussion in the entire book of Hebrews, it would seem that *katapetasma* is here used metaphorically for the sanctuary from which the blessings of the Abrahamic covenant are dispensed.

4. Conclusion

Although commentators are virtually unanimous in saying that *katapetasma* at Hebrews 6:19 is the "second veil" and that *esōteron* is the "inner shrine," these assumptions are called into question by the following facts: (1) In the LXX, the word *katapetasma* is used 34 out of 42 times for all three sanctuary veils; (2) *esōteron,* although a substantive at Hebrews 6:19, cannot be translated as the "inner shrine" because *katapetasma* cannot be identified as the second veil; (3) the context of Hebrews 6:19 does not allow the identification of the second veil, as do the contexts of Leviticus 16:2 and Hebrews 9:3; (4) *katapetasma,* within the context of Hebrews 6:19 and the broader context of the entire book of Hebrews, may be understood metaphorically as the sanctuary in heaven, into which Jesus has entered as our forerunner, into which our hope has entered, and from which Jesus dispenses the blessings of the Abrahamic covenant.

Finally, because the validity of the assumptions regarding *katapetasma* and *esōteron* can be seriously challenged, the assumptions regarding God the Father's presence within the sanctuary and the meaning of *ta hagia* must also come into question.

Index